D1760386

University of Hertfordshire

Learning and Information Services

College Lane, Hatfield, Hertfordshire, AL10 9AB

For renewal of Standard and One Week Loans,
please visit the website: http://www.voyager.herts.ac.uk

This item must be returned or the loan renewed by the due date.
The University reserves the right to recall items from loan at any time.
A fine will be charged for the late return of items.

4827/KM/DS

ADVANCE$ IN INTERNATIONAL INVE$TMENT$

Traditional and Alternative Approaches

ADVANCE$ IN INTERNATIONAL INVE$TMENT$

Traditional and Alternative Approaches

editors

Hung-Gay Fung
University of Missouri, St Louis, USA

Xiaoqing Eleanor Xu
Seton Hall University, USA

Jot Yau
Seattle University, USA

 **World Scientific**

NEW JERSEY · LONDON · SINGAPORE · BEIJING · SHANGHAI · HONG KONG · TAIPEI · CHENNAI

Published by

World Scientific Publishing Co. Pte. Ltd.

5 Toh Tuck Link, Singapore 596224

USA office: 27 Warren Street, Suite 401-402, Hackensack, NJ 07601

UK office: 57 Shelton Street, Covent Garden, London WC2H 9HE

Library of Congress Cataloging-in-Publication Data
Advances in international investments : traditional and alternative approaches /
edited by Hung-Gay Fung, Xiaoqing Eleanor Xu & Jot Yau.
   p. cm.
   ISBN-13: 978-981-270-862-5
   ISBN-10: 981-270-862-6
   1. Investments, Foreign.   2. Capital movements.   3. International economic
relations.   I. Fung, Hung-gay.   II. Xu, Xiaoqing Eleanor.   III. Yau, Jot.
   HG4538.A48   2008
   332.67'3--dc22
                                                2007048502

British Library Cataloguing-in-Publication Data
A catalogue record for this book is available from the British Library.

Typeset by Stallion Press
Email: enquiries@stallionpress.com

Printed in Singapore by World Scientific Printers

To my parents, Linda (wife), Anna (daughter), my brothers and sister.

H.-G. Fung

*To my mom, Jiong (husband), Gloria and Joanna (daughters),
brother, and the loving memory of my dad.*

X. E. Xu

To Marie, my parents, brothers, and sisters.

J. Yau

Preface

In recent years, the globalization of the financial markets has become increasingly accelerated, leading to an integrated world market. At the same time, emerging markets such as China and India have opened up their markets to foreign investors, providing more investment opportunities for the existing investment universe. In addition, more new global investment instruments such as exchange-traded funds are created, enabling investors to fine-tune their investment portfolios. Financial investments are expanded to include real asset investments such as natural resources and real estate investments. Thus, there is a need to better understand the full range of investments available in the global market.

There are two basic approaches that are useful in understanding international investments. The first is presenting and discussing risk/return tradeoffs such as foreign exchange risk, regulatory risks, and different market impediments in global financial markets. The second is identifying different asset classes and current issues pertaining to them in a changing global environment. We adopt the second approach in this book because it contains more relevant information about the current state of global investments. Current hot topics (new financial instruments, innovations, and strategies), are identified and different authors who have expertise in various aspects of international investments are solicited to write for each chapter. Each chapter focuses on the risk and opportunities related to the current topic or the financial instrument, innovation, and/or strategy identified. In addition, alternative investment instruments are included, enabling readers to have a richer and a more complete understanding of the global investment opportunities.

For easy reference and organization, chapters are organized by asset class, which can be labeled as the traditional and alternative investments. The thread that runs through the entire book is: (1) trends (what is the current topic/instrument/strategy in the chosen asset class), (2) opportunities (what is new and/or where to invest or arbitrage, i.e., location); and (3) risks (what are the risks, i.e., peculiar to the location and how international investors can manage/reduce/eliminate the respective risks).

This book has 11 chapters. The first two chapters are the introduction and an overview of global investments. The next two chapters are related to global equity investments, followed by one on global fixed income investments and portfolio management. Four chapters are on alternative investments. The final two chapters are on derivatives and their use in risk management.

About the Editors

Hung-Gay Fung is Dr. Y. S. Tsiang Chair Professor of Chinese Studies at College of Business Administration, University of Missouri–St. Louis. Dr. Fung's research covers international finance, international banking, and Chinese financial markets. He has published over 100 scholarly papers in leading academic journals and in professional journals. He has also published five books. He is the recipient of many grants and academic awards. As a senior expert of Chinese finance studies, Dr. Fung has organized many international conferences and symposiums. He received his PhD in Finance from Georgia State University in 1984 and BBA in Finance from the Chinese University of Hong Kong in 1978.

Xiaoqing Eleanor Xu is Professor of Finance at the Stillman School of Business, Seton Hall University. Her research covers fixed income, venture capital, hedge funds, emerging markets and security market microstructure. She has published over 20 research articles in journals such as *Journal of Banking and Finance, Real Estate Economics, Financial Analysts Journal, Journal of Portfolio Management, Journal of Futures Markets,* and *Financial Review.* She is the recipient of many research grants and academic awards, including the 2006 Seton Hall Researcher of the Year Award and the 2007 New Jersey Bright Idea in Finance Award. She received her PhD in Finance from Syracuse University in 1998 and MBA from Indiana State University in 1994. Dr. Xu is a CFA charterholder.

Jot Yau is Robert D. O'Brien Endowed Chair in Business Administration and Professor of Finance at Seattle University. Since joining Seattle University in 2001, he has served as the chair of the Department of Finance and MSF program director. He has published numerous articles in scholarly and practitioner-oriented finance journals and chapters in professional books. He has been serving on the editorial board of *The Journal of Alternative Investments* since 2001 and served as its Associate Editor from 2001–2005. He has served on the exam and curriculum committees of the CFA Institute and the CAIA Association and has written curriculum materials for the CFA exam program. He has co-founded Strategic Options Investment Advisors Ltd., a Hong Kong-based investment advisory and served as its principal investment advisor and commodity trading advisor from 1998–2005. He is currently the treasurer of the Northwest Hedge Fund Society and a member of the board of directors of GHCU (Group Health Credit Union). Dr. Yau has worked for George Mason University, Independent Research & Consulting, Kidder Peabody, TRS Associates, Shearson/American Express, and Dow Chemical. Dr. Yau holds a PhD degree in Finance from the University of Massachusetts at Amherst. He is a CFA charterholder.

List of Contributors

Sheryl A. Law received a Master of Science in environmental chemistry from the University of Toronto and a Master of Business Administration from Seattle University. She has worked in environmental research at universities, government institutions, and spent many years working at a science and engineering consulting firm. She is the founder of Peregreen Group, a financial research and analytics firm specializing in socially responsible investing and corporate sustainability.

Louis T. W. Cheng, CFP^{CM}, DBA, is an Associate Professor of Finance at the School of Accounting and Finance. From 1989–1998, he was an Associate Professor of Finance at Murray State University in Kentucky. In 2003, he served as the HSBC Fellow of Asian Financial Markets at the University of Exeter in the UK. He is an author of *Fundamentals of Financial Planning* by McGraw-Hill, 2006. Moreover, he has over 60 articles published in top finance research journals including the *Journal of Finance*. He is ranked among the top ten finance professors in the Asia-Pacific in terms of research by articles in the *Pacific Basin Finance Journal* in 2001 and 2005.

Yiuman Tse is Professor of Finance and US Global Investors Inc., Fellow at The University of Texas at San Antonio (UTSA). His research interests are international financial markets and investments. He has papers recently published in *Journal of Financial and Quantitative Analysis* and *Review of Financial Studies*. He received his PhD at Louisiana State University in 1994 and taught at the State University of New York at Binghamton and The University of Memphis. Professor Tse is the recipient of many teaching awards from different universities, including the President's Distinguished Achievement Awards for Teaching Excellence at UTSA.

Grace K. Yeung, CPA, CA, CFA is a Senior Manager at Pricewater-houseCoopers Hong Kong where she serves the investment management industry sector. Grace received her MA in Economics from the University of California at Berkeley. She has been practising public accounting for 10 years. Grace has extensive experience in audit services, compliance matters and internal controls. Her client base includes hedge funds and private equity funds with various investment and trading strategies. She is also closely involved with the fund managers and the service providers to the investment management industry such as fund administrators, trustees and custodians. Grace is a member of the Council of Examiners of the CFA Institute. Her responsibilities include reviewing the CFA Study and Examination Program reading materials as well as writing and proof-reading exam questions. She is also a grader of the CFA exam.

Gary A. Patterson received his PhD in Finance from the University of North Carolina–Chapel Hill. His research interests include real estate investments and studies of market efficiency. He has published in *Journal of Banking, Journal of Alternative Investments, Journal of Futures Markets* and *Journal of International Financial Markets*, and *Institutions and Money*. He currently resides in St. Petersburg, Florida.

Aysegul Ates is an Assistant Professor of Economics at the Akdeniz University. She received her PhD in Economics from American University in Washington DC. Prior to her current position, she worked as an economist at the Commodity Futures Trading Commission. Her research focuses on derivative markets. Her research has been published in *Journal of Futures Markets* and *Review of Futures Markets.*

George H. K. Wang is Research Professor of Finance in the School of Management at George Mason University. He received his PhD in

Statistics and Economics (double majors) from Iowa State University, Ames, Iowa. He was the Deputy Chief Economist and Director of Research at the US Commodity Futures Trading Commission. Dr. Wang was Visiting Professor of Finance, Faculty of Economics and Business, University of Sydney, Sydney, Australia in the summer of 2006 and 2007 and Visiting Professor at National Central University, Taiwan in July 2007. He has published widely in major refereed journals in the areas of derivatives markets, applied time series, econometrics, mortgage markets, and transportation. He is an elected ordinary member of International Statistical Institute and a member of the editorial board of the *Journal of Futures Markets.*

Gaiyan Zhang is Assistant Professor of Finance at College of Business Administration at the University of Missouri–St. Louis. She holds a PhD from the University of California at Irvine, a MS in Finance from Fudan University and a BA in Finance from Nankai University, China. Her research interests include credit risk and credit derivatives, empirical corporate finance, and international finance. Her work has appeared in *Journal of Financial Economics, Journal of Fixed Income,* and *Chinese Economy.*

Anthony L. Loviscek is an Associate Professor of Finance and Chair of the Department of Finance and Legal Studies at Seton Hall University. He has also held appointments at West Virginia University, Indiana University-Purdue University at Fort Wayne, and Princeton University. His research interests are in financial markets and portfolio analysis. His work has appeared in the *Financial Review, The Quarterly Review of Economics and Finance, Financial Services Review, Journal of Real Estate Portfolio Management, North American Review of Economics and Finance,* and *The Southern Economic Journal.*

Contents

Part I: General Issues of International Investments

Chapter 1

International Investment:
Current State and Challenges
from the US Perspective

Hung-Gay Fung, Xiaoqing Eleanor Xu†
and Jot Yau‡*

We discuss the growth of world financial markets with common stocks, bonds, and other new financial instruments such as futures, GDRs and ETFs. We document patterns of international capital flows and discuss their related issues, which include: 1) how capital flows affect economic growth; 2) the cost of capital; and 3) increased linkages among different markets around the world. Home bias in global investment remains an issue that is not easily explained in the light of globalization.

We also discuss patterns of foreign portfolio investments and their implications for US investors. We show the importance of various types of investments in terms of maturity and asset class. The most popular industries for foreign investors are Thrifts and Mortgage Finance, Pharmaceutics, Metals and Mining, Paper and Forest Products, and Media and Insurance.

Keywords: Global investment; home bias; capital flows; global market linkage; cost of capital.

* College of Business Administration, University of Missouri–St. Louis, One University Boulevavd, St. Louis, MO 63121, USA. Email: fungh@msx.umsl.edu.
† Stillman School of Business, Seton Hall University, 400 South Orange Avenue, South Orange, NJ 07079, USA. Email: xuxe@shu.edu.
‡ Albers School of Business and Economics, Seattle University, 901 12th Avenue, Seattle, WA 98122-1090. Email: jyau@seattleu.edu.

1. Introduction

Financial markets across the globe are overflowing with common stocks, bonds, and other financial instruments such as futures and options. In terms of market capitalization, the three largest regions are the US, the Euro area, and Japan, representing US$47.6 trillion, US$26.6 trillion, and US$17.3 trillion of the financial assets, respectively (Table 1). As of 2004, equities were apparently the key driver of the growth of global financial assets and the key component in the financial markets, while bonds accounted for 36% of US$122.6 trillion of the world's financial assets, and 40% of the US$47.6 trillion of US financial assets.

In the past two decades, capital flows across countries have increased substantially, particularly those flows to developing countries, leading to the globalization of financial markets. In 2005, the flows of investment across borders hit US$6 trillion, representing about only 4% of the total financial assets.[1] The relatively small amount of

Table 1. Financial Assets in the World, 2004

Countries and Regions	Total Financial Assets (US$ billion)
US	47,612
Euro area	26,567
Japan	17,323
Emerging Asia	9,581
UK	6,710
Australia, New Zealand and Canada	5,046
Other Western Europe	3,620
Latin America	2,554
Hong Kong and Singapore	1,820
Eastern Europe	1,780
Total	**122,613**

Source: McKinsey & Co., *The Wall Street Journal*, January 10, 2007.

---

[1] Source: *The Wall Street Journal*, January 10, 2007.

international flows (although large in absolute dollar terms) compared to the total size of the entire financial system indeed represents a myth in financial theory that requires further research.

Analysis of international investment can take two approaches. The first one is investigating why investors invest across borders from an issuer's (or investor's) perspective. The reasons behind cross-border investment may include seeking higher returns with lower risk, benefits of diversification, and growth opportunities. The analysis of global investment entails different asset allocation and investment strategies along with risk management in the light of increasing price, exchange rate, and interest rate volatilities. Furthermore, we can examine alternative investment opportunities in the global financial market such as real estate, venture capital, hedge funds and managed futures. Some of the issues are discussed and presented in other chapters in the book.

The second approach to analyzing international investment is taking a broader view of the international investment issues and examining the general patterns of portfolio fund flows and their related economic issues related to cross-border investments. We take this approach in this chapter and discuss: 1) the patterns of cross-border capital investment; 2) the costs and benefits of international capital flows; 3) the limits of financial globalization such as the home bias; and 4) the development of new markets and globalization in Section 2. We will present and discuss the trends in foreign portfolio investments in the US in Section 3.

2. International Portfolio Investment Flows

2.1 *Pattern of International Capital Flows*

Table 2, Panel A, shows the cumulative flows of portfolio investments for different countries/regions, while Panel B indicates the annual flows from 1996 to 2004. The figures of Panel A indicate that industrial countries (such as G7, a group of seven industrialized countries) have registered the most flow of funds in the range of US$12 trillion

Table 2. Global Capital Flows
Panel A. Cumulative Flows of Portfolio Investment 1996–2004 (US$ billion)

		1996	1997	1998	1999	2000	2001	2002	2003	2004
G7 Countries	Outflow	4,284.96	4,921.63	6,007.09	7,304.29	7,473.95	7,225.96	7,612.37	10,087.46	12,002.40
	Inflow	5,477.51	6,295.52	7,557.04	8,922.74	9,129.95	9,155.06	9,843.18	12,704.04	15,326.88
Developed Countries/Territories	Outflow	970.09	1,094.24	1,484.04	1,866.58	2,162.63	2,757.29	4,103.39	5,648.40	3,079.69
(Excluding G7 Countries)	Inflow	1,349.32	1,592.83	2,017.80	2,453.25	2,723.09	3,050.80	4,305.15	5,776.38	3,483.35
Developing Countries	Outflow	40.88	58.44	70.64	108.67	119.60	99.22	110.84	152.20	122.52
	Inflow	185.77	254.94	268.07	307.94	333.26	633.45	638.89	756.57	815.02
Asia	Outflow	943.43	914.14	1,070.41	1,260.21	1,507.51	1,597.03	1,768.97	2,219.36	2,603.12
	Inflow	601.94	657.74	709.82	1,283.54	1,168.75	1,091.28	1,021.16	1,380.04	1,747.23
Europe	Outflow	1,780.05	2,149.28	3,040.70	3,821.75	4,153.49	4,656.66	6,294.51	8,631.15	6,658.10
	Inflow	3,424.97	4,003.12	5,204.95	6,025.23	6,396.36	6,590.09	8,403.06	11,266.76	10,110.37

(Continued)

Table 2. (*Continued*)
Panel A. Cumulative Flows of Portfolio Investment 1996–2004 (US$ billion)

		1996	1997	1998	1999	2000	2001	2002	2003	2004
North America	Outflow	1,566.60	1,842.40	2,172.23	2,676.51	2,564.99	2,320.29	2,249.85	3,147.98	3,648.77
	Inflow	2,607.81	3,089.22	3,532.80	3,919.90	4,187.60	4,484.23	4,682.45	5,695.73	6,763.98
Latin America	Outflow	33.04	40.69	45.35	58.49	60.89	44.63	44.56	59.29	71.69
	Inflow	115.60	141.89	138.87	141.35	131.99	377.74	342.39	406.91	468.16
Oceania	Outflow	47.84	48.88	55.13	79.61	87.25	91.44	105.36	150.16	191.95
	Inflow	238.09	223.33	226.17	272.40	267.45	272.91	306.96	444.82	540.51
Africa	Outflow	3.11	12.39	18.87	42.59	46.79	31.79	32.22	45.69	
	Inflow	25.54	29.52	32.31	44.00	38.11	27.34	37.53	48.66	
Total Cumulative Flows	Outflow	4,374.06	5,007.78	6,402.69	7,939.17	8,420.92	8,741.85	10,495.46	14,253.63	13172.90
	Inflow	7,013.95	8,144.82	9,844.92	11,686.41	12,190.26	12,843.59	14,793.55	19,242.93	19627.33

Table 2. (*Continued*)
Panel B. Annual Change in Flows of Portfolio Investment 1997–2004 (US$ billion)

		1997	1998	1999	2000	2001	2002	2003	2004
G7 Countries	Outflow	636.67	1,085.46	1,297.20	169.66	−247.99	386.41	2,475.09	1,914.94
	Inflow	818.01	1,261.52	1,365.70	207.21	25.11	688.12	2,860.86	2,622.84
Developed Countries/Territories (Excluding G7 Countries)	Outflow	124.15	389.80	382.54	296.05	594.66	1,346.10	1,545.01	−2,568.71
	Inflow	243.51	424.97	435.45	269.84	327.71	1,254.35	1,471.23	−2,293.03
Developing Countries	Outflow	17.56	12.20	38.04	10.93	−20.38	11.63	41.36	−29.68
	Inflow	69.17	13.13	39.87	25.32	300.20	5.44	117.68	58.45
Asia	Outflow	−29.28	156.27	189.80	247.30	89.52	171.94	450.39	383.76
	Inflow	55.80	52.08	573.72	−114.79	−77.47	−70.12	358.89	367.18
Europe	Outflow	369.24	891.42	781.05	331.74	503.17	1,637.84	2,336.64	−1,973.05
	Inflow	578.15	1,201.83	820.27	371.14	193.72	1,812.97	2,863.70	−1,156.39
North America	Outflow	275.80	329.83	504.28	−111.52	−244.70	−70.44	898.13	500.79
	Inflow	481.41	443.58	387.10	267.70	296.63	198.22	1,013.28	1,068.25

(*Continued*)

Table 2. (*Continued*)

Panel B. Annual Change in Flows of Portfolio Investment 1997–2004 (US$ billion)

		1997	1998	1999	2000	2001	2002	2003	2004
Latin America	Outflow	7.65	4.66	13.15	2.40	-16.26	-0.07	14.73	12.41
	Inflow	26.29	-3.03	2.48	-9.36	245.75	-35.35	64.52	61.25
Oceania	Outflow	1.04	6.25	24.48	7.64	4.19	13.92	44.80	41.79
	Inflow	-14.76	2.84	46.23	-4.95	5.46	34.05	137.86	95.69
Africa	Outflow	9.28	6.48	23.72	4.20	-15.00	0.43	13.47	
	Inflow	3.98	2.79	11.69	-5.89	-10.77	10.19	11.13	
Total Annual Change in Flows	Outflow	633.72	1,394.91	1,536.48	481.75	320.92	1,753.62	3,758.17	-1,034.30
	Inflow	1,130.87	1,700.10	1,841.49	503.85	653.33	1,949.96	4,449.38	435.98

Notes:

1. Source of data: International Monetary Fund *IFS* CD-ROM Version 1.1.55.

2. G7 Countries include the US, Canada, France, Germany, Japan, Italy, and the UK; Asia includes China, Japan, and 22 other countries; North America includes the US and Canada; Latin America includes Mexico, Brazil, and 14 other countries; Oceania includes Australia and New Zealand and Africa includes Angola and 22 other countries.

outflows and US$15 trillion inflows of capital. Panel B shows that in 2001, the annual capital fund outflows were abruptly and substantially reduced because of the September 11 terrorist attack in the US. One interesting pattern is that only the G7 countries had experienced growth in foreign portfolio flows, whereas other developed countries, including Europe, experienced a decline in the portfolio flows after September 11. Asian countries had growth in both inflows and outflows of foreign investments.

Table 3 presents the statistics of the capital flows in and out of the equity capital markets for various countries and regions. The equity market is an important driving force behind international fund flows that entail more risk. Figures in Table 3, Panel A, indicate the cumulative flow of funds to the equity market, which in general are quite consistent and stable across time and within geographic regions. The G7 countries are the major recipients of foreign equity funds and key investors in other countries' equity. The Asian market is a growing market. Panel B of Table 3 presents the change in annual flows. Similar to the patterns in Table 2, we find a drop in capital flows to the equity markets (such as G7 and Europe) during 2000–2002.

Panel A of Table 4 shows the cumulative capital flows to the bond market, while Panel B shows the annual flows. Again, the G7 countries are the largest recipients of the inflows and outflows. Investors are primarily interested in government bills and bond markets, which are much safer than equity markets. Panel B of Table 4 shows that the effect of global sentiments of the terrorist attack on the bond market was much less than that of the stock market, most likely due to the nature of the government securities.

2.2 *Costs and Benefits of International Capital Flows*

The dismantling of the restrictions on capital flows during the past three decades has led to growth in the globalization of financial markets and international capital flows. It has been suggested that development of a global financial market reduces the cost of capital worldwide and hence enhances the financial and economic growth of the country. At the same time, there are also costs associated with

Table 3. Capital Flows of Equity

Panel A. Cumulative Flows of Equity 1996–2004 (US$ billion)

		1996	1997	1998	1999	2000	2001	2002	2003	2004
G7 Countries	Outflow	1,907.17	2,273.24	2,821.94	3,979.65	3,940.05	3,484.98	3,100.41	4,414.60	5,410.31
	Inflow	1,729.33	2,198.69	2,921.86	4,227.92	4,015.58	3,516.60	2,978.98	4,228.44	5,003.21
Developed Countries (Excluding G7 Countries)	Outflow	420.13	495.28	673.01	951.01	1,098.93	1,202.05	1,416.79	2,063.44	1,277.86
	Inflow	596.59	759.44	1,049.95	1,382.81	1,529.39	1,615.83	2,402.42	3,201.49	1,569.46
Developing Countries	Outflow	4.12	13.90	21.95	50.03	54.73	46.50	50.38	70.84	40.35
	Inflow	49.18	78.83	74.17	90.47	92.04	210.19	208.20	285.83	315.84
Asia	Outflow	155.31	159.47	211.60	288.46	355.23	360.57	350.10	481.85	636.96
	Inflow	325.55	310.03	332.10	889.06	752.38	655.93	598.87	920.07	1,177.63
Europe	Outflow	1,067.46	1,291.84	1,688.53	2,477.74	2,654.79	2,527.83	2,594.48	3,670.42	3,258.83
	Inflow	1,241.22	1,627.27	2,304.37	3,003.84	3,057.78	2,853.37	3,407.87	4,601.98	3,226.02

(*Continued*)

Table 3. (*Continued*)
Panel A.   Cumulative Flows of Equity 1996–2004 (US$ billion)

		1996	1997	1998	1999	2000	2001	2002	2003	2004
North America	Outflow	1,069.67	1,280.41	1,556.10	2,106.98	1,968.54	1,738.81	1,511.11	2,230.22	2,675.16
	Inflow	706.94	988.86	1,292.38	1,659.39	1,701.28	1,621.33	1,386.87	1,891.41	2,160.91
Latin America	Outflow	0.60	1.87	4.79	9.14	8.96	13.05	15.98	25.80	31.88
	Inflow	25.52	35.35	25.29	20.53	12.78	101.77	79.30	120.94	163.77
Oceania	Outflow	35.93	37.84	41.27	61.49	65.74	67.00	72.67	106.24	132.67
	Inflow	61.41	61.35	73.20	101.00	89.48	93.25	92.98	147.84	158.62
Africa	Outflow	2.47	11.03	15.98	38.55	42.50	28.77	28.07	39.89	
	Inflow	14.59	14.26	18.79	27.73	23.77	17.21	24.64	34.54	
Total Cumulative Flows	Outflow	2,331.44	2,782.46	3,518.27	4,982.36	5,095.76	4,736.03	4,572.41	6,554.42	6,735.50
	Inflow	2,375.23	3,037.12	4,046.13	5,701.55	5,637.47	5,342.86	5,590.53	7,716.78	6,886.95

Table 3. (*Continued*)
Panel B. Annual Change in Flows of Equity 1997–2004 (US$ billion)

		1997	1998	1999	2000	2001	2002	2003	2004
G7 Countries	Outflow	366.07	548.70	1,157.71	-39.60	-455.07	-384.57	1,314.19	995.71
	Inflow	469.36	723.17	1,306.06	-212.34	-498.98	-537.62	1,249.46	774.77
Developed Countries (Excluding G7 Countries)	Outflow	75.15	177.73	278.00	147.92	103.12	214.74	646.65	-785.58
	Inflow	162.85	290.51	332.86	146.58	86.44	786.59	799.07	-1,632.03
Developing Countries	Outflow	9.78	8.05	28.08	4.70	-8.23	3.88	20.46	-30.49
	Inflow	29.65	-4.66	16.30	1.57	118.15	-1.99	77.63	30.01
Asia	Outflow	4.16	52.13	76.86	66.77	5.34	-10.47	131.75	155.11
	Inflow	-15.52	22.07	556.96	-136.68	-96.45	-57.06	321.20	257.56
Europe	Outflow	224.38	396.69	789.21	177.05	-126.96	66.65	1,075.94	-411.59
	Inflow	386.05	677.10	699.47	53.94	-204.41	554.50	1,194.11	-1,375.96
North America	Outflow	210.74	275.69	550.88	-138.44	-229.73	-227.70	719.11	444.94
	Inflow	281.92	303.52	367.01	41.89	-79.95	-234.46	504.54	269.50

(*Continued*)

Table 3. (*Continued*)

Panel B. Annual Change in Flows of Equity 1997–2004 (US$ billion)

		1997	1998	1999	2000	2001	2002	2003	2004
Latin America	Outflow	1.27	2.92	4.35	-0.18	4.09	2.93	9.82	6.08
	Inflow	9.83	-10.06	-4.76	-7.75	88.99	-22.47	41.64	42.83
Oceania	Outflow	1.91	3.43	20.22	4.25	1.26	5.67	33.57	26.43
	Inflow	-0.06	11.85	27.80	-11.52	3.77	-0.27	54.86	10.78
Africa	Outflow	8.56	4.95	22.57	3.95	-13.73	-0.70	11.82	
	Inflow	-0.33	4.53	8.94	-3.96	-6.56	7.43	9.90	
Total Annual Change	**Outflow**	**451.02**	**735.81**	**1,464.09**	**113.40**	**-359.73**	**-163.62**	**1,982.01**	**220.97**
(no double counting)	**Inflow**	**661.89**	**1,009.01**	**1,655.42**	**-64.08**	**-294.61**	**247.67**	**2,126.25**	**-795.29**

Notes:

1. Source of data: International Monetary Fund *IFS* CD-ROM Version 1.1.55.
2. G7 Countries include the US, Canada, France, Germany, Japan, Italy, and the UK; Asia includes China, Japan, and 22 other countries; North America includes the US and Canada; Latin America includes Mexico, Brazil, and 14 other countries; Oceania includes Australia and New Zealand and 22 other countries; Africa includes Angola and 22 other countries.

Table 4. Capital Flows of Bonds

Panel A. Cumulative Flows of Bonds 1996–2004 (US$ billion)

		1996	1997	1998	1999	2000	2001	2002	2003	2004
G7 Countries	Outflow	2,377.80	2,648.40	3,185.15	3,324.62	3,533.89	3,740.96	4,511.97	5,672.86	6,592.09
	Inflow	3,748.18	4,096.84	4,635.18	4,694.84	5,114.40	5,638.48	6,864.19	8,475.60	10,323.67
Developed Countries	Outflow	549.98	598.96	811.04	915.57	1,063.69	1,555.21	2,686.62	3,584.97	1,801.85
(Excluding G7 Countries)	Inflow	752.70	833.35	967.84	1,070.45	1,193.71	1,434.98	1,902.76	2,574.93	1,913.89
Developing Countries	Outflow	35.42	44.46	48.63	58.61	64.89	52.04	59.78	79.01	82.11
	Inflow	136.57	176.08	193.87	217.50	241.18	423.25	430.64	470.75	499.17
Asia	Outflow	788.12	754.64	858.78	971.72	1,152.28	1,236.46	1,418.87	1,737.53	1,966.16
	Inflow	276.39	347.71	377.71	394.49	416.36	435.35	422.28	459.96	569.59
Europe	Outflow	1,642.25	1,934.00	2,523.04	2,699.02	2,850.77	3,488.44	5,060.58	6,631.10	5,465.70
	Inflow	2,183.73	2,375.83	2,900.56	3,021.43	3,338.62	3,736.72	4,995.20	6,664.83	6,884.38

(*Continued*)

Table 4. Capital Flows of Bonds
Panel A. Cumulative Flows of Bonds 1996–2004 (US$ billion)

		1996	1997	1998	1999	2000	2001	2002	2003	2004
North America	Outflow	496.94	562.00	616.13	569.52	596.45	581.47	738.75	917.76	973.61
	Inflow	1,900.88	2,100.36	2,240.42	2,260.51	2,486.33	2,862.90	3,295.56	3,804.32	4,603.07
Latin America	Outflow	32.45	38.80	40.58	49.33	51.91	31.57	28.58	33.50	39.81
	Inflow	90.06	106.54	113.57	120.82	119.21	275.97	263.08	285.98	304.37
Oceania	Outflow	11.92	11.04	13.86	18.11	21.51	24.43	32.69	43.93	59.28
	Inflow	176.68	161.98	152.97	171.40	177.97	179.66	213.98	296.97	381.89
Africa	Outflow	0.64	1.35	2.87	4.04	4.31	2.38	3.46	3.44	
	Inflow	10.94	15.25	13.51	16.27	14.31	10.14	12.86	14.13	
Total Cumulative Flows	Outflow	2,972.32	3,301.83	4,055.26	4,311.74	4,677.23	5,364.75	7,282.93	9,367.26	8,504.56
	Inflow	4,638.68	5,107.67	5,798.74	5,984.92	6,552.80	7,500.74	9,202.96	11,526.19	12,743.30

(Continued)

Table 4. (*Continued*)
Panel B. Annual Change in Flows of Bonds 1997–2004 (US$ billion)

		1997	1998	1999	2000	2001	2002	2003	2004
G7 Countries	Outflow	270.60	536.75	139.47	209.27	207.07	771.01	1,160.89	919.23
	Inflow	348.66	538.34	59.66	419.56	524.08	1,225.71	1,611.41	1,848.07
Developed Countries/Territories (Excluding G7 Countries)	Outflow	48.98	212.08	104.53	148.12	491.52	1,131.41	898.35	−1,783.12
	Inflow	80.65	134.49	102.61	123.26	241.27	467.78	672.17	−661.04
Developing Countries	Outflow	9.04	4.17	9.98	6.28	−12.85	7.74	19.23	3.10
	Inflow	39.51	17.79	23.63	23.68	182.07	7.39	40.11	28.42
Asia	Outflow	−33.48	104.14	112.94	180.56	84.18	182.41	318.66	228.63
	Inflow	71.32	30.00	16.78	21.87	18.99	−13.07	37.68	109.63
Europe	Outflow	291.75	589.04	175.98	151.75	637.67	1,572.14	1,570.52	−1,165.40
	Inflow	192.10	524.73	120.87	317.19	398.10	1,258.48	1,669.63	219.55
North America	Outflow	65.06	54.13	−46.61	26.93	−14.98	157.28	179.01	55.85
	Inflow	199.48	140.06	20.09	225.82	376.57	432.66	508.76	798.75

(*Continued*)

Table 4. (*Continued*)
Panel B. Annual Change in Flows of Bonds 1997–2004 (US$ billion)

		1997	1998	1999	2000	2001	2002	2003	2004
Latin America	Outflow	6.35	1.78	8.75	2.58	-20.34	-2.99	4.92	6.31
	Inflow	16.48	7.03	7.25	-1.61	156.76	-12.89	22.90	18.39
Oceania	Outflow	-0.88	2.82	4.25	3.40	2.92	8.26	11.24	15.35
	Inflow	-14.70	-9.01	18.43	6.57	1.69	34.32	82.99	84.92
Africa	Outflow	0.71	1.52	1.17	0.27	-1.93	1.08	-0.02	
	Inflow	4.31	-1.74	2.76	-1.96	-4.17	2.72	1.27	
Total Annual Change	Outflow	329.51	753.43	256.48	365.49	687.52	1,918.18	2,084.33	-859.26
	Inflow	468.99	691.07	186.18	567.88	947.94	1,702.22	2,323.23	1,231.24

Notes:
1. Source of data: International Monetary Fund *IFS* CD-ROM Version 1.1.55.
2. G7 Countries include the US, Canada, France, Germany, Japan, Italy, and the UK; Asia includes China, Japan, and 22 other countries; North America includes the US and Canada; Latin America includes Mexico, Brazil, and 14 other countries; Oceania includes Australia and New Zealand and Africa includes Angola and 22 other countries.

globalization, such as spillover effects from crises. We discuss these benefits and costs in the following sections.

2.2.1 *Economic Growth*

It has been asserted that financial development through liberalization promotes economic growth. However, previous studies find mixed evidence on this assertion. While some studies provide evidence in support of the positive role of financial development on economic growth, others provide little evidence.

Xu (2000) examines the effects of permanent financial development on domestic investment and output in 41 countries. The results indicate that there is strong evidence that financial development is important to growth and that investment is an important channel through which financial development affects economic growth. Rioja and Valev (2004), using data from 74 countries, find that financial development has a strong positive influence on productivity growth and output.

Love (2003) provides evidence showing that financial development impacts economic growth by reducing financing constraints that would otherwise distort the efficient allocation of investment. The magnitude of the changes in the cost of capital in a country with a low level of financial development is twice as large as in a country with an average level of financial development.

Arestis *et al.* (2001) use time series model from five developed countries (France, Germany, Japan, the UK, and the US) to show that banks play a more important role in promoting growth than the stock market. The results imply that the contribution of the stock market to economic growth has been exaggerated. Similarly, Manning (2003) shows that bank finance is of particular importance for growth in non-OECD member countries, but their tests suffer from the identification problem where the effect of financial development is correlated with factors. From a somewhat different perspective, Andersen and Tarp (2003) provide empirical evidence questioning the assertion that financial development leads to economic growth, because increased competition in the financial sector may disturb prudent bank behavior.

The rational interpretation of these mixed results suggest that there may be limits of globalization on growth, which may probably be due to the home bias in global investments (to be discussed below) and the existence of barriers for global investments that include information barriers and government regulations.

2.2.2 *Cost of Capital*

In the past two decades, a pattern of increasing integration of international markets has emerged. Barriers to international investments among developed economies have slowly and steadily diminished. As a result, the global risk factors are expected to be increasingly important for portfolio selection. Recent empirical evidence has shown that global factors, particularly the exchange rate, affect the pricing of securities. In contrast, the evidence on the lowering of the cost of capital from the stock market is less compelling.

Investors who can move capital freely across countries would probably do so in order to diversify their portfolios. That is, they can form a portfolio with lower risk with the same return or same risk with higher return. DeSantis and Gerard (1997) show that a portfolio diversified internationally among ten major developed countries could have the same volatility with a higher return of 2.5%. Adding emerging markets to this portfolio would lead to more gains from diversification.

If some of the portfolio risks can be diversified away, one would expect the cost of the capital of a firm to be lower. An international capital asset pricing model would be appropriate for evaluating the impact of the global factor on the cost of capital. Koedijk and Dijk (2004) use an international capital asset pricing model to examine if the global risk factor indeed lowers the cost of capital in an integrated financial market. They have presented evidence that global risk factors are not vitally important for practical cost of capital calculations, a surprising result which contradicts expectation.

Bekaert and Harvey (1997) argue that the ratio of the dividend to the share price is a good proxy for the cost of capital. They find that the ratio declines as a country liberalizes, but the decline is relatively small (less than 1%). Their results suggest that the impact of globalization on the cost of capital for a country is limited. Again, this may be the result of limited foreign investments in the liberalized financial market of these countries (home bias).

2.2.3 *Increased Financial Linkages*

Financial markets are linked together if capital flows can move freely from one country to another. It is conceivable that the news from one country could significantly affect a market in another country or location. Xu and Fung (2002) investigate the pricing linkages of dually listed American Depository Receipts in the US and China, while Fung *et al.* (2001) show pricing relationships in futures contracts. Both studies demonstrate strong pricing linkages among the same assets traded in different locations. Thus, it seems clear that the risk premium of an asset would be determined globally, not locally, if the financial market is, indeed, fully integrated. Chan *et al.* (1992) show that the risk premiums on the US and Japanese markets are linked together, inferring a strong co-movement between the two markets.

Goldstein and Folkerts-Landau (1994) document an increased correlation for the 10-year yields in the seven largest developed countries and the US 10-year bond yield. Moreover, Ilmanen (1995) provides evidence that there is a strong common factor in interest rate movements across developed countries. These results indicate that there are common forces driving the debt market in individual countries because of the globalization of financial markets.

Increase in correlation of stock returns across countries over time is less obvious, but the contagion effect across market is apparent. Bekaert and Harvey (1997) find that only nine of the 17 emerging markets show higher correlation over time, implying weak evidence of increased correlation over time. However, it is apparent that there is evidence of a contagion effect among financial markets during a financial crisis. Chan-Lau *et al.* (2004) argue that contagion can be understood as the probability of observing large return realizations simultaneously across different financial markets, but contagion effects are not necessarily related to increased correlation in returns across markets. They show that contagion effects differ significantly across markets. Goh *et al.* (2005) report strong contemporaneous co-movements among five ASEAN countries during the 1997 Asian currency crisis but no increase in correlation across markets over time. Beakert *et al.* (2005) provide evidence of contagion in a model allowing for time variation of market integration.

2.3 *Home Bias*

There is ample evidence that investors overweigh domestic stocks in their investment portfolio, suggesting a home bias in global investments. Various reasons have been suggested to explain the home bias by invoking market imperfections such as departures from purchasing power parity, information asymmetries between domestic, higher transaction cost, investment barriers of trading imposed by foreign governments, and over-optimism of domestic investors toward domestic assets (Karolyi and Stulz, 2003; Lewis, 1999).

As assessts in developing countries are primarily controlled by family owners as the large shareholder, there appears to be a close relation between corporate governance and portfolios held by investors, a result that explains the home bias pattern of global investments (Dahlquist *et al.*, 2003; La Porta *et al.*, 2002).

Stulz (2003) suggests that rulers of sovereign states and corporate insiders pursue their own interests at the expense of the outside investors, constituting the "twin agency problems." The resulting ownership concentration in countries limits the inflows of capital into these countries and thus their economic growth, and financial development.

Table 5, Column (a), shows the US holdings of foreign long-term securities. The amount of foreign holdings increased over time from US$870 billion in 1994 to US$3.57 trillion in 2005. At the same time, the foreign holdings of US long-term financial assets also increased dramatically from US$1.24 trillion in 1994 to US$6.26 trillion in 2005, representing 15.8% of the US long-term securities outstanding. The ratios reflecting the US holdings of foreign assets to total US outstanding securities show an increasing trend from 5.5% in 1994 to 9.0% in 2005. If US investors really intend to diversify fully across the global

Table 5. Holdings of Long-Term Securities by US Investors Offshore and by Foreign investors in the US (US$ billion)

Year	US holdings of foreign L/T securities (a)	Foreign holdings of US L/T securities (b)	a/b % (c)	US L/T securities (d)	a/d % outstanding (e)
1994/12	870	1,244	70	15,700	5.5
2002/06	2,129	3,926	54	32,169	6.6
2003/06	2,367	4,503	53	33,443	7.1
2004/06	3,027	5,431	56	37,499	8.1
2005/06	3,574	6,262	57	39,583	9.0

Column (c) is the ratio (%) of US holdings of foreign long-term (L/T) securities, while column (e) is the ratio (%) of US holdings securities to total US long-term securities outstanding.
Source: Computed from the data from the Department of Treasury, www.ustreas. gov/tic.

securities, we expect these ratios to be large. As they are less than 10% of the US total issues of securities, they are relatively small because the size of the US economy is about one-third of the global economy. The statistics in Table 5 suggest that home bias remains pertinent in the US global investments, although the degree of home bias has declined over time in terms of long-term securities.

2.4 *Development of New Markets and Globalization*

One advantage of globalization is the proliferation of new markets that enable investors to invest abroad and hedge the risks associated with investments. The creation of new markets takes several forms. First, the growth of global depository receipts (GDRs) has enabled investors across the globe to invest in foreign securities. At the same time, securities in emerging markets, once restricted to foreig-
become available to global investors through listing
kets. For example, as of December 31, 2006, 451 of
listed on the New York Stock Exchange are by non-l

Second, the development of exchange-traded funds (ETFs) market has become phenomenal. In particular, ETFs have become increasingly important in the US. For example, they now account for more than half of the daily trading volume on the American Stock Exchange (AMEX). As of March 2007, there are 44 international ETFs tracking equity markets from different countries or regions traded on AMEX. It seems that the product trajectory is upward because these instruments offer lower cost and more flexibility to investors who are interested in investing in international financial markets. In brief, investors can participate in both continuous long and short positions, which are available throughout the trading hours of the day.

Third, for securities such as Eurodollar, currency, and government bond futures that have been traded in different parts of the global market, their pricing has been thoroughly examined by researchers and market participants to ensure consistency throughout the world for profit motives. The round-the-clock trading enhances the price discovery function, synchronized pricing of securities, information flow, and efficiency of the global market.

Fourth, trading methods differ across market types, such as auction and market-makers. In addition, electronic trading across markets has been used to ensure rapid information dissemination and price recovery. The electronic trading offers an efficient way of trading worldwide, enabling transparency of the prices as investors can observe these prices quickly.

Fifth, the globalization of venture capital (VC) funds has allowed US investors to invest in creative innovation and entrepreneurship ventures outside the US, including international venture capital hotbeds in Europe, China, Israel, and India (Table 6).

Finally, new products are created to overcome domestic market impediments. For example, the rise of non-delivery forward contracts (NDFs) is a case in point. The NDFs provide investor a way to hedge risks associated with non-convertible currencies whose prices may be misaligned. These products help globalize the different segments of the world market into one market that offers investors opportunities for risk-taking or hedging purposes.

Table 6. Global Venture Capital Hotbeds (2005)

Country	VC Investments (US$ billion)	VC Investing Rounds
US	22.1	2239
Europe	4.3	1020
UK	1.2	307
France	0.8	213
Germany	0.6	106
Sweden	0.3	96
China	1.1	233
Israel	1.1	171
India	1.1	92

Source: Ernst & Young Global Venture Capital Report 2006.

3. Foreign Portfolio Investments in the US

In recent years, securities have replaced bank lending as the primary means for cross-border fund flows (Bertaut and Griever, 2004). When the US needs external financing, the US government and corporations can directly issue securities (debts and stocks) to raise external funds, instead of relying on global bank loans. As a result, the percentage of foreign ownership of US securities has sharply increased as shown in Table 7.

The resulting foreign holdings of US securities reveal several interesting characteristics. First, foreign investors hold more US debts than US equities. Second, the visible foreign holding of short-term US debts is only a recent phenomenon because the debts held by foreign investors are largely long-term. The long-term debts issued are primarily the US Treasurys, US agencies, and corporates. Third, in recent years, foreign investors appear to be more interested in holding corporate bonds, whose amount exceeds that of the US Treasurys since 2002.

Table 8 shows the value of foreign holdings of US securities by countries. The total amount of foreign investments in the US market was about US$6.86 trillion. Most of the foreign funds were invested in the US equity market (US$2.1 trillion). The second category was in the corporate bonds market, which amounted to US$1.73 trillion.

Table 7. Foreign Holdings of US Securities (US$ billion)

Types	1984/12	1989/12	1994/12	2000/3	2002/6	2003/6	2004/6	2005/6
Long-term securities	268	847	1,244	3,558	3,926	4,503	5,431	6,262
Equities	105	275	398	1,709	1,395	1,564	1,930	2,144
Debt	163	475	846	1,849	2,531	2,939	3,501	4,118
US Treasury	118	333	464	884	908	1,116	1,426	1,599
US agency	13	48	107	261	492	586	619	791
Corporate	32	191	276	703	1,130	1,236	1,455	1,729
Short-term debt	n/a	n/a	n/a	n/a	412	475	588	602
US Treasury	n/a	n/a	n/a	n/a	232	269	317	284
US agency	n/a	n/a	n/a	n/a	88	97	124	150
Corporate	n/a	n/a	n/a	n/a	92	110	147	168
Total	n/a	n/a	n/a	n/a	4,338	4,979	6,019	6,864

Note: n/a denotes not available.
Source: Department of Treasury, www.ustreas.gov/tic.

Table 8. Value of Foreign Holdings of US Securities by Countries, June 30, 2005 (US$ billion)

| Country | Total | Equity | Long-Term Debt | | | Short-Term Debt |
			Treasury	Agency	Corporate	
Japan	1,091	178	572	140	103	100
UK	560	260	45	23	215	16
China, PR	527	3	277	172	36	40
Luxembourg	460	151	30	33	208	37
Cayman Islands	430	151	30	42	180	26
Belgium	335	18	13	51	248	5
Canada	308	221	14	4	55	13
Netherlands	262	161	17	18	58	8
Switzerland	238	129	29	11	55	15
Bermuda	202	59	24	28	70	20
Country unknown	196	2	*	*	193	1
Rest of world	2,254	811	546	266	310	322
Total	**6,864**	**2,144**	**1,599**	**791**	**1,729**	**602**

Note: *denotes amount less than $500,000.
Source: Department of Treasury, www.ustreas.gov/tic.

The third category was the US Treasury and Agency debts, which totaled about US$1.6 trillion. Japan and China were the two largest investors in the US Treasury and Agency debt markets, while the UK and Japan were the two largest countries investing in the US equity market.

In light of the heavy investment of foreign money in the corporate equity and debt market, it is interesting to see which industries have attracted most foreign investors. Table 9 shows the top ten foreign holdings of US securities by individual countries in 2005. The top five popular industries ranked by foreign investors with the amount of investment in parentheses are: Pharmaceuticals (US$133.2 billion), Thrifts and Mortgage Finance (US$130.9 billion), Media (US$120.0 billion), Oil and Gas (US$110.6 billion), and Insurance (US$107.1 billion).

Pharmaceuticals and Oil and Gas were also two popular industries for foreign investors in 2005, while the corporate debt instruments were in the Thrifts and Mortgage Finance (US$117.7 billion) and

Table 9. Top 10 Foreign Holdings of US Securities by Industry, June 20, 2005 (US$ billion)

Industry	Total	Equity	ST Debt	LT Debt
Pharmaceuticals	133.2	122.1	0.0	11.1
Thrifts and mortgage Finance	130.9	13.0	0.2	117.7
Media	120.0	84.4	0.0	35.5
Oil and Gas	110.6	107.2	0.3	3.1
Insurance	107.1	81.8	0.0	25.3
Metals and Mining	78.8	21.6	0.7	56.6
Software	73.4	72.0	0.0	1.5
Specialty Retail	58.7	44.9	0.6	13.3
Paper and Forest Products	57.3	13.8	0.0	43.5
Personal Products	37.1	31.8	0.4	4.9
All foreign holdings	6,864.3	2,143.9	602.0	4,118.4

Source: Department of Treasury, www.ustreas.gov/tic.

Metals and Mining (US$56.6 billion), reflecting the attractiveness of steady cash flows from these industries to bondholders.

4. Conclusions

This chapter discusses the growth of the world financial markets with common stocks, bonds, and other new financial instruments such as GDRs, ETFs, and derivatives. In terms of market capitalization, the three largest regions are the US, the Euro area, and Japan. We document patterns of international capital flows and discuss various issues related to capital flows. That is, how capital flows affect economic growth, the cost of capital, and increased linkages among different markets around the world. However, home bias remains an issue that is not easily explained in light of globalization.

We also discuss patterns of foreign portfolio investments in the US, and vehicles of investment in terms of: 1) maturity — short-term versus long-term investments; and 2) asset class — equities versus debt instruments. Finally, we discuss which US industries have attracted the interest of foreign investors. We find that the most popular industries for foreign investors have been Thrifts and Mortgage Finance,

Pharmaceutics, Metals and Mining, Paper and Forest Products, and Media and Insurance.

Although we have observed an increasing growth of capital flows in the past two decades, there have been renewed barriers established restricting foreign direct investments in recent years in different countries from Canada to China, because of the fear of intense competition and national security issues (*The Wall Street Journal*, July 6, 2007). The extent of the adverse effects rising from these restrictions of foreign investments on the overall capital flows across borders merits investigation. In addition, the ebbs and flows of market impediments related to capital flows across countries represent an interesting phenomenon that is worth studying in future research.

References

Andersen, T. B. and F. Tarp, 2003, Financial liberalization, financial development, and economic growth in LDCs, *Journal of International Development*, 15, 189–209.

Arestis, P., P. O. Demetriades, and K. B. Kuintel, 2001, Financial development and economic growth: The role of the stock market, *Journal of Money, Credit, and Banking*, 33(1), 16–41.

Bekaert, G. and C. R. Harvey, 1997, Emerging equity market volatility, *Journal of Financial Economics*, 43, 29–77.

Bekaert, G., C. R. Harvey, and A. Ng, 2005, Market Integration and contagion, *Journal of Business*, 78(1), 39–69.

Bertaut, C. C. and W. L. Griever, 2004, Recent developments in cross-border investments in securities, *Federal Reserve Bulletin*, Winter, 19–31.

Chan, K. C., G. A. Karolyi, and R. M. Stulz, 1992, Global financial markets and the risk premium on US equity, *Journal of Financial Economics*, 32, 137–168.

Chan-Lau, J. A., D. J. Mathieson, and J. Y. Yao, 2004, Extreme contagion in equity markets, *IMF Staff Paper*, 51(2), 386–408.

Dahlquist, M., L. Pinkowitz, R. M. Stulz, and R. Williamson, 2003, Corporate governance and the home bias, *Journal of Financial and Quantitative Analysis*, 38(1), 87–110.

DeSantis, G. and B. Gerard, 1997, International asset pricing and portfolio diversification with time-varying risk, *Journal of Finance*, 52, 1991–1913.

Fung, H. G., W. K. Leung, and X. Xu, 2001, The information role of US futures trading in a global financial market, *Journal of Futures Market*, 21, 1090–2001.

Goh, K. L., Y. C. Wong, and K. L. Kok, 2005, Financial crisis and intertemporal linkages across the ASEAN-5 stock markets, *Review of Quantitative Finance and Accounting*, 24, 359–377.

Goldstein, M. and D. Folkerts-Landau, 1994, International capital markets: Development, prospects, and policy issues, *International Monetary Fund*, Washington, D.C.

Ilmanen, A. 1995, Time-varying expected returns in international bond markets, *Journal of Finance*, 50, 481–506.

Karolyn, A. and R. M. Stulz, 1997, Are financial assets priced locally or globally? In *Handbook of the Economics of Finance*, G. Constantinides, M. Harris, and R. Stulz (eds.), Amsterdam, The Netherlands: North-Holland, 2003.

Koedijik, K. G. and M. A. Van Dijk, 2004, Global risk factors and the cost of capital, *Financial Analysts Journal*, 60(2), 32–38.

La Porta, R., F. Lopex-de-Silanes, A. Shleifer, and R. Vishny, 2002, Investor protection and corporate valuation, *Journal of Finance*, 57, 1147–1170.

Lewis, K. K., 1999, Trying to explain home bias in equities and consumption, *Journal of Economic Literature*, 37, 571–608.

Love, I., 2003, Financial development and financing constraints: International evidence from the structural investment model, *Review of Financial Studies*, 16(3), 765–791.

Manning, M. J., 2003, Finance causes growth: Can we be so sure? *Contribution to Macroeconomics*, 3(1), 1–22.

Rioja, F. and N. Valev, 2004, Finance and the sources of growth at various stages of economic development, *Economic Enquiry*, 42(1), 127–140.

Stulz, R. M., 2003, The limits of financial globalization, *Journal of Finance*, 60(4), 1595–1638.

Xu, X. and H. G. Fung, 2002, Information flows across markets: Evidence from Chinese stocks dually listed in Hong Kong and New York, *Financial Review*, 37, 563–588.

Xu, Z. 2000, Financial development, investment, and economic growth, *Economic Inquiry*, 38(2), 331–34.

Chapter 2

Socially Responsible Investing: Growth and Development in International Financial Markets

Sheryl A. Law* and Jot Yau[†]

"Socially responsible investments" (SRI) is a broad term for investments that meet certain environmental, social, and corporate governance (ESG) benchmarks. Portfolios based on SRI either screen out companies with poor performance in these three areas, or actively seek out firms that meet pre-established thresholds. Investors have embraced socially responsible investing as a way to meet personal or institutional values, fulfill fiduciary responsibilities, and seek profitable and sustainable investments over the long-term horizon. Several factors such as the business case for ESG, engagement of institutional investors, and regulations have proven to be favorable for SRIs and its upward momentum in the near future.

Keywords: Ethical investing; green investing; principles for responsible investment (PRI).

1. Introduction

As the world becomes more globalized, people are becoming aware that their actions at home affect not only their own communities but

* Peregreen Group, 3414-161st Court SE, Bellevue, WA 98008, USA. E-mail: sheryllaw@ peregreen.com.
† Albers School of Business and Economics, Seattle University, 901 12th Ave, Seattle, WA 98122, USA. E-mail: jyau@seattleu.edu.

also those around the world. In the past, stakeholders such as activists, non-governmental organizations (NGOs) and consumers have voiced their opinions on environmental issues, boycotted unhealthy and dangerous products, and campaigned for human rights. However, the increasingly inter-related world makes it almost impossible to separate our actions from the undesirable effects and ramifications they have on the environment and social development. Thus, it is not surprising that investors are concerned about their investment choices and are becoming more active in making decisions that balance positive financial returns while minimizing environmental and social damages.

Investors who want their portfolios to have positive social and environmental impact as well as profit can incorporate social, environmental, and ethical considerations (SEE) in their investments. Socially responsible investing (SRI) is an umbrella term investors have used to refer to investments and/or investment decisions that account for some aspects of either screening out or including investment options that adhere to a set framework of SEE or environmental, social, and corporate governance issues (ESG). Investors who are concerned about the moral implications of their portfolio, the investment returns resulting from these decisions, and are acting in the best interest of beneficiaries (in the case of fiduciaries), have turned to SRI as a practical way to embrace these considerations. Despite the increasing pressures to consider ESG or SEE in the investment process, there is limited information available as to how analysts and fund managers can practically and quantitatively incorporate these criteria into the valuation of equities. Developing an institutional framework to address ESG and SEE criteria is left to the discretion of individual fund managers.

The appeal of SRI has reached a high level of expectation as evidenced by the active involvement of institutional investors. In step with corporate leaders, institutional investors have instituted some ESG metrics as a means of documenting and monitoring non-financial data to achieve risk reduction, sustainability and subsequently, long-term financial returns. Public pension funds in various countries have integrated SRI initiatives, expectations, and criteria (UNEP FI

AMWG, 2007). Government agencies that manage funds, securities regulators, and retail investors are all increasingly gravitating towards scrutiny of non-financial data and evaluating the adequacy of investment research and analysis that go into investment decisions. Investment in a firm with a poor environmental record or less-than-reputable labor practice represents a big risk in the portfolio. Therefore, whether SRI is an ethical decision or an act of prudence, investors and fiduciaries should give serious consideration to it in their decision processes. SRI is becoming imminently important to the financial industry.

Previous studies have examined the two-sided argument over the financial trade-offs of SRIs. A review of prior work (Hamilton *et al.*, 1993; Statman, 2000; Bello, 2005; Hudson, 2006; Renneboog *et al.*, 2006) indicates that the financial performance of funds that used SRI strategies was comparable to those of traditional portfolios in most studies. A few studies (e.g., Rudd, 1981; Grossman and Sharpe, 1986), however, show that SRI may have been disadvantaged because profitable options are screened out. In addition, the discussion on whether or not fund managers using SRI strategies are meeting their fiduciary duties and acting in the best interest of the beneficiaries seems to be prevalent in recent literature. Kinder (2005) has noted that the revised SEC standard will require fiduciaries to factor into their judgments social and corporate responsibility issues. Despite the absence of definitive financial benefits or resolution of fiduciary duties, SRI has transcended from niche concept to mainstream acceptance practised by large pension and mutual fund managers.

In this chapter, we focus on the how institutional investors incorporate ESG issues into their SRI investment decision-making process. In Section 2, we discuss SRI concepts and rationales for SRI. In Section 3, we explain the common screening strategies used in various SRI investments and indices. In Section 4, we discuss the development and growth of SRI in the international financial markets. In Section 5, we describe the favorable factors that fuel the growth of SRI. In the final section, we conclude with suggestions for future research.

2. What is SRI?

Socially responsible investing has been broadly identified as investment decisions based on environmental and social standards. For instance, the Social Investment Forum (SIF)[1] defines SRI as "...investing in companies that meet certain baseline standards of social and environmental responsibility; actively engaging those companies to become better, more responsible corporate citizens; and dedicating a portion of assets to community economic development." This definition attempts to be all-encompassing without specifically alluding to "ethical investing." However, some SRIs are based on ethical standards that were originally derived from religious institutional beliefs and/or personal core values and morals. SRI criteria are more objective and standardized than ethical standards, which are harder to define. Thus, "SRI" tends to be a more popular term that may sometimes embrace "ethical investing."[2]

SRI strategies are not a new phenomenon. The concept behind the strategy dates as far back as the early 20th century. In the 1920s, the Methodist Church in the UK began screening out the "sin" stocks, such as tobacco, alcohol and gambling, from their portfolio (White, 2005). Investments in these industries did not adhere to their general belief systems. By the 1940s, labor unions and some government organizations began excluding firms charged with unfair labor practices or firms without proper union worker representation (Shank *et al.*, 2005). Moving forward another 20 years, European countries adopted SRIs, and the United States was not far behind in the 1960s when unions began voicing their concerns about the decisions made for their pension funds (White, 2005). In the 1970s, investors began excluding the stocks of any firm that had ties to the Vietnam War. This deliberate resolution gave momentum to divestment activities in the 1980s in companies that had even the most ephemeral ties with South Africa during the apartheid movement (Hussein and Omran, 2005). A Ralph Nader-sponsored "Campaign GM" was one of the first to

---

[1] Social Investment Forum is an online clearinghouse of SRI information (www.socialinvest.org).
[2] For example, Beal *et al.* (2005) use the term "socially responsible investment (SRI)" and "ethical investment" interchangeably.

convince churches, university endowments and pension funds to become active in issues such as corporate governance, pollution control, and automobile safety (Lamb *et al.*, 1995).

Desmadryl (2007) presented a broader definition of SRI to the United Nations Environment Program Finance Initiative (UNEP FI). "SRI" is "sustainable and responsible investing," defined as "an investment strategy that takes into account a company's performance in the three pillars of sustainable development, in addition to its financial performance, when selecting and managing investment portfolios."[3] This definition is focused on the concept of "sustainable development," a term used to describe economic viability in the long-term horizon that "enables present generations to satisfy their needs without threatening the ability of future generations to satisfy theirs," a concept originally described in *Our Common Future*[4] in 1987.

Both SIF and Desmadryl's definitions of SRI describe the concept of using a framework that links financial returns to good environmental practices and respecting the dignity of fellow humans.

Sometimes, SRI refers to portfolios resulting from a deliberate inclusion or exclusion of specific investments. "Green investing" usually refers to the exclusion of firms with poor operations (e.g., strip mining), or products (e.g., hazardous chemicals) that lead to environmental pollution. "White investing" subscribes to the concept of making investment choices based on religious grounds, such as excluding companies that produce weapons, tobacco, and alcohol (the "sin" stocks). Additional white screens can exclude the entertainment industry (e.g., casinos and pornography), and other adherences to specific religious rules. Finally, "red investing" defines the strategies that consider labor and human rights in the decision. Red-screened investments scrutinize the working conditions and employee treatment in both the actual firm in question and its supply chain. Companies that turn a blind eye to deplorable work environments or child labor in other countries are omitted from the portfolio. More screening strategies will be discussed in Section 3.

---

[3] The three "pillars" are people, planet, and profit.
[4] Also popularly known as *The Brundtland Report to the United Nations* (1987).

With so many definitions and nuanced terms used for socially responsible investing, we use "SRI" to refer to the collection of investments resulting from a decision-making process that has taken into account ESG and/or SEE criteria in the deliberation.

2.1 *Why SRI?*

In Section 1, we suggest that individuals engage in SRI because of their personal values, morals and beliefs. We allude that since individuals are concerned about SRI, financial advisors, money and pension managers should consider SRI seriously because they have the fiduciary duty to act in the best interest of their beneficiaries. Due to the sheer size of their assets under management (AUM) and large bearing on capital markets, institutional investors should be appropriately concerned and consider SRI. Mutual funds and pension funds hold such a large market share of equities, that ignoring the impact of their own investment decisions (such as externalizing SEE costs) on the economy can subsequently affect the values of their own portfolios (Sethi, 2005; Hawley and Williams, 2000).

At the institutional level, there are three main reasons to consider SRIs: 1) client mandates; 2) voting of proxies; and 3) long-term investing.

2.1.1 *Client Mandates: Financial and Non-Financial*

Many investors are motivated by non-financial reasons in their investments. They are looking for a "feel-good satisfaction" that they are doing the "right thing." Researchers have discovered that people who participate in certain activities or events will experience pleasure when they maximize their "experience utility" or "net affective experience" (Beal *et al.*, 2005). These activities can just as well include investing decisions as much as participating in their favorite hobbies. Results of a survey indicated that only 46.6% of equity investors ranked expected corporate earnings as significant factors in choosing stocks, and surprisingly, emotional and non-rational decision drivers such as "feelings for firm's products and services" ranked third in the list of variables (Beal *et al.*, 2005).

In our globalized world where our actions affect distant communities, some investors want to make a difference and incite global change through their investments. People in this group are willing to pay a premium on their SRI investments, just as they would for fair trade products or organic produce. They believe that managers of large funds can use shareholder advocacy to pressure companies to change their business strategies to create a better world.

With increasing deregulation of industries, increasing government transfers of vital services to the private sector, and decreasing of barriers to international trade, some investors believe that corporations are the greatest force for social and environmental change (Lydenberg, 2005). Global issues such as climate change and water shortages affect everyone, and some shareholders believe that they should have some influence with companies with power and money to make these changes.

Still other investors have embraced a new definition of a firm's "wealth creation", considered to be different from "profit maximization." These new definitions of wealth creation include items such as increased productivity, product innovation, and creating less impact on the environment (Lydenberg, 2005). Investors want to see public companies increase their value with this idea of corporate wealth.

However, traditional definitions of wealth are still at the core of most client mandates and SRI is considered purely for positive financial returns. Although the evidence is inconclusive on whether SRIs outperform traditional investments and indices, some studies show SRIs are at least competitive with traditional market returns. For example, the returns of Australian SRI funds were not found to be significantly different from that of normal market returns (Bauer *et al.*, 2004). A comparison of SRI funds to "vice" funds (those that included tobacco, gambling, entertainment, weapons, and alcohol) found no statistically significant difference in excess returns over a 3-year period, but found better returns over a 5- and 10-year period (Shank *et al.*, 2005). Statman (2000) found that SRI mutual funds underperformed in comparison to the S&P 500, but performed just as well as conventional mutual funds for the period May 1990–September 1998. In addition, he found that the Domini Social Index (an index of stocks of socially responsible companies) also performed comparably well to the S&P 500 Index. Orlitzky *et al.* (2003) found a slight positive correlation (R^2 of 0.36) between corporate social performance and financial performance across several studies and industries over 30 years. They concluded that there is no tradeoff between social performance and financial performance. A study found that Islamic indices provided a positive return over a bull market but seemed to underperform over a bear market (Hussein and Omran, 2005). To these investors, SRI is yet another strategy to increase financial return and minimize risk.

In summary, there are several reasons why individual investors are requesting SRI strategies, and it is the fund managers who are obliged to act on those requests on behalf of their beneficiaries.

2.1.2 *Voting of Proxies*

Given the various reasons for SRI in client mandates, one reason that fund managers are embracing SRI is the voting of proxies. In the US, the Securities Exchange Commission (SEC) requires fund managers to publish their proxy voting guidelines and their voting records of all resolutions. This disclosure requirement means that managers are obligated to vote their clients' proxies in accordance with their investment objectives. Institutional investors can achieve their requirements for transparency by using SRI as a framework (Kinder, 2005). As investors take on more active roles, they demand fund managers to disclose their positions on ESG issues and will quite often question their decisions (Lydenberg, 2005). Smith (2005) suggests fund managers use SRI to fulfill their fiduciary responsibilities and "thoughtfully vote the proxies they oversee."

2.1.3 *Long-Term Investment Horizons*

Inherent in most institutional investments, especially pension funds, is the long-term investment horizon. Investors are interested in companies that promote sustainability by proactively working on ESG factors. Investors seek long-term success of companies and not those that overlook long-term risk because of short-term goals (Sethi, 2005). They equate these sustainable companies as being financially viable in the future by having a long-term view (Lydenberg, 2005). Firms with internal sustainability directives and long-term business strategies are considered valuable, and are favored by investment analysts because of their good corporate management.

In summary, institutional investors can accomplish fiduciary requirements, acknowledge their client mandates through proxy voting, and fulfill the financial need to invest for the long-run horizon by investing in SRI vehicles.

3. SRI Screening Strategies and Indices

There are numerous ways SRI portfolios can be created. In this section we describe screening strategies commonly used in SRI investments and indices and summarize the practices from different countries in Table 1.

3.1 *Screening Strategies*

SRI investing strategies can range widely amongst financial vehicles, investors and geographic regions. In general, the commonly employed strategies are categorized into two groups — exclusionary (negative screening) and inclusive (positive screening). Historically, SRI leaders in the US and UK have predominately used negative screens. However, recent advances in positive screening have included methods such as the best-in-class approach. Both screening strategies require the fund manager to decide on a subjective grouping of preferences for their investors (Farmen and van der Wijst, 2005).

3.1.1 *Exclusionary Screens*

Portfolios that use exclusionary screens are those that omit companies that fall into specific groups. Strategies that omit an entire sector (such as the tobacco industry) is often referred to as "simple screens" or "simple exclusions." Religious screens exclude all the "sin" products such as alcohol, tobacco, gambling, pornography, and weapons. Two of the most prominently used religious screens are based on Catholic and Islamic beliefs. In 1986, the US Conference of Catholic Bishops issued "Economic Justice for All" that incorporated Catholic teachings with investing theory (Kurtz and diBartolomeo, 2005) and excluded firms involved with traditional sin products, as well as gay rights for employees and abortion. Islamic funds do not allow the receipt and payment of interests so they are usually equity-based and omit fixed income vehicles. In addition, they also avoid firms associated with the sin products and pork, hotel and leisure industries, conventional financial services and firms with a debt-to-equity ratio greater than 33% (Hussein and Omran, 2005).

Exclusionary screening based on environmental issues is also a popular strategy. Companies with poor environmental management practices are omitted from the portfolio. Factors that are scrutinized can include production of hazardous waste (e.g., nuclear energy), operations with negative impact on the environment (e.g., natural resource extraction), non-renewable energy (e.g., oil and gas), and greenhouse gas emissions (e.g., automobile and utilities). Excluding these types of companies will prevent additional portfolio risk if these companies are held accountable for their actions through litigation and regulatory compliance. A survey by the UK Environmental Agency found that 51 out of 60 companies had a positive correlation between its environmental performance and their financial returns (Smith, 2005).

Social factors used in exclusionary screens fall into two categories — labor and human rights. SRI fund managers will use labor criteria such as supply chain monitoring, codes of conduct, use of child labor, sweatshop conditions, employment diversity, women and minority rights, and fair wages. Human rights criteria include affiliations to warring countries, treatment of workers, and access to health care and education. While human rights screens are common among SRIs, they have also been used in conventional investment decisions.[5]

---

[5] Examples of traditional investment decisions that have applied human rights screens include the divestments in companies and financial institutions that do business in countries with human rights violations, such as South Africa during the apartheid movement, Myanmar during military regime repression, and most recently, Sudan with the crisis in the Darfur region.

Another negative screening approach is the norm-based method. This approach screens against firms that do not comply with certain international standards, such as those implemented by the United Nations or the Organisation for Economic Co-Operation and Development (OECD). Popular norms-based standards include the Equator Principles or the Global Compact (discussed in Section 5).

3.1.2 *Inclusive Screens*

In general, inclusive screens are methods in which investment decisions are based on choosing companies that will positively affect the financial returns of a portfolio. While the use of negative screening is an easier and a more basic approach because companies are simply excluded, inclusive screens are more complex. Fund managers using a positive screen need a method framework to justify those companies are to be included in the portfolio. Fund managers using positive screens will seek companies with good corporate social responsibility (CSR) practices, those that give back to the community, have demonstrated good ESG practices, promote employee diversity, have good labor relations, and produce products with quality and safety in mind. They believe that firms with best practices will outperform industry competitors in the long run and that it is a decision inherent to the overall risk-based investment strategy.

One approach fund managers use to provide clarity in applying criteria to a positive screen is the "best-in-class" method (Eurosif, 2004). The fund manager first rates companies from a universe of equities (such as a large-cap index) on ESG issues. Then, depending on the agreed upon threshold, the top percentage of performers based on the ESG ratings will be retained. The third and final step is to apply a traditional financial analysis to these companies and balance the portfolio by adjusting sector weightings so that they reflect the original index weightings.

Another approach in inclusive screening is the use of engagement. Engagement is essentially the use of an investor's shareholder rights to influence the operations and business strategies of a firm. Institutional investors can leverage ESG issues by virtue of its large portion of holdings (and votes) in the equity market (Smith, 2005). Many fund managers already focus on corporate governance in traditional investing strategies, but are increasingly adding SRI dimensions. Fund managers have many engagement options open to them, such as questioning company management, writing to other shareholders to express concerns, creating a dialogue with the company in question, proposing shareholder resolutions, exercising voting rights, calling on extraordinary general meetings, and possibly even issuing press briefings. Many companies would welcome engagement practices over divestment.

Similar to engagement practices, fund managers can use opportunities to vote on ESG issues. In the past, shareholders, including institutional investors, have voted along with management. However, shareholder activism has become increasingly apparent in recent years and remains an effective way to communicate to firms about their ESG-related policies and activities.

Other strategies that are used, mainly in European Union (EU) countries, include pioneer screening or thematic investments. These two strategies include companies whose operations are based primarily on ESG issues, such as clean technology, renewable energy, or drinking water technology.

Table 1 summarizes the differences in screening strategies as practiced in different selected countries and geographical regions. There are several noteworthy patterns. First, as discussed above, negative screens appear to be the predominant method used in most countries.[6] In cases where both types of screens are prevalent (France, Germany, Italy, the Netherlands, the UK and Canada), negative screens are the predominant approach. This pattern is consistent with the evidence that less than 1% of EU pension assets use positive screens (White, 2005).

Second, the best-in-class approach was the most popular form of inclusion screening. Although the US SRI AUM is the largest in the world, they come second in terms of using inclusive screening

---

[6] In 2005, positive screened funds accounted for €64 billion, combination positive screened and ethical exclusions accounted for €32 billion, and ethical exclusions accounted for €73 billion for European countries (Eurosif, 2006).

Table 1. Screening Strategies in Different Regions and Countries

Region	Country	Screening Approach#		Major Criteria Applied#***
		Positive/ Inclusive*	Negative/ Exclusionary**	
Europe				
	Austria		6	c
	Belgium	1		
	France	1, 2	6	**a1**, c
	Germany	1, 2, 3, 5	6	c
	Italy	1, 3	6	
	Netherlands	1, 3	6	
	Spain		6	
	Switzerland	1		a, b, c
	United Kingdom	**1, 2, 3**	6	
North America				
	United States	2,3	6	a1, b, e1, **e2, e3**, e4
	Canada	3, 4	6	**a2, b, e2, e3, e4**
Asia and Pacific Rim				
	Japan		6	**a2, b**
	Australia		6	**a2, b, e2, e3, f**

Notes:

The predominant screen approach used and major criteria applied in each country are bolded.

* Positive Screening Approaches: 1) Best-in-class; 2) SEE Integration; 3) Engagement; 4) Proxy voting; 5) Pioneer/thematic screening

**Negative Screening Approaches: 6) Simple

***Criteria: a) social (human + labor); a1) Labor; a2) Human rights; b) environmental; c) ethical; d) religious; e1) alcohol; e2) tobacco; e3) gambling; e4) non-weaponry; f) sustainable development

Source: Ali (2006), Baue (2004a, 2004b), Carpenter (2004), Desmadryl (2007), EIA (2007), Eurosif (2006), SIO (2007), White (2005), Whitten (2004), Stewart (2006).

strategies to EU countries. Many American institutional investors use engagement practices, such as shareholder advocacy to communicate ESG issues. Engagement and integration strategies are also used widely in the EU because they are compatible with institutional investors' perspectives of their fiduciary duty. Most notable are investors in the

UK that frequently integrate ESG issues with their traditional financial analysis.

Third, almost half of the countries surveyed have used both types of screens. However, more European countries are adopting positive screens as their major method in contrast to their North American or Asian counterparts.

Fourth, among the major criteria used in the negative screens, human rights, environment, and tobacco are the most prevalent factors used in these surveyed countries.

Combinations of negative and positive screening strategies may provide a practical way to integrate ESG issues in SRI portfolios, minimize risks, and increase financial returns. Portfolios based on the FTSE4Good and DJSI indices (discussed below) are examples of portfolios using mixed screening strategies. Renneboog *et al.* (2006) found that SRI mutual funds employing a higher number of screens to model their investment universe received larger money-inflows and performed better in the future than focused funds.

3.2 *SRI Indices*

The proliferation of various SRI indices in recent years is a *prima facie* evidence of the surging demand for SRI investments. These indices represent the performance of the SRI investments. Table 2 presents the performance of a sample of SRI indices. One of the first indices that are specific to ESG, sustainability, and other SRI factors are the Dow Jones Sustainability Indexes (DJSI) launched in 1999. The DJSI family includes the Dow Jones Sustainability World Index, North American Index, United States Index, STOXX® Sustainability Index, EURO STOXX® Sustainability Index, STOXX® Sustainability 40 Index, and EURO STOXX® Sustainability 40 Index. The DJSI was a response to the growing rise of corporate sustainability and the need for a benchmark that investors can use for analysis in portfolio management. All DJSI comprised the leading companies based on ESG criteria, such as codes of conduct, corporate governance, eco-efficiency, philanthropy, and human capital development. Closely related to DJSI is the Dow Jones Islamic Market Index that seeks to provide a benchmark that

Table 2. Performance of Selected SRI Indices (In Percentages; As of July 2007)

Index	Inception Date	Total Assets	Return Since Inception	Standard Deviation	1-Year Return	3-Year Return*	5-Year Return*
KLD Broad Market Social Index (BMSI),	2001	US$10.7 trillion	2.98	15.18	15.29	11.44	12.25
Domini 400 Social Index (DS400)	1990	US$6.6 trillion	11.82	4.69	15.59	9.51	10.65
KLD Global Climate 100 Index	2005	US$2.5 trillion	22.03	11.59	24.8	NA	NA
KLD CV400	1998	US$6.4 trillion	4.35	15.74	15.67	9.55	10.7
DJSI EURO STOXX® Sustainability Index	2001	€2.1 trillion	52.42	19.98[a]	23.72	26.05	16.73
Dow Jones Islamic Market World Index	NA	NA	168.42	NA	19.6[b]	18.28[b]	17.67[b]
DJSI STOXX® Sustainability Index	2001	€4.7 trillion	39.51	15.16[a]	17.12	22.65	15.48

Notes:
[a] Since inception.
[b] As of August 2007.
* Annualized.
Sources: www.kld.com; www.sustainability-indexes.com; www.djindexes.com.

complies with Shariah, or Islamic law. The key attribute of these indices is the exclusion of "sin" stocks as well as companies involved in pork-related products and financial services.

The FTSE Group has created three types of indices that can be used for SRI analysis and research. The FTSE Corporate Governance Index Series tracks corporate performances such as compensation systems, stock ownership, equity structure, Board independence and the audit process. The FTSE4Good Index, launched in 2001, was created specifically for SRI. It uses criteria such as corporate responsibility, SEE issues, and excludes the traditional "sin" stocks. Eligible companies that are included in this index must meet five criteria: 1) work towards environmental sustainability; 2) develop positive relationships with stakeholders; 3) uphold universal human rights; 4) ensure good labor standard within the supply chain; and 5) counter bribery. The FTSE4Good Environmental Leaders Europe 40 Index was created specifically to track the top 40 European companies with leading, best environmental practices. In the light of the growing concerns of climate change, the FTSE indices have recently included five new climate change criteria based on a company's policy to address climate change impacts, management of the impact, disclosure of greenhouse gas emissions, performance measures for assessing their response actions, and the scope in which they reduce their climate change impacts.

KLD Research and Analytics, a focused social research company for institutional investors, created a family of indices to address SEE factors in 1990. Among the indices are the Domini 400 Social Index (DS400), KLD Broad Market Social Index (BMSI), and KLD Catholic Values 400 Index (CV400).[7] The DS400 is based on the S&P 500 index (comprising mainly US equities), excludes the "sin" stocks, and includes companies with positive ESG records based mainly on community relations, diversity, employee relations, human

---

[7] Other indices in the KLD family include the KLD Dividend Achievers Social Index; KLD Global Climate 100 Index, KLD Large Cap Social Index, KLD Large Cap Sudan Free Social Index, and the KLD Select Social Index.

rights, and product quality and safety. The BMSI is based on the Russell 3000 Index (which represents 98% of the US capitalization in equities), screens out companies involved in the "sin" industries and chooses the top 65–75% performers based on ESG criteria. The CV400, which represents the large-cap US equities segment, meets the eligibility requirements of the United States Conference of Catholic Bishops Socially Responsible Investment Guidelines.[8] Specifically, the index does not include companies that produce tobacco, anti-personnel landmines, firms that derive more than 5% of their revenue from weapons and companies involved with nuclear power generation (although companies with notable involvement in alternative energy are given consideration). It also excludes companies that are counter to the Catholic Church's views on abortion, embryonic stem cell/fetal tissue research, human cloning, and contraception. It seeks to include companies that are instrumental in promoting human dignity such as health care and pharmaceuticals and opportunities for women and minorities, and exclude companies with a history of discrimination. It includes firms that pursue economic justice without sweatshop manufacturing, predatory lending, and poor labor conditions. In addition, it includes companies that provide affordable housing, protect the common environment, promote environmentally beneficial technologies, reduce greenhouse gas emissions, and develop alternative energies.[9]

In addition, there are numerous investment and finance research firms which provide their own benchmarks that account for social and environmental factors, such as the Morningstar Responsible Investment Index, Goldman Sachs Energy Environment and Social Index (GSEES), the Ethibel Sustainability Index in Europe, the Jantzi Social Index in Canada, and the OWW Responsibility SRI Asia Index.

---

[8] The United States Conference of Catholic Bishops Socially Responsible Investment Guidelines in general endorse investments which give consideration to: 1) respecting human life; 2) promoting human dignity; 3) reducing arms production; 4) pursuing economic justice; 5) protecting the environment; and 6) encouraging corporate responsibility.

[9] See www.kld.com.

4. The Growth of SRI in the International Financial Markets

The SRI strategies being implemented and integrated with traditional investment decisions have seen an admirable growth in both acceptability by investors and assets under management with a SRI mandate. The growing significance of SRI is taking center stage in the global financial industry and is consistent with the movement of economic prosperity from the US to other nations, as suggested by Cohen (2006) and evidenced by the proliferation of various SRI indices and products as well as initiatives taken by international companies and investment practitioners discussed in Section 5.

4.1 *The Growth of SRI*

The growing amount of assets allocated to SRI investment products by both institutional and individual investors is a *prima facie* evidence of the popularity of SRI. Growth in SRI is categorized as either "core" or "broad" SRI. Core SRI includes strategies that are more elaborate and contain both negative and positive screening (such as best-in-class and pioneer screening). Broad SRI is defined as strategies that include the core SRI, but also simple exclusions, engagement practices, and explicit integration of ESG into the analysis (Eurosif, 2003). In 2005, core SRI AUM in EU countries reached €105 billion and broad SRI AUM was €1.033 trillion whereas the US SRI market was still the largest with over US$2.3 trillion in SRIs, constituting 9.4% of the US$24.4 trillion in all AUM. Desmadryl (2007) estimates the global SRI market to be at least US$3.58 trillion, with about 64% of the AUM in the US, 34% in Europe and less than 1% in Asia and the emerging markets. All countries with a developed financial market have seen increases in SRI retail products because of the overwhelming demand by environmentally and socially concerned investors. Countries that are on the fringe of SRI (for example, South Africa) are following the lead of the European countries that have provided the impetus for the movement. A summary of the size and growth of SRI, and types of investors and investments in selected countries and geographic regions is presented in Table 3. In the following discussion, we highlight the differences in regulations and philosophy that drive the regional growth in SRI.

4.2 *Drivers of Growth*

Eurosif (2006) identifies the drivers for SRI growth as: 1) the business case for SEE issues among investors; 2) business regulations (e.g., REACH Directives that require transparency in the chemical sector); 3) fiduciary and pension regulations in the UK, Italy, Austria, Germany, and Belgium; and 4) large investors such as the FRR in France, the Environment Agency in the UK, Superannuation Fund in New Zealand, and CalPERs in the US, that lead the momentum for other SRI investors.[10]

4.2.1 *Business Case*

Among the major drivers for growth of SRI, the need to integrate SEE concerns into business operations for long-term sustainability in business (voluntary or mandatory) has been recognized by many multinational corporations, such as the members of the World Business Council for Sustainable Development (WBCSD), and financial institutions and pension funds, which are members of the United Nations Environment Program Finance Initiative (UNEP FI), respectively.[11]

4.2.2 *Regulations*

The policy stance and philosophy of regulators towards SRI will also determine the future growth of SRI. The stricter the policy and the more stringent the regulations, the greater the impetus to growth of SRI. In contrast, countries with less regulation will have less SRI growth. This can be seen in Australia where 2002 disclosure

---

[10] Although the drivers are identified for Europe, the discussion that follows also applies to all regions. We will include the discussion of unique growth drivers for other regions if appropriate.
[11] See UNEP FI AMWG (2004).

Table 3. Summary of Regional SRI AUM, Growth, Investor and Investment Types

Region	Country	Size of SRI AUM* and Growth	Major Investor Types	Investment Types
Europe				
	Austria	€1.2 billion (0.5% of the total Austrian securities market); up over 1,000% from 2002	Religious institutions are the greatest investors, followed by occupational pension funds, insurance companies, and corporations.	About 80% of the SRI capital from institutional investors are in mutual funds.
	Belgium	€9.5 billion (almost 4% of total invested capital); up 111% since 2002	70% are institutional investors and the remaining are retail investors.	Retail SRI vehicles are composed of 50 SRI mutual funds and very little SRI savings products.
	France	€8.2 billion in core SRI market and €13.8 billion in broad SRI market; up 162% and 663%, respectively since 2003	Institutional investors make up 74% and retail 17% of the SRI market. Largest institutional investors are churches, NGOs and charities, although Fonds de Réserve pour les Retraites has lead the way for trade unions to invest in SRI.	Nearly 74% of institutional investors favor European SRIs, choosing large-cap equities.

(*Continued*)

Table 3. (*Continued*)

Region	Country	Size of SRI AUM* and Growth	Major Investor Types	Investment Types
	Germany	Nearly €5.3 billion SRI AUM (0.3% of the total capital); up 45% since 2002	Major investors are religious organization, followed by NGOs and foundations.	"Spezialfonds", which account for 0.4% of all spezialfonds, are SRI exclusive mutual funds for institutional investors. More than €3 billion of the SRI assets are invested in funds that are managed abroad and €800 million are invested in alternative banks and micro credit organizations.
	Italy	€2.89 billion, where 87% is made up of broad retail (€2.5 billion)**; up about 100% by retail investors and 58% by institutional investors since 2002	Retail investors are the majority. Institutional investors only make up 13% of the market, where pension funds are the majority.	Retail mutual funds.

(*Continued*)

Table 3. (*Continued*)

Region	Country	Size of SRI AUM* and Growth	Major Investor Types	Investment Types
	Netherlands	Over €47 billion in retail SRI (about 4.3% of the total AUM); over 1,500% since 2003	Mainly dominated by institutional investors, with pension funds the largest followed by insurance companies and other institutional investors.	Nearly 75% of the SRI vehicles are self-managed pension funds, followed by 11% "other", and 7% mutual funds. 93% of SRI funds focus on large caps, 63% have extended SRI practices to corporate bonds, and 13% to government bonds. Approximately 60% of assets are European SRIs and 28% in North America.
	Spain	€1.5 billion in core SRI and €25 billion in broad SRI	Main investors are the occupational pensions (44% of core SRI) but the public sector makes up less than 4% of SRI assets.	Guaranteed funds and indexed deposits (total €850 million or 40% of the SRI market). Almost 43% of the retail SRI funds are indexed to the DJSI or FTSE4Good Indices.

(*Continued*)

Table 3. (*Continued*)

Region	Country	Size of SRI AUM* and Growth	Major Investor Types	Investment Types
	Switzerland	Approximately €7.45 billion are in broad SRI assets (0.3% of the total Swiss investment market); up 350% since 2002	Nearly 80% of the SRI market is dominated by public pension funds and reserve funds, followed by NGOs, foundations, and corporate pension funds.	Most of the SRI market is made up of SRI mutual funds (€3.3 billion) and make up 2.3% of the total mutual fund market. However, Swiss mandates make up 48% of the SRI assets (€3.364 billion). Nearly €30 billion in SRI investments in the UK and US are managed by Swiss invetsment companies.
	United Kingdom	£6.1 billion (€3.5 billion) with SRI mandates	Approximately 96% of SRI assets are held by institutional investors, with public pension funds being the largest, followed by NGOs/foundations and corporate and occupational pension funds. However, most investment companies serve public	SRI vehicles were made up of approximately 47% mandates and 41% mutal funds in 2005.

(*Continued*)

Table 3. (*Continued*)

Region	Country	Size of SRI AUM* and Growth	Major Investor Types	Investment Types
			pension funds (80% of their client base), followed by religious and insurance institutions. Nearly 6% in SRI AUM are from high-net-worth individuals.	
North America	Canada	C$503.6 billion SRI AUM in 2006; up about 770% since 2004	Public pension funds holds the majority assets in broad SRI assets. The majority SRI mutual fund investors are retail investors (C$7.6 billion), and institutional investors mostly are: corporate pension funds (C$3.1 billion), insurance companies (C$197.9 million), foundations (C$166.8 million) and public sector pension funds (C$151.8 million).	SRI assets represented 19.6% of the retail mutual fund market and institutional investment market (due to Broad SRI inclusion into the public pension funds). Over 20% of all venture capital assets (C$449 million) between 2004–6 were in sustainable capital venture.
	United States	US$2.29 trillion (9.4% of all AUM); up 258% since 1995	Institutional investors make up the greatest involvment in SRI with $1.49 trillion in AUM, followed by retail mutual funds of $179 billion in AUM.	SRIs are available through 151 mutual funds, 22 variable annuities, and 28 other pooled products (such as closed end funds, ETFs, and hedge funds).

(*Continued*)

Table 3. (*Continued*)

Region	Country	Size of SRI AUM* and Growth	Major Investor Types	Investment Types
Asia and Pacific Rim	Japan	Over ¥200 billion (US$ 1 billion) in AUM 2004.	High-net worth investors hold more than $700 billion in SRI AUM.	Over 100 billion yen is invested in 11 domestic SRI funds.
	Australia	A$11.98 billion; up 3,587% since 2000	Institutional investors	The Australian SRI market is dominated by a fes funds:
			The bulk of Australian SRI assets reside in investments by religious organizations and employer superannuation funds using SRI overlays.	Tower Life's Ethical Fund was the first national ethical investment fund (opened in 1986) and screened out the sin products, firms involved with armaments, or had South African involvement.
	New Zealand	SRI AUM were estimated to be NZ$37.2 million as of 2006, an increase of 18% from 2005. This total does not include Crown Financial	NA	Asteron launched New Zealand's first SRI trust in 2002 investing in New Zealand listed companies with negative screens. The

(*Continued*)

Table 3. (*Continued*)

Region	Country	Size of SRI AUM* and Growth	Major Investor Types	Investment Types
		Institutions, such as the the Superannuation Fund or the Government Superannuation Fund. The Superannuation Fund AUM is NZ$10.6 billion AUM (as of 2006).		Quaker Investment Ethical Trust was created in 1989 to reflect Quaker concerns.
Africa	South Africa	US$1.4 billion AUM in 2003 by 21 SRI funds; SRI market was R18.6 billion (1.55% of the total investment market) in 2001	Individual and institutional investors.	Since 1992, 20 SRI funds track companies SEE performances. The most notable is Nedbank's Green Trust (with World Wlife Fund of South Africa) that funds community-based wildlife conservation and counter unsustainable development. Starting with US$770,0

Notes:
* As of 2005 unless noted otherwise.
**Figures do not include the Catholic Church and other religious groups.
Source: Ali (2006), Baue (2004a, 2004b), Crowe (2004), Davids (2007), Desmadryl (2007), EIA (2007), Eurosif (2006), George *et al.* (2006), Lozano *et al.* (2006), SIF (2006), SIO (2007), Taylor (2007), Tippet (2001), Visser (2005), Whitten (2004), UNEP FI (2006), www.asria.org, and www.nedbank.co.za

regulations for occupational funds, and mandates over mutual funds[12] increased SRI. In France, institutional investors are required to abide by the Employee Savings Plan and this subsequently helped the growth of SRI.

Sometimes regulations are unnecessary when institutional investors are aware of their social and fiduciary responsibilities to their beneficiaries. For instance, the Netherlands does not have SRI regulations, but the majority of their pension funds considers SRI in their decisions and provides a greater push for SRI than statutory regulations.[13]

Another case in point is Germany. In 2004, Germany mandated regulations for all pension funds to report their SRI policies to their members. However, funds that had contractual agreements with members that stated they were not considering SRI in their investments were exempted. Unfortunately, many of the funds decided to utilize this exemption (Statman, 2005). Compared to other EU countries, Germany has very little regulation for SRI activities[14] and there is limited information on whether ESG transparency is broadly accepted yet (White, 2005). Likewise, SRI has gained little acceptance by Spanish institutional investors who have not advanced in adopting engagement activities.

In general, European regulations have provided momentum for SRI, especially when competition is used as the incentive (Statman, 2005). For example, Swedish investors use SRI regulations in the Swedish National Pension Funds as a vehicle for a competitive marketplace by requiring the funds to consider SRI without decreasing the overarching goal of high investment returns. Unlike Germany, this approach gives each fund the flexibility to choose how to implement SRI in their investments, and use only exclusionary screening as a final resort (Statman, 2005).

---

[12] The Pension Reserve Fund (2001) distributed money between six SRI asset managers and are assessed over five years (George *et al.*, 2006).

[13] 74% of Dutch pension funds expect to be using social or environmental criteria in investment decisions in the near future (Whitten, 2004).

[14] It provides incentive rather than regulation in supporting SRI, e.g., "green investing" ever since the 1991 Renewable Energy Act that allowed tax-advantaged closed-end funds to create wind farms.

The driving forces of SRI in Australia (where there has been a SRI growth of 3,587% between 2000 and 2006) are regulations mandated by the Australian Securities and Investment Commission,[15] industry groups (such as Investment and Financial Services Association and Australia Council of Superannuation Investors), Australia's Superannuation funds and the formation of the Ethical Investment Association.

In the US, the SEC adopted mutual fund proxy disclosure regulations in 2003 that require mutual funds to disclose their voting on proxy issues. US institutional investors initiated the momentum to develop proxy-voting policies, and active endowments (e.g., universities) have developed policies for voting on ESG policies. The Federal Employees Responsible Investment Act (introduced in 2005), if passed, would require government pension funds to offer an SRI option under the Thrift Savings Plan. Similar to the development in the US, SRI is not currently mandatory in South African pension funds. However, fund managers are required by law to declare their SRI policies. Future mandatory allocation to SRI is imminent.[16]

Surveys of Central and Eastern European countries found that most countries in the region are challenged by environmental issues such as urban air pollution, low energy efficiency, and deteriorating water and sewage systems (UNEP FI, 2004a). However, these countries have been striving to improve these issues in an effort to adopt EU environmental regulations since the majority felt that sustainability was both a business risk and opportunity, and it would be particularly important in the financial sector. However, SRI is still an emerging field in this region. They feel that the most important drivers for implementing sustainability practices are enhanced reputation, social responsibility, cost savings, competitive advantage, and industry trends.

---

[15] The Financial Services Reform Act (2002) requires all investment firms to disclose the extent to which their socially responsible investment issues are taken into account. Since March 2005, every Australian ethical investment fund is required by law to have a product disclosure statement that describes the way they select, retain, and sell their investments.

[16] Recent proposals issued by the South African National Treasury Department have outlined that a maximum of 10% of retirement assets be allocated to SRI (Davids, 2007).

4.2.3 *Engagement of Institutional Investors*

The California Public Employees' Pension System (CalPERS), one of the largest pension funds in the US, was instrumental in demonstrating how SRIs can be incorporated into pension fund strategies and what their impact can be in the SRI space. In 2004, the State Treasurer of California proposed that pension funds adopt an environmentally-focused investing strategy such as environmental technologies that are either more efficient (such as recyclable products or products made with less natural resource damage) or less polluting (such as clean energy) (Kurtz, 2005). CalPERS committed to a broad and flexible scope in choosing opportunities with environmental benefits, while diversifying the funds by sector, geography, stage and structure. CalPERS assigned a separate risk benchmark to these investments to measure their portfolio performance over the long-term horizon by specifically stating that they would expect negative returns in the short-term but that would increase to "attractive" returns in the long run as the environmental market evolves (CalPERS, 2004). By 2005, CalPERS initiated the development of a greenhouse gas reporting project that would improve data transparency in the electric power and utilities industry. In that same year, they signed on to the Carbon Disclosure Project[17] and joined the other 154 institutional investors with a combined assets under management (AUM) of US$41 trillion[18] (CalPERS, 2006).

Likewise, commitments made by other large pension funds in different countries may serve the same purpose in helping the growth of SRI. For instance, the Canada Pension Plan Investment Board, the Caisse de depot et placement du Quebec of Canada, and the New Zealand Superannuation Fund's sign on with the Principles of Responsible Investment (PRI) has provided a boost to the growth of SRI.

---

[17] The Carbon Disclosure Project (www.cdproject.net) is an NGO that provides information about business risks and opportunities to institutional investors regarding the implications for shareholder value and commercial operations presented by climate change and works to create open dialogue between policymakers, corporations, and shareholders.

[18] As of August 2007 (www.cdproject.net).

The development of SRI in Malaysia and Indonesia would probably come from funds based on Islamic law. Malaysia's government has created a favorable environment to develop Islamic funds, and the Securities Commission has maintained a list of companies that are Shariah compliant for trading on the Kuala Lumpur Stock Exchange. In addition, the Institute of Islamic Understanding, a Malaysian think-tank that pursues alternatives to establish standards for halal certification, provides SRI research in Malaysia. In Indonesia, the creation of the Jakarta Islamic Index is a step towards SRI.

4.3 Obstacles to the Growth of SRI: Under Developed Financial Markets

Under developed financial markets may be an obstacle to the growth of SRI in emerging countries. A case in point is South Africa, which has many of the infrastructures set up for success for SRI.[19] Although there is some SRI in some emerging economies (e.g., South Africa), it is not a primary consideration. The greatest focus in the African region is the availability of low cost credit and insurance to low-income, rural people. SRI is not popular because most African pension fund managers are restricted by regulations and investment policies, and because of indifference from beneficiaries on ESG issues. Some exchanges require bond issues to be guaranteed by third-parties. Some of these bond issues can obscure the consensus value of the company debt. Additionally, there is a lack of listed equities for fund managers to invest in. All these reasons point to a lack of SRI considerations because the financial markets are not developed enough to include SRI (World Bank, 2007).

---

[19] South Africa has a framework for SEE reporting described in The King Report on Corporate Governance which was revised and updated in 2002. Although adherence to the King Code is voluntary, the Johannesburg Securities Exchange (JSE) requires all listed companies to follow it. In 2002, the South African Sustainability Index was launched and ranked the top 40 listed companies based on their sustainability criteria in 2002. In 2004, JSE launched a tradable SRI Index (based on the FTSE4Good), the first of its kind in an emerging market.

5. Other Supporting Factors for the Growth of SRI

In addition to the growth drivers mentioned above, several other factors that favorably support the growing popularity of SRI in the world economy. The increasing corporate reporting of corporate sustainability and responsibility reporting, the emergence of standards and guidance frameworks, and the increasing research made available by international agencies and research groups are three main factors.

5.1 *Increasing Corporate Non-Financial Reporting*

The increasing popularity of corporate sustainability and responsibility (CSR) reports produced for shareholders and stakeholders is indicative of the sustainable growth in SRI. Increasingly, public companies are providing additional non-financial disclosure about their environmental practices and social performances. Investors and stakeholders use this information as a supplement to analyze financial disclosures. However, unlike financial reporting, disclosure of potential risks arising from environmental and social practices in many countries, (e.g., the US), is not mandatory. Companies have the freedom to report any of their environmental and social sustainability information in any format, using any metrics and criteria they feel would help the transparency of their activities. The Global Reporting Initiative (GRI)[20] provides a "Sustainability Reporting Framework" with "Sustainability Reporting Guidelines" that is currently the global *de facto* standard for reporting performances.

France was the first country to mandate French corporations to report on their environmental and social performance in their financial reports when they passed the "nouvelles régulations économiques" (new economic regulations) in 2002 (Lydenberg, 2005). The new economic regulations require reporting based on nearly forty social and environmental indicators, such as employment diversity, engagement with

---

[20] The Global Reporting Initiative (www.globalreporting.org) is an organization that brings together multiple stakeholders to facilitate consistent, regular, and comparable sustainability reporting and provides a consensus approach to environmental and social disclosure framework.

communities and stakeholders, volunteerism or donations, energy usage, carbon emissions, and responsible procurement policies with suppliers.

British corporations are also required to include information about their social and environmental responsibility factors in their operations, along with a financial review in annual reports to their shareholders (Lydenberg, 2005). The London Stock Exchange requires listed companies to adhere to a standardized CSR reporting format that is integrated into their financial reporting requirements through the Corporate Responsibility Exchange which provides a single point of contact for listed companies to demonstrate compliance with domestic and global codes, and for investors to analyze, benchmark, and compare CSR data.

The increase in CSR reporting[21] demonstrates that corporations and their stakeholders agree that non-financial reporting is essential to characterize fully all risks and wealth creating potential of a firm. Knowledge of environmental and social issues that are being dealt with at the corporate level, along with financial data, encourages a more efficient market and subsequently more accurate pricings of equities and firm values.

5.2 *Emergence of Standards and Guidance Frameworks*

The emergence of standards and guidance frameworks at both the domestic and international level purports the growing importance of SRI. Corporations that subscribe to the rigors of these standards will often voluntarily disclose them in their CSR reports. From a practicality point of view, firms find it advantageous to adhere to a specific code because the guidelines are explicit and often provide explanations of the criteria they can use to measure their performance in SEE arenas. The business case for adopting a standard includes recognition, enhanced reputation, and opportunities to collaborate with other adhering companies.

Two examples of the many forerunners of CSR reporting frameworks are the International Organization for Standardization (ISO) and the UN Global Compact.

---

[21] The GRI reports nearly 1,000 organizations in over 60 countries using the Reporting Framework.

ISO launched the guidelines for social responsibility known as the ISO 26000. Although ISO 26000 is not a certification standard, it was developed to encourage voluntary commitment to social responsibility by providing guidance on concepts and methods of evaluation for social factors. The UN Global Compact is a non-regulatory, voluntary, and non-enforceable instrument based on ten principles categorized by human rights, labor standards, environment, and anti-corruption.[22] It aims to help companies and organizations find practical solutions for corporate responsibility issues involving multiple stakeholders. Although there is no certification, the UN Global Compact Office permits participants to use the Global Compact logo in communications that outline participation in the program. Companies that participate in the Global Compact develop a reputation for demonstrating leadership in its industry by advancing corporate responsibility and by managing risks by taking a proactive stance on critical ESG issues.

Parallel to the CSR framework initiatives spearheaded by corporations, institutional investors such as pension funds, have adopted the Principles for Responsible Investment (PRI), a guidance framework for institutional investors to consider ESG issues that have impacts on investment decisions.[23] There are six Principles for Responsible Investment: 1) incorporate ESG issues into investment analysis and decision-making processes; 2) be active owners and incorporate ESG issues into their own policies and practices; 3) seek appropriate disclosures on ESG issues by the entities in which they invest; 4) promote acceptance and implementation of the Principles within the investment community; 5) work together to enhance our effectiveness in implementing the Principles; and 6) report their activities and progress towards implementing the Principles.[24] As with frameworks for corporations, adoption of the PRI is not mandatory. The act of adoption simply demonstrates that the signatories recognize and support environmental and social factors that can lead to positive financial

---

[22] For the details of the ten principles, please go to www.unglobalcompact.org.
[23] The PRI was developed in partnership with the UNEP FI and UN Global Compact and launched in 2006.
[24] Source: www.unpri.org.

returns in the long run. Institutional investors who commit to PRI principles believe that they are meeting their fiduciary duty of acting in the best interests of their beneficiaries by taking into account the ESG factors that affect companies, industry sectors, geographic regions, and time, which ultimately affects their portfolio performance. Although PRI is compatible with SRI instruments, it is applicable to all traditional investment strategies that operate in a fiduciary framework.

PRI signatories can be divided into three categories: asset owners (e.g., pension funds), investment managers (e.g., firms retailing financial instruments), and professional service partners (e.g., investment researchers and consultants). Only one year after PRI's launch, more than 150 signatories with assets under management of greater than US$6 trillion (as of August 2007)[25] have embraced the six Principles as a method of aligning their investment decisions with the concerns of their beneficiaries and simultaneously contributing to the UN's goal of a stable global economy with social progress and sustainable development. Financial institutions that provide funding for projects, especially in emerging markets, have adopted the Equator Principles as a guidance framework to evaluate a corporation's social and environmental management practices, as well as provide a benchmark for use in the analysis and decision process of funding global projects with capital costs greater than US$10 million.[26] Equator Principles Financial

---

[25] Source: www.unpri.org.

[26] Source: www.equator-principles.com. The ten principles with which projects are evaluated by the EPFIs are: 1) review and categorize the impacts and risks in accordance with environmental and social screening criteria developed by the International Finance Corporation; 2) assess the social and environmental impacts and risks; 3) assess the project with applicable social and environmental standards based on whether or not the project is located in an OECD country; 4) review the project's Action Plan and Management System that addresses the impacts, risks, and corrective actions required to comply with host country's social and environmental laws and regulations; 5) determine whether the borrower has consulted and disclosed the project to the local community, government and other stakeholders and adequately addressed their concerns; 6) determine whether the borrower has a mechanism in place to engage with stakeholder grievances; 7) check that an independent review was performed to assess compliance to the Equator Principles; 8) incorporate covenants linked to Equator Principle in the financing documentation; 9) ensure that an independent environmental and social reviewer monitors and reports activities throughout the life of the loan; and 10) each EPFI commits to annual disclosures of its Equator Principles implantation processes and experiences.

Institutions (EPFIs) adopt ten principles to ensure that the projects they finance are developed in a socially and environmentally responsible manner. Projects that do not meet the Equator Principles are not funded by EPFIs. More than 50 major international financial institutions have signed on to the Equator Principles.[27]

5.3 *Involvement of International Non-Governmental Organizations and Research Groups*

The emergence and involvement of large international agencies such as the United Nations Environment Program Finance Initiative (UNEP FI), CERES, and the World Business Council for Sustainable Development (WBCSD) is indicative of the growing significance of SRI at the supranational level.[28] A special UNEP FI Asset Management Working Group (AMWG) that comprised fund managers was established to study the materiality of ESG issues in institutional portfolio management because beneficiaries had requested approaches in asset management that would include any non-financial information that becomes relevant to investment decisions. In 2003, AMWG carried out a research project to identify SEE factors (such as climate change, occupational and public health issues, human labor and political rights, and corporate trust and governance) that would significantly affect a company's competitiveness and reputation in seven industry sectors, and to quantify the impacts on the stock price. Their research findings show: 1) ESG issues affect long-term shareholder value and may be significant in some cases; 2) due to non-standardized ESG reporting, comparative analysis between companies is difficult; and 3) it is easier to do an analysis if there is clear government policy on ESG issues. The AMWG concluded that because ESG issues can contribute to shareholder value, non-financial information should be integrated as an important part of fundamental financial analysis (UNEP FI AMWG, 2004).

---

[27] For example, JPMorgan Chase, Bank of America, HSBC, Rabobank, and Citigroup, to name a few.

[28] The WBCSD is made up of CEOs from 200-plus companies working towards sustainability. CERES is a network of investors and public interest groups.

Other NGOs, like CERES and the WBCSD and private firms such as Innovest, Investor Responsibility and Research Center, Institutional Shareholder Services, and Sustainable Investment Research International (SiRi), provide independent research, analysis, and consulting to investors in the area of SRI, ESG issues, and sustainability. The sheer number of reports produced by NGOs and private researchers in the last few years indicates that SEE factors warrant thorough research and serious consideration by investors.

6. Concluding Remarks

SRI is increasingly becoming an important consideration in the global financial industry as both retail and institutional investors demand proactive integration of ESG issues into investment considerations. In this chapter, we focused on how institutional investors incorporate the ethical, social, environmental, and corporate governance issues into their SRI investment decision-making process. We discussed SRI concept is and rationales for SRI. We explained the common screening strategies used in various SRI investments and indices, identified the growth drivers of SRI, and discussed the development and growth of SRI in the international financial markets. We described the three supporting factors that help fuel the growth of SRI. In summary, the SRI trend in many countries seems to indicate that consideration of non-financial issues is gaining momentum but has not yet become popular practice. Some countries, particularly those in Asia, are still grappling with the conflict of interest between maximizing financial returns and screening out potentially profitable sectors.

Out of all ESG issues, climate change seems to be gaining the most traction. Nearly every industrialized country (except the US and Australia) has signed the Kyoto Protocol and many economic markets have launched a cap-and-trade greenhouse gas scheme. Other growing ESG issues that have gained acceptance in the financial world are biodiversity or restoration banking (credit-trading schemes that have market value) and the enormous potential growth of Islamic finance.

As noted in various surveys and reports, active SRI integration is not a straightforward process. SRIs require a lot of non-financial information. This information is not regulated, sometimes not required, and can be vague or as specific as the discloser would like. Even if the information were available, it can be hard to quantify and there are no established metrics to compare data from different sources with each other. To support these reasons and others, further research is warranted.

Aside from a few empirical studies (e.g., Orlitzy *et al.*, 2003), very little research at the corporate level has been done to examine the relationship between the proactive integration ESG issues in management and operations and their financial performance, while controlling for other factors that contribute to financial performance. Thus, development of usable SRI metrics that can be applied broadly across sectors and geographic regions is necessary. In addition, data is needed to assess whether engagement and proxy voting by fiduciaries, such as pension funds, will have any impact on financial returns. Moreover, the efficacy of different screening strategies needs to be studied at the portfolio level in terms of optimization. This implies that the risk involved in a portfolio optimized under ESG criteria may require taking into consideration risk measures that go beyond volatility.

On the international front, as new vehicles become available (e.g., SRI exchange traded funds [ETFs] and SRI hedge funds), they provide opportunities to examine the efficacy of SRI vis-à-vis unscreened investments, including those from other asset classes (e.g., the fixed income securities, venture capital, and private equity) as well as in different geographic markets such as the emerging economies. It would be interesting to see whether different market structures and cultures create differences in the financial performance of SRI. If there were differences, the behavioral finance theory may be helpful in explaining why and how they differ given cultural environments. Research can focus on comparing the differing financial performance caused by behavioral differences in how managers relate and incorporate SEE considerations to the ethical considerations that are requested by their beneficiaries in different cultures. Although financial research on SRI is not a new topic area, interest and importance in this line of research will continue to grow as SRI is assimilated into mainstream investing.

References

Ali, P., 2006, Investing in the environment: Some thoughts on the new breed of green hedge funds, *Derivatives Use, Trading & Regulation*, 12(4), 351–357.

Baue, W., 2004a, Daiwa launches Japan's newest socially responsible investment fund. Accessed at www.socialfunds.com.

Baue, W., 2004b, Socially responsible investment assets on the up and up down under. Accessed at www.socialfunds.com.

Bauer, R., R. Otten, and A. Tourani-Rad, 2004, Ethical investing in Australia: Is there a financial penalty? EFA 2004 Maastricht Meeting Paper, Paper #1224.

Beal, D. J., M. Goyen, and P. Phillips, 2005, Why do we invest ethically? *The Journal of Investing*, 14(3), 66–77.

Bello, Z. Y., 2005, Socially responsible investing and portfolio diversification, *Journal of Financial Research*, 28(1), 41–57.

CalPERS, 2004, Alternative Investment Management (AIM) Program presentation presented to the Members of the Investment Committee, March 15, 2004. Accessed at www.calpers.ca.gov.

CalPERS, 2006, Corporate governance environmental strategic plan update presented by the Global Equity program to the Members of the Investment Committee, March 13, 2006. Accessed at www.calpers.ca.gov.

Carpenter, J., 2004, Advising SRI — Presentation to EIA Australia. Accessed at www.eia.org.au.

Cohen, A. J., 2006, Challenges for the next generation of investors, in *Global Perspective on Investment Management: Learning from the Leaders*, Sullivan, ed., The CFA Institute.

Crowe, R., 2004, Risk returns and responsibility, Association of British Insurers. Accessed at www.abi.org.uk.

Davids, D., 2007, SRI-Investing for the future, Old Mutual Investment Group, March 2007. Accessed at www.omigsa.com.

Desmadryl, X., 2007, SRI & ESG inclusion: Does it pay after all? Presentation made at ANBID/UNEP FI Roundtable in Sao Paolo, HSBC, March.

EIA (Ethical Investment Association), 2007, 2006 SRI benchmarking study. Accessed at www.eia.org.au.

Eurosif, 2003, Socially responsible investment among European institutional investors. Accessed at www.eurosif.org.

Eurosif, 2004, Pension programme SRI toolkit. Accessed at www.eurosif. org.

Eurosif, 2006, European SRI study 2006. Accessed at www.eurosif.org.

Farmen, T. E. S. and N. van der Wijst, 2005, A cautionary note on the pricing of ethics, *The Journal of Investing*, 14(3), 53–56.

George, A., N. Edgerton, and T. Berry, 2006, Mainstreaming socially responsible investment (SRI): A role for government? Institute for Sustainable Future, University of Technology, Sydney.

Grossman, B. R., W. F. Sharpe, and W. F. 1986, Financial implications of South African divestment, *Financial Analysts Journal*, 42(4), July/August, 15–29.

Hamilton, S., H. Jo, and M. Statman, 1993, Doing well while doing good? The investment performance of socially responsible mutual funds, *Financial Analysts Journal*, 49(6), November/December, 62–66.

Hawley, J. and Williams, A. 2000, *The Rise of Fiduciary Capitalism: How Institutional Investors Can Make Corporate America More Democratic*, Philadelphia: University of Pennsylvania Press.

Hudson, J., 2006, *The Social Responsibility of the Investment Profession*, Research Foundation of the CFA Institute.

Hussein, K. and M. Omran, 2005, Ethical investment revisited: Evidence from Dow Jones Islamic Indexes, *The Journal of Investing*, 14(3), 105–124.

Kinder, P. D., 2005, New fiduciary duties in a changing social environment, *The Journal of Investing*, 14(3), 24–37.

Kurtz, L. and D. diBartolomeo, 2005, The KLD Catholic Values 400 Index, *The Journal of Investing*, 14(3), 101–104.

Kurtz, L., 2005, Answers to four questions, *The Journal of Investing*, 14(3), 125–138.

Lamb, W. B., R. E. Wokutch, and R. Kumar, 1995, The financial impact of the end to South African sanctions: An event history analysis, *Academy of Management Journal: Research Library*. 391.

Lozano, J. M., L. Albareda, and M. Rosario Balaguer, 2006, Socially responsible investment in the Spanish financial market, *Journal of Business Ethics*, 69, 305–316.

Lydenberg, S., 2005, Social and environmental data as new tools, *The Journal of Investing*, 14(3), 40–46.

Orlitzy, M., F. L. Schmidt, and S.L. Rynes, 2003, Corporate social and financial performance: A meta-analysis, *Organization Studies*, 24(3), 403–441.

Renneboog, L., J. R. ter Horst, and C. Zhang, 2006, "Is ethical money financially smart? ECGI — Finance Working Paper No. 117/2006. Accessed at SSRN: http://ssrn.com/abstract=887162

Rudd, A., 1981, Social responsibility and portfolio performance, *California Management Review*, 23(4), 55–61.

Sethi, S. P., 2005, Investing in socially responsible companies is a must for public pension funds — Because there is no better alternative, *Journal of Business Ethics*, 56, 99–129.

Shank, T. M., D. K. Manullang, and R. P. Hill, 2005, Is it better to be naughty or nice? *The Journal of Investing*, 14(3), 82–87.

Social Investment Forum (SIF), 2006, 2005 Report on socially responsible investing trends in the United States, 10-year review, January 24, 2006. Accessed at www.socialinvest.org.

Smith, T., 2005, Institutional and social investors find common ground, *The Journal of Investing*, 14(3), 57–65.

Social Investment Organization (SIO), 2007, Canadian socially responsible investment review 2006. A comprehensive survey of socially responsible investment in Canada, March 2007. Accessed at www.socialinvestment.ca.

Statman, M., 2000, Socially responsible mutual funds, *Financial Analysts Journal*, 56(3), May/June, 30–50.

Statman, M., 2005, The religions of social responsibility, *The Journal of Investing*, 14(3), 14–22.

Steward, G., 2006, Socially responsible investing: transforming to the mainstream, Mercer Investment Consulting, 27 September 2006.

Taylor, M., 2007, SRI: Changing times and climates, March 8, 2007. Accessed at www.moneymanagement.com.au.

Tippet, J., 2001, Performance of Australia's ethical funds, *The Australian Economic Review*, 34(2), 170–178.

UNEP FI AMWG, 2004, The materiality of social, environmental and corporate governance issues to equity pricing, June 2004. UNEP Finance Initiative.

UNEP FI AMWG, 2007, Responsible Investment in Focus: How leading public pension funds are meeting the challenge, 2007 Report, UNEP Finance Initiative AMWG and the United Kingdom Social Investment Forum, Sustainable Pensions Project, 2007.

UNEP FI., 2004a, Finance and sustainability in Central and Eastern Europe. Accessed at www.unepfi.net

UNEP FI., 2004b, The materiality of social and corporate governance issues to equity pricing, June 2004, UNEP Finance Initiative.

UNEP FI., 2006, Environment and Finance. Accessed at http://www.unepfi.org/regional_activities/asia_pacific/japan/index.html

UNEP FI., 2007, Responsible investment in focus: How leading public pension funds are meeting the challenges, 2007 report, UNEP Finance Initiative, April 2007.

Visser, W., 2005, Corporate citizenship in South Africa: A review of progress since democracy, *The Journal of Corporate Citizenship*, 18, 29–38.

White, C. F., 2005, SRI best practices: Learning from the Europeans, *The Journal of Investing*, 14(3), 88–93.

Whitten, D., 2004, Socially responsible investment pays in Japan: the latest investment boom elsewhere finally gains traction in Japan — Upfront, February. Accessed at http://findarticles.com/p/articles/mi_m0NTN/is_52/ai_113526684/

World Bank, 2007, Making finance work for Africa, November 2006. Report by the Africa Region of the International Bank for Reconstruction and Development.

Part II: Traditional Investments

A. Global Equity Investments

Chapter 3

Global Equity Investments and Analysis

*Louis T. W. Cheng**

Owing to the rapid globalization of equity markets, equity returns from different international markets have become more correlated. This synchronization of markets makes diversification more challenging than ever. The recent popularity of wealth management services, especially in Asia, allows less wealthy individuals to gain access to advanced structured products and alternative investments. While sophisticated portfolio strategies are used to enhance performance, cultural behavior and home-bias must be considered in making international equity investments.

Keywords: Asset allocation; international equity; ETFs.

1. The New Challenge

The international equity markets have become more unified in the past ten years. Owing to the globalization of business trade, especially in the Asia Pacific region, business and economic cycles of different countries have gradually been moving together in harmony. Such an increasing synchronization of international economic cycles is affecting the equity markets as well. Institutional investors and fund managers have realized that, due to the more rapid price adjustment of

---

* Hong Kong Polytechnic University.

international markets to local and overseas information recently, conducting profitable arbitrage activities among international equity markets are getting more and more difficult.

The traditional static asset allocation strategy used to achieve international diversification may not be effective anymore as the correlations among different equity markets are getting stronger. This also explains the recent development and popularity of Tactical Asset Allocation (TAA), which adopts a more dynamic approach in asset allocation than the Strategic Asset Allocation (SAA). Of course, there are many ways to conduct TAA, from a pure quantitative approach to subjective market timing strategy. Adding the dimension of foreign exchange fluctuation, international diversification using some sort of TAA has become a critical and yet challenging ingredient for institutional investors and portfolio managers in managing a global investment portfolio.

The increasing momentum of alternative investments in mainstream portfolios held by traditional investors such as pension funds, foundations, and family offices of ultra-high net worth individuals is definitely affecting the role of international equity investments. Recent evidence has shown that even alternative investment indices are getting more correlated with the major US market indices (correlation coefficient of 0.48 as reported by Credit Suisse/Tremont Hedge Fund return statistics in February 2006). Finally, the surge of structured products in the form of equity derivatives being offered at both the institutional and retail level (e.g., Equity-Linked Notes [ELN] in Hong Kong) is also making a significant impact on the liquidity and pricing of the underlying equity. As time passes, the cross-selling of these structured products in the international markets will be more imminent, which in turn will affect the volatility of the domestic as well as the international markets.

Under such an increasing variety of channels for international equity investments, institutional investors and wealth managers need to conduct a thorough review at their current international equity investments and see if they have adopted the most efficient strategies to conquer these new challenges.

2. Chapter Design

The focus of this chapter is not the statistics or the institutional features of all the major stock markets as there are plenty of published and web-based materials to cover just that. The objective of the chapter is to examine the current status of product development and investment strategies for global equity as an asset class.

First, we review the role of international equity in an investment portfolio from the perspective of wealth management. Section 4 looks at the investment channels designed for global investments. Section 5 first explores various investment strategies suitable for global equity. Then we examine the hottest emerging market and its investment environment: China. In short, we start with concept and theories, place products and strategies in the middle, and finish up with an international equity market with great profit potential.

3. The Role of International Equity in a Portfolio

3.1 *Increasing Linkage of Global Equity Markets*

Empirical evidence from portfolio diversification indicates that a small dosage of international equity can bring substantial risk diversification benefit to a domestic portfolio. However, the underlying principle of international risk diversification rests on the level of correlation between the international securities (equity in most cases) and the domestic assets. Through the recent years, due to globalization of businesses and consequently equity markets, the correlation between international and domestic assets has been strengthened positively. This increased correlation weakened the diversification benefit for international investments.

In the past, equity market linkage exists in the form of transmission from well-established markets to developing markets. Recently, we have seen a growing importance of multi-directional global linkage in equity market movements. US investors for the first time experience a substantial price effect from an Asian emerging equity market.

On February 27, 2007, a mini stock market crash in Mainland China set off a chain reaction in equity markets all over the world. The Chinese

CSI 300 index dropped 260.32 points from 2717.81 to 2457.49 in one day. This 9.58% decline in the Chinese market results in a 412.66 point (or 3.27%) loss in the Dow (from 12,628.9 to 12,216.24) which opened a few hours later. This event illustrates that there may exist a close bi-directional connection between the US and Asian emerging markets, which substantially reduces the diversification benefits of international equity.

3.2 *Home Bias and International Investments*

It is clear that practicing international investment to achieve risk diversification is easier said than done. Financial research has shown that investors are subject to home (location) bias. In other words, domestic investors tend to underweigh the riskiness of local equity and over weigh the riskiness of international equity. Location bias is an interesting topic in behavioral finance. No matter what the reasons are, home-market bias leads to market segmentation and reduces the international capital flows needed to achieve international diversification.

Such a home bias partially explains why in the 1970s, a worker at General Motors might choose to invest all his retirement money in GM stock; and why in the 1980s, many US small investors were not interested in investing in international equity mutual funds. The same home bias may help to explain why many Hong Kong investors are more interested in investing in small local stocks than in well-known blue-chip US stocks such as Microsoft cross-listed on the Hong Kong Exchanges (HKEx) (see Appendix 1 for a list of the international securities listed on HKEx). Home bias may be stronger in the early stage of the investment experience. When the investors become more mature and educated, the benefits of international investments would be better understood and more widely employed.

3.3 *Investment Culture and International Investments*

It is common knowledge among financial services firms that Asian investors are more into direct investments (buying stocks directly) while North American and European investors prefer to invest in equity indirectly through mutual funds and pension funds.

Furthermore, Asian investors are more active equity investors (measured by turnover) than their Western counterparts. Thus, it is logical to expect that investment culture would affect international investment activities of that region or country.

If the local investors enjoy direct equity investment, it will be more difficult for them to invest overseas due to possible language barrier and investment restrictions, among other challenges. Thus Asian investors would have less incentive or interest in international investments. On the other hand, Western investors have learned to depend on fund managers for their investment. Therefore, when these institutional investors engage in international diversification and start to invest globally, small investors would naturally have a piece of the action in the international arena.

For high-net-worth investors, there appears to be a move towards international investments. Recently, hedge funds have become an essential component (around 10% to 20%) in the investment portfolios for wealthy individuals and institutional investors (even for charitable foundations and pension funds). As international investments are a common strategy for hedge funds, it is logical to expect that hedge funds would accelerate the level of international investments.

In conclusion, we can make some key observations for the development of international equity in the context of wealth management. First, globalization of trade and business certainly has an impact on the formation of multinational companies (MNCs). Similarly, the globalization of equity investments is driven by global investors such as international mutual funds, hedge funds, and even private equities. Second, the level of international investments is deeply affected by home bias and local investment culture. Finally, with the growing wealth cumulated in Asia, especially mainland China, it is expected that, pending the relaxation of currency and capital control, international equity investments from China will pick up quickly in the coming years. All these factors would make the synchronization of various equity markets more obvious. Consequently, international investors would be more vulnerable to unexpected volatility set off by one of the international equity markets.

Two decades ago, chaos theory was popular and people kept saying that the tiny air flow created by a butterfly at one end of the earth could induce a major current at the other end on earth. Well, in a way, the international equity markets are experiencing something similar to what the butterfly story mentioned above. For instance, the recent Asian market drop in February 2007 partly caused by hedge funds unwinding their carry-trades in Japan actually set off global market turbulence in no time.

Looking ahead, international equity investments are getting more volatile and sophisticated as structured products using international equity as underlying assets are gaining momentum in Asia. The recent popularity of Exchanged Traded Funds (ETFs) further speeds up the globalization of equity investments. In the next chapter, you will learn more about the role of ETFs in international investment. For now, let us turn our attention to the products suitable for international investments.

4. The Channels for International Equity Investments

The appropriate channel for international equity investments depend on the type of investors and the size of the investment. Of course, these two characteristics are often closely related. A professional or institutional investor usually makes international investments in a much larger scale than those by smaller investors.

4.1. *Institutional Investors and Their Role in International Equity Investments*

The goal of participating in international equity investments depends on the need of the investors. For active professional investors such as fund managers, seeking investment opportunities with a unique risk-return trade-off that does not exist in the domestic market may be a key reason to invest overseas. Active managers constantly shift their investment choices and adjust their asset weights to take advantage of market ineffi-ciencies. Expanding into international equity investments, especially in the emerging markets, allow them to better explore these pricing errors.

This is certainly true due to the recent rapid expansion of hedge funds. As hedge funds are not regulated by the SEC the way that mutual funds are, objectives of many hedge funds can be relatively flexible (such as Event-Driven and Global Macro, and Emerging Markets, to see a sample list of hedge fund categories, please refer to Appendix 3). These hedge funds can trade in any equity and securities market for their "best buys". In addition, these international equity investments made by hedge funds are usually large in size and attract media attention.

Due to the flexibility of investment banks and hedge funds in their investment strategies, their participation in international equity range from very short term to long term.

Short-term Investment: Hedge funds can engage in risk arbitrage involving equity and currencies driven by program trading and the time period can be a few days before unwinding.

Medium-Term Investment: Investment banks and hedge funds can serve as strategic investors in pre-IPO financing activities. The investment lock-up period is usually two years after IPOs. Thus, they can participate in the pre-IPO advisory and hold the equity for around three years (one year before and two years after IPO) before selling some or all of the shares for profit. There are ample examples in the recent IPOs in China that overseas investment banks have engaged in this form of investment activities and made good profit.

Long-Term Investment: Institutional investors can buy substantial equity ownership in large international firms and serve as a long-term investor. In mid-April 2007, Saudi Arabia's Saad group bought 3.1% interest (worth around US$6.57 billion) in HSBC and became its second largest investor after Barclays. The group claims that this is a long-term investment. (See www.ft.com/cms/s/45df6590-ebf8-11db-a12e-000b5df10621.html).

4.2 *International Markets and Investment Channels*

While the US equity markets remain the largest in the world, the Asian markets are catching up in size. Appendix 4 lists the market capitalization of the NYSE, Toronto Stock Exchange, and those of a few Asian markets. Notice that the market value of the largest Exchange, NYSE, is more than five times the size of the second-placed Tokyo Stock Exchange. Also, the size of the Toronto Stock Exchange is similar to that of the Hong Kong Exchanges. The rapid expansion of the Hong Kong market is mainly due to the H-share IPO listings from huge mainland firms such as China Construction Bank. The improved market capitalization and liquidity of the Asian markets allow the US and European funds to trade Asian stocks without worrying about price pressure or liquidity.

Owing to the sophistication of investment strategies employed by fund managers, the products used for international equity investments are getting more and more complicated. We briefly introduce some of the major channels and products for international equity investments in the context of wealth management.

Direct Investments: With the international expansion of brokerage houses, subject to securities regulations and ownership restrictions, local investors can go through domestic brokers to purchase international stocks. Normally, the commission would be higher due to the limited economies of scale and more layers of transaction and administrative costs involved. Thus, using this channel to conduct speculative and intra-day trading would not be cost efficient. Such a channel would be acceptable for a buy-and-hold strategy focusing on the diversification benefits and long-term growth. For high-net-worth clients (i.e., investable assets of US$1 million or more) of international private banks, the brokerage arm of the parent investment banks normally help their clients buy foreign shares as part of the service. Recently, large US discount brokers such as E*Trade and Charles Schwab have gradually expanded into selective overseas markets. E*Trade has about a dozen international sites while Schwab currently has operations in Hong Kong, the UK and Switzerland. These overseas US brokers help small international investors diversify into the US equity and bond markets with much lower capital requirement and cheaper transaction costs. Eventually, direct international equity investments are an economically viable option for global investors whether they reside in the East or the West.

Open-end Mutual Funds: International equity has been a fund category for a long time. There are two types of mutual funds investing in overseas equity. The first type is International Fund, which invests in international markets but excludes US securities. The second type is Global Fund, which invests in equity globally, including US stocks. In the old days, international and world funds mostly pursued a passive strategy by maintaining relatively stable weights among geographical regions. Later, international asset allocation funds adopted a more active strategy in asset allocation or timing in international equity markets. Gradually, regional and country funds have become more popular as more mature investors are interested in making bets on specific regions such as Europe or a country such as China. More recently, Brazil, Russia, India and China — the BRIC economies have gathered enormous investors' interest. Mutual funds designed for selective emerging markets such as BRIC are the latest international equity fund choice for small investors.

Exchange Traded Funds: Exchange Traded Funds (ETFs) are regarded as a great innovation for average investors to diversify into various international equity markets and even alternative investments. ETFs are portfolios of securities managed by investment managers such as State Street but listed in the exchanges. Thus ETFs are traded like a stock. ETFs always track an index. The first ETF was the Standard and Poor's Deposit Receipt (SPDR) established in 1993. It allows investors to invest in the S&P 500 without buying an index mutual fund. However, nowadays many ETFs tracks non-diversified indices such a single industry (e.g., Energy) and selective international market segment (e.g., Japan high yield equity). Thus, ETFs are no longer limited to investments on market-wide indices. Nevertheless, ETFs are a great channel for international equity investments, especially for small investors due to their low transaction costs and convenience in trading (relative to mutual funds).

Hedge Funds: According to the World Wealth Report 2006 by Capgemini and Merrill Lynch (www.capgemini.com/industries/financial solutions/wealth/worldwealth report), High-Net-Worth Individuals (HNWIs) increased their allocations to alternative investments from around 3% in 2000 to 20% in 2005. A common channel to invest in alternative investments for middle-income investors would be hedge funds. As mentioned before, hedge funds are flexible in investment choices and some hedge funds such as Global Macro and Emerging Markets pursue international equity in their strategy.

Investment-linked Insurance Plans: In some economies like the UK, Australia and Hong Kong, savings plans using mutual funds but packaged as an insurance product are very popular. These investment-linked insurance plans include a wide selection of international equity funds for consideration. As most of these plans have a minimum five-year saving period (to exempt from penalty) and normally designed for ten years of monthly savings, investments on international equity in these plans can be relatively long-term. Most investors of investment-linked plans are middle-income families who use these plans to save for retirement.

One may wonder why people are willing to invest in mutual funds through the help of insurance agents or financial planners instead of going directly to mutual funds. The main reason is "service". Many middle-income investors know little about equity investments, let alone asset allocation and international diversification. Unfortunately, middle-income investors cannot afford high-end wealth managers from private banks, and they do not have the time or knowledge to construct an appropriate investment portfolio themselves either. Investment-linked products serviced by insurance professionals fill the needs of these middle-income clients by providing investment advice for retirement savings. International equity is a major component in these plans.

5. Investment Strategies for International Equity

5.1 *Asset Allocation*

Asset allocation in international equity investments is a very important issue. In this case, the distribution and weights of asset classes will be replaced by equities from different geographical regions. Betting on different regions of equity markets can be done with or without hedging the exchange rate risk. According to our understanding, most international equity managers treat investment decisions on the international equity market and the currency risk as a joint decision. That means many asset allocation managers will form a view on the net expected gains for the regional markets, including the currency bets. It is not common that they care to hedge the currency risk while investing in a particular international equity market. Therefore, international asset allocation can be highly complicated and risky. This is also why superior fund managers can truly differentiate themselves from the pack by engaging in international asset allocation in order to prove that they can outperform their peers in such a sophisticated investment competition!

There are several strategies for international asset allocation.

5.1.1. *Strategic Asset Allocation*

Based on some long-term predicted risk-return relation, risk tolerance of the investors, limitations and mandates of the investors, SAA constructs a constant mix of assets and pursue a relatively static investment strategy (usually at least a five-year investment horizon). Re-balancing is conducted when substantial deviation (e.g., more than 5% from its benchmark) from the original policy mix occurs.

In its website, UBS AG describes that there are four components in its strategic asset allocation: 1) disciplined team approach that develops an individual allocation based on risk profile and goals; 2) securities selection from a range of global equity and fixed income product; 3) active management of assets by shifting allocations according to market and personal goals; and 4) ongoing global review of industry trends and currency activities (www.ubs.com/1/e/wealth_mgmt_ww/u_s/growng_wealth/total_wealth.html). SAA is a relatively more rigid strategy due to the practice of a constant weighting of assets based on the predicted rates of return for each asset class.

5.1.2 *Tactical Asset Allocation*

TAA can be defined as active strategies that aim to enhance returns by shifting asset mix in reaction to the changing opportunities. Lee (2000) defines TAA as an active strategy which attempts to deliver a positive information ratio by systematic asset allocation shifts. The value may be in terms of higher return and/or lower risk. TAA strategies can be qualitative or quantitative. A qualitative approach focuses on how the global issues such as inflation, political and economic stability, and terrorism may affect the investment opportunities in different geographic regions. On the other hand, a quantitative approach mainly employs the econometric and statistical modeling to forecast asset returns which are used as inputs in the optimization process to construct portfolios. Lee (1998; 2000) suggests that TAA strategy is more popular among the global fund managers than the domestic fund managers.

5.1.3 *Dynamic Asset Allocation*

By employing high frequency adjustment of asset weights, DAA concentrates on the dynamic approach of capturing market inefficiencies and market timing. Any active asset allocation strategy must employ certain time-varying strategies and result in a non-constant portfolio mix over time. Thus, the portfolio insurance and the tactical asset allocation approaches can both be labeled as DAA. Of course, in theory, the adjustments to asset mix should be very frequent for DAA. Unfortunately, there is no consensus on how high the frequency of adjustments should be classified as DAA, leaving room for subjective interpretation in using the terminology.

While asset allocation is a popular investment approach, the practical implementation of asset allocation is not easy. Campbell (2002) suggests that the asset allocation approach should be determined by the financial goals, tax code (tax brackets and tax shelters), investment horizon (short-term, medium-term and long-term), age (young and old), return expectation (aggressive and conservative) and risk tolerance (risk-averse and risk-taking) of the investors. TAA is an investment approach developed by Wells Fargo Investment Advisors in the US in the 1970s. Today, the rapid expansion of TAA is a consequence of the growing trend of investment globalization.

5.2 *Measuring Performance of Asset Allocation Strategies*

To evaluate the performance of the asset allocation managers, we need a benchmark portfolio. There are several indicators, namely alpha, tracking error, information ratio and hit ratio, to evaluate the performance of asset allocation managers. Aggressiveness in making bets can be evaluated by measures such as alpha and tracking error, in which the frequency of winning affects the performance measures.

5.2.1 *Alpha*

"Alpha" refers to the excess return due to active asset allocation. In mathematical term:

$$\text{Alpha}_t = \text{Return of Portfolio}_t - \text{Return of Benchmark Portfolio}_t.$$

For easier comparison of performance among the asset allocation managers, the usual practice is to compute alpha over a certain horizon. The most frequently used alpha measure is the annualized alpha. Alpha seeking strategies are popular among international fund managers. For instance, at Barclays Global Investors (BGI), research analysts may examine valuation inefficiencies in non-Japanese Asian banks listed in Hong Kong, South Korea, Indonesia and India to enhance alphas.[1]

5.2.2 *Tracking Error*

The performance of an asset allocation strategy can also be measured by the consistency of performance, which can be reflected by the volatility of alpha, or commonly known as "tracking error". To ensure that the portfolio managers have followed the benchmark asset allocation strategy and to avoid extensive deviations, tactical ranges are imposed. Tactical ranges are the constraints on deviations from benchmark weights and serve as boundaries for percentage deviation of weight differentials between the actual portfolio and the benchmark portfolio. There are different ways to estimate tracking error. The simplest measure of tracking error is the standard deviation of alphas:

$$\sqrt{\frac{1}{T-1}\sum_{t=1}^{T}\left(\text{alpha}_t - \frac{1}{T}\sum_{t=1}^{T}\text{alpha}_t\right)^2}$$

---

[1] See "Outsmarting the Market", *Business Week*, January 22, 2007, pp. 58–63.

Similar to alpha, we may quantify the tracking error in an annualized form too. If the alphas are estimated on a monthly basis, the annualized tracking error is the product of the square root of 12 and the monthly tracking error.

There are other ways to compute the tracking error. Ammann and Zimmermann (2001) use the square root of the non-central second moment of return deviations. Mathematically, it is defined as:

$$\sqrt{\frac{\sum_{\text{period } k}^{\text{sample size}} \left(\begin{array}{c}\text{return of tracking portfolio in period } k \\ - \text{ return of predetermined benchmark} \\ \text{portfolio in period } k\end{array}\right)^2}{\text{sample size} - 1}}$$

The third measure is the residual volatility of the tracking portfolio relative to the benchmark (Treynor and Black, 1973). In mathematical terms, it is defined as:

$$\text{volatility of tracking portfolio} \times \sqrt{1 - (\text{return correlation of portfolio and benchmark})^2}.$$

Tracking errors can be actively managed to exploit the profit from a portfolio. There must be a balance between following the benchmark asset allocation and allowing for some tracking errors to maximize alphas. In international equity investments, alphas can be a result of home currency depreciation (assuming profit is measured by domestic dollar). Thus, the weightings for the appreciated markets can be the same in terms of the foreign currency but actually increased in terms of the domestic currency. As the bottom line of investment is to make profit, most fund managers do not mind having positive tracking errors in the domestic dollar term. In this case, tactical ranges have to be established with the consideration of currency fluctuation.

5.2.3 *Information Ratio*

While alpha and tracking error are aggressiveness dependent (i.e., how much risk the managers are willing to take in making bets), information ratio better reflects the skill rather than the aggressiveness of the managers in making bets. Information ratio is defined as the ratio of alpha to tracking error.

5.2.4 *Hit Ratio*

The hit ratio is the proportion of times that the managers add value to the portfolio. It measures the frequency rather than the degree of success. Although a high percentage of the hit ratio (e.g., more than 50%) means that the number of positive alphas is larger than that of negative alphas, it does not mean that the asset allocation manager is able to add value to the portfolio managed as the magnitude of the positive alphas may not exceed that of the negative alphas.

5.3 *Empirical Evidence of Portfolio Performance due to Asset Allocation*

As suggested by Dahlquist and Harvey (2001), there are three levels of asset allocation strategies. The first level is the benchmark asset allocation or indexing which replicates some well-known market indices such as the MSCI World Index. At the second level, a longer-term SAA (conventionally at least a 5-year investment horizon) employs a tracking error strategy. Finally, at the third level, TAA with a shorter-term perspective (conventionally a 30 days to 4 months investment horizon) aims to deviate from the strategic weights and induce tracking errors.

Concerning the profitability of the TAA, Brinson *et al.* (1986) and Brinson *et al.* (1991) find that, on average, the asset allocation strategy explains more than 90% of the variability of the portfolio returns (in terms of R^2 or variance) of pension plans. In the UK, Blake *et al.* (1999) find a slow mean reversion in the portfolio weights towards a common time varying strategic asset allocation. In addition, SAA explains most of the variation in the portfolio returns.

5.4 *Investment Opportunities in the Global Equity Market*

It is well understood that investment performance varies substantially across geographical regions such as North America, Europe and Asia. Another commonly used perspective in differentiating risk-return trade-offs is to look at the maturity and sophistication of the equity market. Using this perspective, we can divide the world into developed and emerging markets. Even though there are equity markets from different geographical regions in a group under such a classification, this gives us a simple way to identify two equity asset classes with similar risk-return characteristics within a class while very different risk-return characteristics across classes.

5.4.1 *Developed Market*

Using MSCI Barra's definitions, we have selected three regional indices to examine the performance of the developed markets. Panel A of Appendix 5 shows the 1-Year, 3-Year and 5-Year annualized returns for the North American, Pacific and European regions. First, as expected, short-term returns are better than longer-term performance for all regions, indicating that the bull market phenomenon is growing strong and accelerating. The best performance belongs to the developed markets (such as France, Germany, Spain and the UK) in the European region. The 1-Year return for Europe is 29%, while the world's average is 21.4%. The second place belongs to the Pacific region (countries including Australia, Hong Kong and Japan) when a five year period is used (5-Year return = 13.81%), while North America is ranked second (1-Year return = 18.97%) when performance is measured by one year. Overall, compared with the past, developed markets have recently provide excellent returns with a relatively safe environment for investors.

5.4.2 *Emerging Market*

If an investor is willing to take additional risk, then emerging markets would definitely be a viable choice in his portfolio. Panel B of Appendix 5 shows four different combinations under the emerging market category. They are Emerging Market Asia (including China, India and Thailand), Emerging Market Eastern Europe (including Czech Republic, Hungary, Poland, Russia), Emerging Market Latin America (including Argentina, Brazil, Mexico) and the famous BRIC (Brazil, Russia, India, China). No matter which investment period we use, the returns for these emerging markets are extremely impressive. For instance, the 3-Year annual return for EM Latin America is 52.31%. Its 1-Year annual return is even higher (58.52%). The 3-Year annual returns are 37.86% and 30.72% for EM Eastern Europe and EM Asia, respectively.

For EM Eastern Europe, there appears a slow down in performance as the 1-Year return is reduced to 22.05%, while the other regions are still earning returns beyond 40% in the same year. If an investor has 20% or more of his portfolio invested in emerging markets, the overall performance of the entire portfolio can be enhanced significantly. Of course, the underlying risk for the emerging market is also high. Thus, proper asset allocation is critical to maintaining risk control.

5.4.3 *China*

Panel C of Appendix 5 shows the returns for China and USA. For the 1-Year period, the USA provides an excellent return of 18.43%. Even so, that is only about one quarter of the total return provided by China (75.80%). Let us explore the reasons and the prospects of investing in China.

It is well recognized in the investment and wealth management arenas that China is the place for equity investments this decade. In the Asia-Pacific Wealth Report 2006 by Capgemini and Merrill Lynch, it is estimated that Chinese High-Net-Worth Individuals

(HNWIs) are in charge of US$1.59 trillion, or 20.9% of all wealth owned by HNWIs in Asia. Owing to regulatory restrictions, Chinese investors have limited opportunity in international investments. While some of the Chinese wealth would be exported to overseas investments through the Qualified Domestic Institutional Investor (QDII) scheme authorized by the government, most of the money, however, remains in the domestic equity market.

Therefore, we can expect that, due to strong home-bias and internal demand for Chinese equity, the value of Chinese equity will remain high. For instance, the average P/E ratio for the Chinese CSI 300 index is around 44 times on May 4, 2007. Such a high P/E ratio (compared with the P/E multiple of 15 times for HK stocks in March 2007 and a P/E of 16 times for Dow Jones Industrial Average in April 2007) may alert international investors to stay cautious in the seemingly over-valued Chinese equity market.

For international investors, the real issue is how long before this run-away Chinese bull is stopped by a bear. In the light of the strong international consumption and gigantic foreign reserve (US$1.2 trillion as of April 2007) that the Chinese government holds, it seems unlikely that the Chinese government will let the stock market suffer a substantial free-fall and risk the international investors' confidence in its equity markets. While the equity market may not experience the rapid growth as it did in 2006 (the equity value of China's stock markets had more than doubled), it will certainly be the focus of international investors for the next year (at least till the Beijing 2008 Summer Olympics Games are over). Eventually, the financial world does evolve around the "Middle Kingdom", an ancient name of a country now called China.

Appendix 1: International Securities Listed Under the Pilot Program on the Main Board of HKEx (May 4, 2007)

Stock code	Name of listed securities
04332	AMGEN-T
04336	APPL MATERIAL-T
04333	CISCO-T
04331	DELL-T
04335	INTEL-T
04362	ISHARES KOR-TR
04363	ISHARES TWN-TR
04338	MICROSOFT-T
04337	STARBUCKS-T

Source: www.hkex.com.hk/tradinfo/stockcode/eisdnadq.htm.

Appendix 2: List of Fund Categories for Credit Suisse/Tremont Hedge Fund Index

Convertible Arbitrage
Dedicated Short Bias
Emerging Markets
Equity Market Neutral
Event Driven
Distressed
Multi-Strategy
Risk Arbitrage
Fixed Income Arbitrage
Global Macro
Long/Short Equity
Managed Futures
Multi-Strategy

Source: www.hedgeindex.com/hedgeindex/en/default.aspx?cy=USD.

Appendix 3: Market Capitalization of Selective Stock Markets as at December 2006

Country	Market capitalization (US$ million)
Australia (Australian Securities Exchange)	1,160,511 (domestic only)
Canada (Toronto Stock Exchange)	1,826,540
Hong Kong Exchanges	1,698,566
Japan (Tokyo Stock Exchange)	4,636,923
USA (New York Stock Exchange)	25,000,000

Sources: www.asx.com.au; http://www.tsx.com; http://www.hkex.com.hk/ index.htm; http://www.tse.or.jp/english; http://www.nyse.com.

Appendix 4: Equity Return Performance of Selective Regions and Countries (All Returns are Annualized and Measured by MSCI Indices Ending on June 29, 2007)

	1 Yr (%)	3 Yr (%)	5 Yr (%)
Panel A: Developed Markets			
The World Index	21.400	14.680	12.030
North America	18.970	10.900	9.660
Pacific	14.020	15.510	13.810
Europe	29.000	21.270	15.620
Panel B: Emerging Markets			
EM Asia	43.450	30.720	22.000
EM Eastern Europe	22.050	37.860	35.500
EM Latin America	58.520	52.310	38.680
BRIC	48.360	47.020	36.510
Panel C: Selective Countries			
USA	18.430	9.940	8.940
China	75.800	41.030	30.840

Sources: www.mscibarra.com/products/indices/stdindex/performance.jsp.

References

Ammann M. and H. Zimmermann, 2001, Tracking error and tactical asset allocation, *Financial Analyst Journal,* 57, 32–43.

Blake, D., B. N. Lehmann, and A. Timmermann, 1999, Asset allocation dynamics and pension fund performance, *Journal of Business,* 72(4), 429–461.

Brinson, G. P., L. R. Hood, and G. L. Beebower, 1986, Determinants of portfolio performance, *Financial Analysts Journal,* 42(4), 39–44.

Brinson, G. P., B. D. Singer, and G. L. Beebower, 1991, Determinants of portfolio performance II: An update, *Financial Analysts Journal,* 47(3), 40–48.

Campbell, J. Y., 2002, Strategic asset allocation, Invited address to the American Economic Association and American Finance Association, Atlanta, Georgia, January 4.

Dahlquist, M. and C. R. Harvey, 2001, Global tactical asset allocation, *Emerging Markets Quarterly,* Spring, 6–14.

Lee, W., 1998, Risk and return characteristics of TAA under imperfect information, *Journal of Portfolio Management,* 25(1), 61–70.

Lee, W., 2000, *Theory and Methodology of Tactical Asset Allocation,* Hoboken, NJ: Wiley.

Treynor, J. L. and F. Black, 1973, How to use security analysis to improve portfolio selection, *Journal of Business,* 46, 66–86.

Chapter 4

Exchange-Traded Funds

*Yiuman Tse**

Exchange-traded funds (ETFs) are a basket of securities or commodities that can be traded throughout the day. ETFs are flexible investments for asset allocation, diversification and market tracking performance with low fees and tax efficiency. The growing popularity of ETFs is evident from the rapid growth in trading volume and the increasing expansion in product coverage over the past few years. ETFs track a wide variety of investment options across domestic and global markets, market capitalization, investment styles, and sectors. While ETFs that track the US broad-market indexes are the most popular class, US investors are ever more interested in ETFs that cover international indexes.

Keywords: Exchange-traded funds; international investments; asset allocation; diversification.

1. Introduction

Exchange-traded funds (ETFs) are rapidly becoming a popular investment tool for both individual and institutional investors. ETFs represent diversified portfolios of securities and commodities that have the best qualities of closed-end and open-end mutual funds. Like closed-end mutual funds, ETFs can be traded throughout the day, but unlike

* College of Business, 501 West Durango Blvd, University of Texas at San Antonio, San Antonio, Texas 78208, USA. Email: yiuman.tse@utsa.edu.

open-end mutual funds, they allow for the creation and redemption of securities. ETFs are used to execute a variety of tactics including asset allocation, diversification, and long-short arbitrage. ETFs generally have lower expense fees than mutual funds and are also more tax efficient. They have fewer security transactions than an actively managed mutual fund and, in contrast to open-end mutual funds, trading activity of other investors will not generate distributable capital gains.

The first ETF in the US was the S&P's Depository Receipt, which tracks the S&P 500 (SPDR or commonly known as the "Spider"), introduced by the American Stock Exchange in 1993. SPDR is now the most actively traded security in the world with an average daily volume of US$9.15 billion in 2006. The next most actively traded security is also an ETF, QQQQ, which tracks the Nasdaq 100 Index., with an average daily volume of US$4.35 billion in 2006.

Total assets invested in the more than 400 US ETFs grew 40% in 2006 to US$422 billion, according to Investment Company Institute, as the investor demand for trading flexibility, cost efficientcy, and transparency increased. Figure 1 shows the increasing trend in

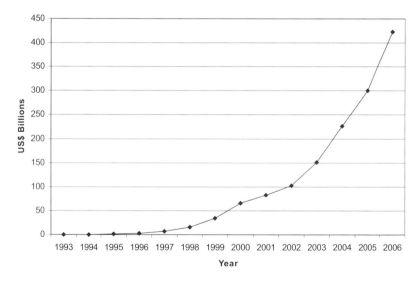

Figure 1. ETF Asset Growth: 1993–2006.

Source: Investment Company Institute.
The first ETF started trading in 1993.

Table 1. Different Classes of iShares Products as of March 2007

A. Market Capitalization	D. International
Small Cap	Europe
Mid Cap	Asia
Large Cap	Americas
Broad US Market	Global
	Regional
B. Style	Emerging Markets
Value	
Growth	E. Specialty/Real Estate
C. Sector/Industry	F. Fixed Income
Basic Material	Broad Market
Consumer Services	Government/Credit Bond
Consumer Goods	Credit/Corporate Bond
Energy	Treasury Bond
Financial	Mortgage
Healthcare	
Industrial	G. Commodities
Natural Resources	Broad Based
Technology	Precious Metals
Telecommunications	
Transportation	
Utilities	

There are more than 120 iShares ETFs managed by Barclay Global Fund Advisors.
Sources: www.iShares.com.

ETF asset growth. Asset managers such as Barclays Global Investors, the largest ETF manager, and State Street Global Investors launch new ETFs every year. Most ETFs are passively managed, tracking a wide variety of sector-specific, country-specific, and broad-market indexes. As shown in Table 1, iShares funds managed by Barclays Global Investors is the world's largest family of ETFs. The ETFs in this family cover almost every sector, market cap, country and style.

Although ETFs still have a smaller market share than the conventional stock and bond mutual funds (which have a total asset value of US$7.5 trillion), the rapid growth of ETFs has forced the Vanguard Group and other large mutual funds to lower fees and launch their own ETFs.

2. How Are ETFs Created, Redeemed, and Traded?

Investors can trade ETFs on an exchange throughout the day like a single stock and, unlike mutual funds, the money does not go directly to the fund company. Instead, Authorized Participants (the market makers and large institutional investors who are authorized to create and redeem shares of an ETF) loan an entire portfolio of shares to the fund manager. The stocks are placed in a trust and shares of the ETF are created and redeemed in multiples of 50,000 shares. The ETF requires in-kind transactions; i.e., units of the fund are swapped for the underlying stocks. Only institutional and wealthy investors can afford to deal directly with the fund companies. Most investors go through a broker to trade ETF shares.

As described by Traulsen (2000) and Chamberlain and Jordan (2006), by permitting large investors to buy or redeem shares in kind, ETFs should trade close to the net asset values (NAV) of their underlying holdings. If an ETF traded at a discount to its NAV, institutional investors could buy 50,000-share units in the open market at the discounted price, redeem them for the underlying stocks, and sell those stocks at a profit. If the ETF trades at a premium, institutional investors will buy the underlying stocks, create new ETF units in kind, and sell these units at the premium price.

These arbitrage activities close the gap between the market price of ETFs and their NAV, providing small investors assurance that they can trade at equitable prices. Moreover, liquidity comes from ETFs being created and redeemed as needed to match investor demand. This enables both large and small orders to be "filled" intraday at prices that represent close tracking to the intraday NAV of the ETFs.

Elton *et al.* (2002) show that the differences between the market price and NAV of SPDR are small (less than 1.8 basis points per year) and short-lived (not more than a day). However, Lauricella and Gullapalli (2007) contend that when markets are fast-moving and volatile, the difference can be significant. For example, February 27, 2007 was one of those exceptional days when stock prices tumbled first in China, and the Russell 2000 Index of small-company shares fell 3.75% that day, but the corresponding ETF that tracks that index fell 4.7%, and 89 ETFs tracked by Morningstar fell short of their portfolio value by more than 1%. Investors who sold amid the turmoil got significantly less for their ETF shares than the underlying assets were worth. This mispricing problem is more severe for the US traded ETFs whose underlying stocks are traded overseas.

3. Advantages of ETFs

ETF shares can be bought and sold on an exchange anytime during regular trading hours, and may often be traded after-hours on Electronic Communications Networks (ECNs) through any brokerage account. Investors can use all investment strategies that are associated with stocks, such as market orders, limit orders, stop orders, short sales, and margin trading. ETFs are powerful and flexible instruments that provide asset allocation, diversification and market tracking performance with low fees and tax efficiency.

3.1 *Asset Allocation*

Asset allocation, or determining what percentage of a portfolio to devote to various asset classes, is the most important decision an investor must make. ETFs are the ideal tool for asset allocation. They represent almost every asset class available and are cheap, liquid, and reliable. The asset classes in which ETFs are available include major index funds, value and growth funds, small-, mid- and large-cap funds, sector and industry funds, individual country and global region funds, Treasury and corporate bond funds, real estate funds, commodity (including gold, silver, and oil), and currency funds. Using ETFs, investors can easily build a portfolio suited to their investment goals.

ETFs are also useful for cash equitization. In particular, if investors want to hold some cash to give them flexibility in their investment decisions, they can hold very liquid ETFs, such as SPDR and QQQQ. This allows them, particularly institutional investors, to remain in the market, and, if necessary, they can convert the ETFs to cash easily for reinvestment.

3.2 *Diversification*

ETFs provide efficient and diversified exposure to an entire asset class because they track the composition and performance of some of the world's major market indexes. ETFs can also be used to diversify an entire portfolio. For example, the DB Commodity Index Tracking Fund (DBC) works like a commodity pool. This is the most recent ETF-like product offered on a US stock exchange providing direct exposure to a diverse basket of commodities, such as oil, gold, agricultural products. Global commodities have one of the lowest correlations to US stocks. Including ETFs of commodities in a stock portfolio is an easy way to reduce the portfolio's volatility and increase its risk-adjusted returns.

3.3 *Tax Efficiency*

Traditional mutual funds are subject to specialized tax rules. In particular, when some investors sell their shares, fund managers may have to sell holdings to raise cash. If that trading generates capital gains, they must pass through realized capital gains to the remaining (buy-and-hold) investors, regardless of the fund's performance. That is why investors may still receive capital gains tax distributions even if that fund has lost value. Nevertheless, managers of tax-managed mutual funds can employ many strategies to avoid taxable distributions, such as limiting the number of transactions and selling trailing stocks for a loss to offset gains.

In contrast, ETFs are traded on an exchange, not from a fund company. ETFs are not redeemed by shareholders. The creation and redemption activity using the in-kind transfer does not create capital gains and, accordingly, tax burden for the remaining ETF holders. Investors only realize capital gains when they sell their own ETFs shares. However, some ETFs, such as gold, silver, and currency ETFs, are taxed at the collectibles tax rate (28%) instead of the long-term capital gains rate of 15%. Bond ETFs are also taxed at a less desirable income tax rate.

3.4 *Low Expense Ratios*

Because of the passive nature of most index ETFs, their expense ratios are lower than those of actively managed funds and most traditional index mutual funds. In 2006, the expense ratios of iShares S&P 500 (IVV) was 0.09%, while the average expense ratios of the most active large-blend funds was 1.3%. The average ratio of large blend index funds was 0.62%, while the lowest ratio among those funds was 0.18%, for the Vanguard 500 mutual fund (VFINX).

It is important to note that ETF transactions will result in brokerage commissions. For large trades of above $10,000, this transaction fee is immaterial, but for small trades, it becomes significant. ETF's cost advantages are not always as attractive as they show. Therefore, a traditional mutual fund is a better choice than an ETF for investors who buy regular small amounts of shares, such as with 401(k) monthly contributions. Recently, the industry is also making ETFs easier to use in 401(k) plans, as fund managers can lower expenses by bundling trades from different accounts and then executing them once a day.

4. Recent Developments of ETFs and Conclusions

ETFs continue to grow in popularity with the asset percentages of 60% in the broad US market, 26% in international, 9% in sector US, and 5% in the bonds in 2006. While all classes are growing, international leads the trend with 71% increase. Figure 2 shows the increasing growth of international ETFs traded in the US in recent years. In particular, international iShares ETFs of Barclays Global Investors, including Asian, European, and American ETFs, allow investors to diversify their holdings in international markets by using investment vehicles that represent diversified baskets of international assets which can be traded in dollars on US markets. US investors who are interested in purchasing stocks of international companies can purchase ETFs rather than worrying about trading in local currencies through overnight markets and holding undiversified positions in international stocks (see Tse and Martinez, 2007).

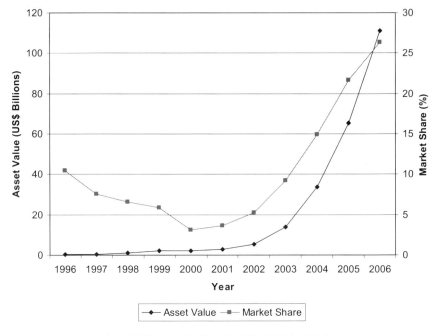

Figure 2. International ETFs traded in the US: 1996–2006.

Source: Investment Company Institute
No international ETFs were traded in the US before 1996.

China ETFs were the best investments in 2006 because of booming economic growth in China. iShares FTSE/Xinhua China 25 Index (FXI) and PowerShares Golden Dragon Halter USX China (PGJ) returned 81% and 51%, respectively. The growing Russian economy is also attracting investor interest. Investment manager Van Eck Global recently launched Market Vectors-Russia ETF (RSX), a new exchange-traded fund. The fund is the first ETF listed in the US that enables investors to gain exposure to a wide spectrum of Russian companies.

Single-country iShares also provide targeted exposure to different economic sectors. Understanding sector exposures is the primary step in designing investment strategies that incorporate both geographical and sector preferences in a single investment product. Table 2 summarizes the iShares Single-Country ETFs.

Table 2. Top Five Single-Country iShares within Each Sector as of March 2007

Country	Ticket Symbol	Sector %
A. Consumer Discretionary		
Japan	EWJ	21.2
Netherlands	EWN	15.4
Malaysia	EWM	15.3
France	EWQ	14.6
Germany	EWG	14.3
B. Consumer Staples		
Netherlands	EWN	19.0
Mexico	EWW	18.4
Malaysia	EWM	12.8
Switzerland	EWL	12.5
Belgium	EWK	12.0
C. Energy		
Canada	EWC	29.3
Brazil	EWZ	25.1
Italy	EWI	17.2
UK	EWU	16.2
France	EWQ	12.7
D. Financials		
Belgium	EWK	61.7
Singapore	EWS	55.0
Hong Kong	EWH	52.6
Australia	EWA	48.2
Italy	EWI	47.9
E. Healthcare		
Switzerland	EWL	30.6
UK	EWU	8.1
France	EWQ	8.04
Belgium	EWK	5.9
Japan	EWJ	5.8
F. Industrial		
Sweden	EWD	29.0
Singapore	EWS	21.7
Malaysia	EWM	18.0
Japan	EWJ	16.6
Hong Kong	EWH	14.8

(Continued)

Table 2. (*Continued*)

Country		Ticket Symbol	Sector %
G.	Information Technology		
	Taiwan	EWT	57.9
	South Korea	EWY	26.4
	Sweden	EWD	18.1
	Japan	EWJ	12.6
	Germany	EWG	6.2
H.	Materials		
	South Africa	EZA	27.0
	Brazil	EWZ	26.1
	Australia	EWA	20.5
	Mexico	EWW	18.7
	Canada	EWC	15.6
I.	Telecommunications Services		
	Mexico	EWW	39.0
	Spain	EWP	17.1
	Austria	EWO	13.6
	Singapore	EWS	12.6
	South Africa	EZA	11.1
J.	Utilities		
	Spain	EWP	14.7
	Germany	EWG	14.4
	Hong Kong	EWH	13.0
	Malaysia	EWM	12.4
	Italy	EWI	10.8

Source: www.iShares.com.

The currency ETFs such as the Euro Currency Trust (FXE) from Rydex Investments allow investors to gain exposure to the currency markets. Currency ETFs are similar to money-market funds but denominated in foreign currencies. A declining dollar has increased the popularity of these ETFs since they were introduced in 2006. However, like the international ETFs, currency ETFs have a higher expense ratio (ranging from 0.4% to 0.8%) than most US index ETFs. Investors should also beware of the notoriously unpredictable currency markets.

A series of ETFs introduced by ProShares in 2006 do not merely attempt to merely achieve the same return as their underlying indexes. Ultra QQQ ProShares (QLD) seeks daily investment results that correspond to twice (200%) the daily performance of the Nasdaq-100 Index, while UltraShort QQQ(R) ProShares (QID) doubles the *inverse* of the Nasdaq index. Another example of an innovative ETF is the oil futures ETF, USO, which is like a traded commodity. The fund invests primarily in futures contracts for light and sweet crude oil that are traded on the New York Mercantile Exchange.

A continuous array of fundamentally weighted, timeliness-seeking, dividend-focused and other specialty exchange-traded funds are rolling out. These ETFs have been launched with the same premise: market-cap weighted indexes are inefficient because they get caught up in market bubbles; one can outperform the market by using an alternate methodology. However, it takes more time to evaluate the performance of these specialty ETFs. The SEC is also considering the applications for actively managed ETFs. Despite higher transaction costs, some fund managers expect actively managed ETFs to outperform their counterparts tied to market indexes. However, many studies have shown that it is difficult to outperform or add value above indexes. Moreover, big mutual-fund companies are likely to continue to dominate because of their plentiful marketing resources and powerful distribution networks.

In conclusion, ETFs offer investors many advantages. They are flexible, transparent, liquid, and low-cost. The popularity of ETFs is soaring among institutional and individual investors as advisors are using more ETFs to provide various strategies to clients. However, it is worth noting that if the strategy is erroneous, ETFs will also make it easier for investors to more efficiently lose money.

References

Chamberlain, M. and J. Jordan, 2006, *An Introduction to Exchange Trade Funds*, iShares Publications.

Elton, E. J., M. J. Gruber, G. Comer, and K. Li, 2002, Spider: Where are the bugs? *Journal of Business*, 75, 453–427.

Lauricella, T. and D. Gullapalli, 2007, Fast-money crowd embraces ETFs, adding risk for individual investors, *The Wall Street Journal*, A1, March 17.

Traulsen, C. J., 2000, Exchange-traded funds: What you should know, *Morningstar Articles*, id=3503, August 24, 2000.

Tse, Y. and V. Martinez, 2007, Price discovery and informational efficiency of international iShares funds, *Global Finance Journal* 18.

Part II: Traditional Investments

B. Global Fixed Income Investments

Chapter 5

Global Fixed Income Markets and Portfolio Management

*Xiaoqing Eleanor Xu**†

The globalization and innovation of the world's fixed income markets in the past two decades have created tremendous opportunities for investors and portfolio managers who are seeking more investment alternatives, return enhancement, and risk diversification. This chapter discusses recent advances in global fixed income markets, focusing on four areas that deserve the most attention: the creation of the Euro and its impact on the global bond market, securitized debt and covered bonds, inflation-linked bonds and emerging market bonds. Finally, I discuss the risk management of fixed income portfolios in a global context.

Keywords: International bonds; securitized debt; inflation-linked bonds; emerging market debt; risk management.

---

* The author thanks Sherwood Kuo and Nick Gendron of Lehman Brothers Fixed Income Research for providing data on Lehman Brothers Fixed Income Indices, Matthew Cocup of Barclays Capital for providing data on World Government Inflation-Linked Bond Index, Conor Coughlan of International Capital Market Association for providing data on international bond market size and composition, and Anthony Loviscek of Seton Hall University for comments and suggestions.
† Stillman School of Business, Seton Hall University, 400 South Orange Avenue, South Orange, NJ 07079, USA. Email: xuxe@shu.edu.

1. Introduction

Although bonds have traditionally attracted less attention than stocks, the globalization and innovation of the world's fixed income markets in the past two decades have created tremendous opportunities for investors and portfolio managers who are seeking more investment alternatives, return enhancement, and risk diversification. Predictable cash flow streams make bonds well suited to fund predefined liability for institutional investors such as pension funds, life insurance companies, and endowment funds.

According to the Irish Association of Pension Funds (IAPF), the size of the world global bond market was US$45 trillion in 2004, with a US composition of 48%. As shown in Table 1, the size of the world bond market is far greater than that of the equity market. For example, the Eurozone and Japan's bond markets are both around three times the size of their respective equity markets. The US, with the most developed equity market, also has a bond market that is 45% larger than its equity market.

The latest statistics from the Lehman Brothers Global Aggregate Bond Index indicate that 61% of the world's bonds are denominated in currencies other than the US dollar (see Table 2) and 64% are

Table 1. Size of Bond Markets, Equity Markets, and Bank Assets, Year-end 2003

Country/Region	Bond Markets	Equity Markets	Bank Assets
Panel A. Size in USD billions			
Eurozone	12,005	4,098	21,377
EU-15	14,941	6,321	24,966
US	18,587	12,787	8,004
Japan	7,250	2,647	6,259
Panel B. Size as a Percentage of GDP			
Eurozone	146%	50%	260%
EU-15	142%	60%	237%
US	169%	116%	73%
Japan	169%	62%	146%

Source: European Capital Markets Institute, Casey and Karel (2005).

Table 2. Composition of the Global Fixed Income Market by Currency and Sector, June 2007

Sector	Sub-sector\Currency	United States Dollar (USD)	European Euro (EUR)	Japanese Yen (JPY)	UK Pounds (GBP)	Canadian Dollar (CAD)	Korean Won (KPW)	Swedish Krona (SEK)	Australian Dollar (AUD)	Other Currencies	Total
Treasury	Total	9.20	17.90	12.79	2.57	0.87	1.32	0.31	0.16	2.52	47.64
Government-Related	Agency	4.92	1.91	1.42	0.46	0.40	0.07	0.01	0.05	0.04	9.28
	Local Authority	0.33	1.37	0.47	0.01	0.83			0.19	0.00	3.20
	Sovereign	0.66	0.40	0.05	0.05				0.01	-0.01	1.16
	Supranational	0.53	0.42	0.02	0.38	0.02		0.00	0.05	0.03	1.45
	Total	**6.44**	**4.09**	**1.97**	**0.90**	**1.25**	**0.07**	**0.01**	**0.30**	**0.06**	**15.09**
Corporate	Industrial	3.75	1.73	0.19	0.49	0.11	0.00	0.01	0.01	0.00	6.29
	Utility	0.67	0.34	0.24	0.20	0.02			0.00	0.00	1.47
	Financial Institutions	3.67	2.67	0.64	1.21	0.23	0.02	0.05	0.06	0.03	8.58
	Total	**8.08**	**4.75**	**1.08**	**1.89**	**0.36**	**0.02**	**0.06**	**0.07**	**0.03**	**16.34**
Securitized	MBS Pass-through	13.58								0.00	13.58
	ABS	0.21	0.15	0.01	0.22					-0.01	0.58
	CMBS	1.38	0.00		0.08					0.00	1.46
	Covered	0.13	4.68	0.02	0.05			0.29	0.00	0.13	5.30
	Total	**15.30**	**4.83**	**0.03**	**0.34**			**0.29**	**0.00**	**0.13**	**20.92**
Total	**Total**	**39.02**	**31.57**	**15.87**	**5.71**	**2.48**	**1.41**	**0.67**	**0.54**	**2.73**	**100.00**

Note: All figures represent the composition of market size in percentages, both country domestic and international bond markets.
Source: Lehman Brothers Global Fixed Income Aggregate Index.

Table 3. Composition of the Global Fixed Income Market by Country and Maturity, June 2007

Country	Total	Maturity in Years					
		1 to 3	3 to 5	5 to 7	7 to 10	10 to 20	20 +
United States	36.21	6.86	7.20	5.27	12.78	2.03	2.06
Japan	15.90	4.45	4.04	2.09	3.10	1.81	0.40
Germany	9.76	3.35	2.42	1.36	1.45	0.34	0.83
France	6.23	1.62	1.23	0.93	1.14	0.79	0.52
United Kingdom	5.19	0.81	0.78	0.37	0.91	1.01	1.31
Italy	4.83	1.12	0.84	0.35	0.82	0.76	0.93
Spain	3.28	0.62	0.59	0.59	0.75	0.42	0.31
Canada	2.89	0.59	0.67	0.28	0.37	0.36	0.62
Netherlands	2.03	0.65	0.39	0.32	0.40	0.13	0.14
South Korea	1.56	0.81	0.32	0.12	0.26	0.04	0.00
Supranational	1.45	0.42	0.26	0.21	0.24	0.18	0.14
Belgium	1.26	0.28	0.19	0.25	0.30	0.10	0.14
Austria	0.99	0.16	0.13	0.23	0.23	0.17	0.07
Sweden	0.97	0.44	0.23	0.12	0.10	0.07	0.00
Greece	0.90	0.22	0.13	0.17	0.11	0.18	0.08
Australia	0.62	0.18	0.18	0.08	0.14	0.04	0.00
Mexico	0.58	0.12	0.11	0.07	0.13	0.09	0.06
Denmark	0.54	0.21	0.14	0.07	0.07	0.05	0
Portugal	0.53	0.12	0.14	0.07	0.11	0.07	0.03
Ireland	0.51	0.12	0.07	0.09	0.14	0.07	0.02
Others	3.77	0.82	0.85	0.55	0.80	0.58	0.23
Total	**100.00**	**23.97**	**20.91**	**13.59**	**24.35**	**9.29**	**7.89**

Note: All figures above are composition of market size in percentage.
Source: Lehman Brothers Global Fixed Income Aggregate Index.

issued outside of the US (Table 3). As for non-domestic international bond markets, statistics from the International Capital Market Association (Table 4 and Figure 1) show that Euro-denominated bonds occupied a larger market share (46%) than US dollar-denominated bonds (37%) in 2006. This is in dramatic contrast with the composition of international bond markets in 2002, when the share of the USD-denominated bonds (49%) clearly outweighed the share of Euro-denominated bonds (32%).

Table 4. International Bond Market Size by Currency and Year

Year\ Currency	European Euro (EUR)	US Dollar (USD)	UK Pounds (GBP)	Switzerland Francs (CHF)	Japanese Yen (JPY)	Other	Total
Panel A. International Bond Market Size in USD billions							
2002	2,037	3,150	515	111	161	482	6,456
2003	2,652	3,420	624	121	158	402	7,377
2004	3,369	3,579	763	139	157	396	8,403
2005	4,131	3,770	916	163	148	414	9,542
2006	4,836	3,892	1,043	191	149	434	10,545
Panel B. International Bond Market Size %							
2002	31.55	48.79	7.98	1.72	2.49	7.47	100
2003	35.95	46.36	8.46	1.64	2.14	5.45	100
2004	40.09	42.59	9.08	1.65	1.87	4.71	100
2005	43.29	39.51	9.60	1.71	1.55	4.34	100
2006	45.86	36.91	9.89	1.81	1.41	4.12	100

Source: International Capital Market Association (ICMA) Limited.

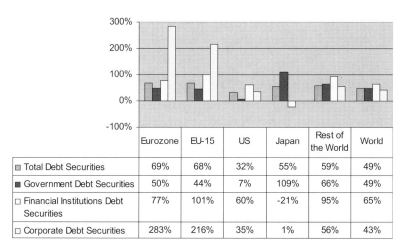

	Eurozone	EU-15	US	Japan	Rest of the World	World
Total Debt Securities	69%	68%	32%	55%	59%	49%
Government Debt Securities	50%	44%	7%	109%	66%	49%
Financial Institutions Debt Securities	77%	101%	60%	-21%	95%	65%
Corporate Debt Securities	283%	216%	35%	1%	56%	43%

Figure 1. Growth in Amount Outstanding of Debt Securities from 1999 to 2004.

Note: EU-15 refers to Austria, Belgium, Denmark, Finland, France, Germany, Greece, Italy, Luxembourg, Netherlands, Portugal, Spain, Sweden, and the UK
Source: Europe's Hidden Capital Markets, Center of European Policy Studies, 2005.

The dramatic growth and sheer size of non-US bond markets can be largely attributed to the end of the Cold War, the transition to a market economy, deregulation, disintermediation, creation of Euro, advancement of information technology, and global integration. Given this new global debt market structure, ignoring non-US bonds is no longer a sensible option for investors because it limits investors to less than 40% of the available bonds worldwide.

The global fixed income market is composed of domestic bonds (bonds issued by domestic issuers denominated in the issuing country's official currency) and international bonds (bonds issued by foreign issuers and/or denominated in foreign currency). Excluding all the domestic bond markets around the world, the international bond market is estimated to be US$10.5 trillion as of year-end 2006 (see Figure 2), which is equivalent to 5.5 times of its size in 1993 and 2.6 times its size in 1999. International bonds consist of foreign bonds, Eurobonds, and global bonds.

A foreign bond is a bond issued in a country's national bond market by an issuer from another country. A foreign bond is called a *Yankee* bond in the US, a *Samurai* bond in Japan, a *Bulldog* bond in the UK, a *Matador* bond in Spain, and a *Rembrandt* bond in the Netherlands.

International Bond Market Size by Currency (December 2006)

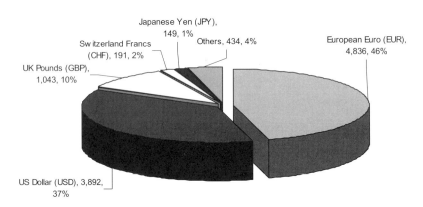

Figure 2. International Bond Market Size by Currency as of December 2006 (figures in USD billions).

Source: International Capital Market Association.

Typically, a foreign bond is subject to regulations from the country where the bond is issued. The *Yankee* bond market was the most popular place for foreign companies to issue dollar-denominated bonds in the 1950s and early 1960s. However, the interest equalization tax imposed by the US government in 1963 led to the decline in *Yankee* bonds. Foreign bonds represent the earliest form of international bonds, but their markets have experienced substantial declines due to the growth in the Eurobond market.

A Eurobond is a bond issued in one country's currency but is traded outside of that country. Eurobonds are named after the currency they are denominated in. For example, Eurodollar and Euroyen bonds are denominated in US dollar and Japanese yen, respectively. Eurobonds may also be denominated in Euros. They are underwritten by international syndicates and issued outside the jurisdiction of any single country.

A global bond is one that is issued in two or more countries at the same time, and typically by multinational corporations or governments to raise large amounts of funds at one time in global financial markets. Most of the global bonds are offered both domestically and internationally as domestic bonds and Eurobonds (see Amira and Handorf, 2004).

To discuss recent advances in global fixed income markets, I will focus on four areas that deserve the most attention: the creation of the Euro and its impact on the global bond market, securitized debt and covered bonds, inflation-linked bonds, and emerging market bonds. Finally, I will discuss the risk management of fixed income portfolios in a global context.

2. The Creation of the Euro and Its Impact on the Global Bond Market

The Euro was introduced to the world as the official currency of the Eurozone (initially including 11 European nations of Austria, Belgium, Finland, France, Germany, Ireland, Italy, Luxembourg, the Netherlands, Portugal, and Spain) in January 1999 and managed by the European Central Bank (ECB). With the launch of the Euro, these eleven bond markets consolidated into one: a unified market for Euro-denominated bonds. The addition of Greece in 2002 and

Slovenia in 2007 brings the total Eurozone membership to thirteen. The UK and Denmark are also widely expected to adopt the Euro within the next decade.

The impact of the creation of the Euro on the global fixed income market has been threefold. First, the creation of the Euro eliminated the thirteen member national currencies and stimulated M&A activities across country borders within the Eurozone. This has resulted in explosive growth in corporate bond issuance in Europe. While the US remains the dominant corporate bond market, the explosive growth rate in issuance of Euro-denominated corporate bonds has made the international credit market even more important. Between 1999 and 2004, outstanding corporate debt securities grew by 283% in the Eurozone, while in the US and Japan, they grew by 35% and 1%, respectively (see Figure 3). Second, the rise of the Euro has fostered a deeper, more innovative, and more integrated European bond market. Finally, the creation of the Euro has transformed the landscape of the world bond market into three major currency blocs: 39% in the US dollar, 32% in the Euro, and 16% in the Japanese yen (see Table 2). Although the remaining 13% are denominated in other

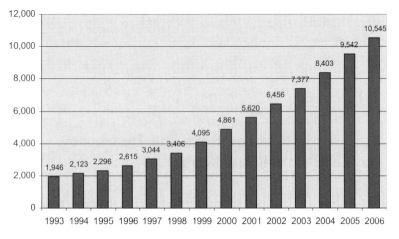

Figure 3. International Bond Market Size from 1993 to 2006 (figures in USD billions).

Source: International Capital Market Association.

currencies, they are typically associated with one of the above three currency blocs. For example, UK, Sweden and Denmark bonds are benchmarked to Euro-denominated bonds, and Canada and Australia bonds are benchmarked to the US bond market.

3. Securitized Debt and Covered Bonds

Securitized debt involves mortgage-backed securities (MBS) and other asset-backed securities (ABS). They are typically off-balance-sheet transactions in which financial institutions package homogeneous loans in special purpose vehicles (SPVs) and issue bonds funded by the loan pool's cash flow. A MBS is a security in which cash flows are backed by the principal and interest payments of a pool of mortgage loans. Other types of ABS include securitization products of credit card receivables, account receivables, car loans, home equity loans, and student loans. This securitization process removes the loans and the associated interest rate risk, prepayment risk and credit risk from financial institutions' balance sheets. Securitized debt currently represents the largest sector in the US bond market and the second largest sector in the global bond market. As of March 2007, the value of US MBS and other ABS outstanding amounted to US$6.6 trillion and US$2.2 trillion, respectively, accounting for 37% of the US bond market (see Table 5). Advances in financial engineering and structured finance techniques, increased availability of consumer credit information, and standardization and credit support from government agencies are credited for the success of the US securitized debt market.

Covered bonds are debt instruments secured by a cover pool of mortgage loans or public-sector loans. Based on the high quality of the collateral loans in the cover pool and the credit strength of the issuing financial institutions, most covered bonds are rated as AAA or AA. Germany first introduced covered bonds, known as *Pfandbriefe*, back in 1770. Covered bonds are also known as mortgage bonds, *Obligations Foncières* (in France), *Lettres de Gage* (in Luxembourgeois), and *Cédulas Hipotecarias* (in Spain). Covered bonds play a critical role in the European financial system. From the issuers' perspective, covered bonds enable financial institutions to obtain a

Table 5. A Comparison of Securitized Debt Issuance Volume in US and Europe

	US			Europe		Europe/ US
	MBS	ABS	Total	Euro billions	Converted to USD billions	
1999	1,046.1	287.1	1,333.2	73.2	77.98	5.8%
2000	708.1	337.0	1,045.1	78.2	72.19	6.9%
2001	1,671.4	383.3	2,054.7	152.6	136.61	6.6%
2002	2,219.2	469.2	2,688.4	157.7	149.09	5.5%
2003	3,071.0	600.2	3,671.2	217.3	246.01	6.7%
2004	1,779.1	869.8	2,648.9	243.5	302.87	11.4%
2005	1,966.3	1,172.1	3,138.4	327.0	407.08	13.0%
2006	2,002.6	1,251.9	3,254.5	458.9	576.52	17.7%

Note: All figures are in USD billions. European data are converted to US dollar from Euro using the annual EUR-USD exchange rate provided by the Federal Reserve.
Source: Securities Industry and Financial Markets Association (SIFMA), European Securitisation Forum.

lower cost of funding to finance mortgage or public loans. From the investors' perspective, covered bonds provide government-like credit quality and enhanced return potential. To attract investors, Germany and many other European countries have modified their covered bond laws in recent years. For example, Germany reformed the Mortgage Banking Act in 1998, 2002, and 2004. In the past decade, the once domestic covered bond markets have become international due to the excellent safety record of these bonds, the emergence of the Euro, the increasing need for mortgage financing, the enhanced investor protection provided by new legislations, and greater liquidity brought by Jumbo *Pfandbriefe*. As of year-end 2005, the value of covered bonds outstanding amounted to 1.8 trillion Euros, making it the second largest sector of the European bond market, after government bonds. With more than 976 billion euros outstanding as of year-end 2005, the German *Pfandbriefe* represents 54% of Europe's covered bond market, while the other twenty-four covered bond issuing countries in Europe represent the remaining 46% of the market (see Figure 4).

Mortgage-covered bonds are similar to MBS in that they both play important roles in the funding of mortgage loans, but there is

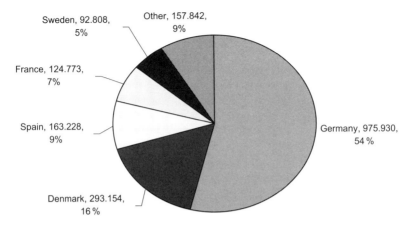

Figure 4. Composition of the European Covered Bond Market (as of December 2005).

Note: Figures are in billion Euros. Total market size: 1,808.735 billion Euros.
Source: European Covered Bond Council.

one major difference: loans backing the covered bonds remain on the balance sheet, while loans backing the MBS are off the balance sheet. In addition, covered bonds are bullet bonds that are direct obligations of the issuing financial institutions, while MBS are amortized bonds that are funded by the mortgage pool's monthly principal and interest payments and guaranteed either by state agencies (such as Ginnie Mae, Fannie Mae, and Freddie Mae in the US) or private agencies. Securitization in Europe has also developed quickly since the introduction of the Euro. As shown in Table 5, annual securitized debt issuance in Europe increased rapidly from 73 billion Euros in 1999 (equivalent to 5.8% of the issuance volume in US) to 459 billion Euros in 2006 (equivalent to 17.7% of the issuance volume in US). However, asset securitization in Europe is still in its infancy. As of 2005, the European covered bonds issuance (479 billion Euros) is still larger than the securitized debt issuance (327 billion Euros). In addition, securitization debt in Europe is largely dominated by the UK, which accounts for 51% of the issuance in 2006 (see Table 6, Panel A). Residential MBS represents 53% of the securitized debt issuance in Europe, followed by collateralized debt obligations and commercial MBS (see Table 6, Panel B).

Panel A. World ILB Market Size from 1997 to 2007

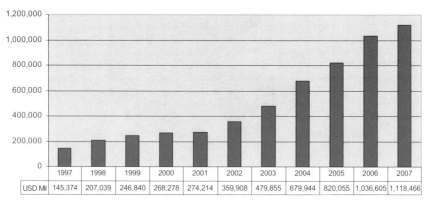

Panel B. World ILB Market Composition from 1997 to 2007

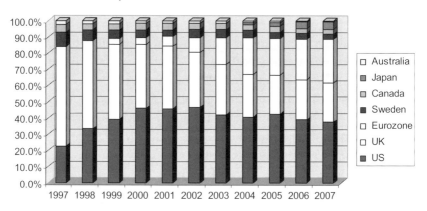

Figure 5. Global Inflation-Linked Bonds (ILBs).

Note: 2007 figures are as of June 30, 2007. All other annual figures are based on year-end data.
Source: Barclays Capital World Government Inflation-Linked Bond Index.

4. Inflation-linked Bonds

Inflation-linked bonds (ILBs) offer bond investors a guaranteed inflation-adjusted yield. From an investor's perspective, ILBs provide an
explicit hedge against the erosion of purchasing power from inflation

Table 6. European Securitization Issuance by Country of Collateral and Asset of Collateral

Country	In Euro Billions		Percent of Total	
	2006	2005	2006	2005

Panel A. European Securitization Issuance by Country of Collateral (excluding Credit Derivative Obligations (CDOs))

UK	192.2	126.4	51.8%	45.5%
Spain	44.0	40.5	11.9%	14.6%
Germany	37.7	15.5	10.2%	5.6%
Italy	30.2	32.7	8.1%	11.8%
Netherlands	28.6	39.2	7.7%	14.1%
Ireland	10.6	0.5	2.9%	0.2%
France	7.7	7.5	2.1%	2.7%
Portugal	5.8	7.6	1.6%	2.7%
Others	14.1	8.2	3.8%	2.9%
Total	**370.9**	**278.1**	**100.0%**	**100.0%**

Note: Excluding CDOs in the above country composition table. A substantial percentage of CDOs are backed by multi-jurisdictional collateral.

Asset	In Euro Billions		Percent of Total	
	2006	2005	2006	2005

Panel B. European Securitization Issuance by Asset of Collateral

Residential MBS	244.6	144.9	53.3%	44.3%
CDO[a]	88.0	48.9	19.2%	15.0%
Commercial MBS	60.1	38.6	13.1%	11.8%
Loans[b]	15.7	46.9	3.4%	14.3%
Auto Loans	11.7	4.1	2.5%	1.3%
Receivables[c]	6.0	4.0	1.3%	1.2%
Leases[d]	5.9	8.2	1.3%	2.5%
Credit Cards Receivables	3.4	11.7	0.7%	3.6%
Other	23.5	19.7	5.1%	6.0%
Total	**458.9**	**327.0**	**100.0%**	**100.0%**

[a] CDO securities issued in Euros.
[b] Includes leveraged, commercial, consumer, corporate and other loans.
[c] Includes account, health care, insurance, utility and other receivables.
[d] Includes equipment and other leases.
Source: European Securitisation Council.

and a diversification in a portfolio due to their low correlation with other asset classes. From an issuer's perspective, ILB removes the required inflation premium from the required yield on the bonds, lowers the borrowing cost of the issuer, and allows for better matching of interest payment with the inflation-linked revenues that the issuer generates.

An inflation-linked bond's face value and coupon payment are typically adjusted periodically to compensate investors for inflation risk. While there are some inflation-linked issues in the European corporate bond market, ILBs remain highly dominated by government bond issues. A consumer price index from the issuing country has been historically used as the benchmark for the ILB's inflation adjustment. European countries, such as France, Germany, Italy and Greece, have recently issued ILBs that are linked to the core inflation index in the Eurozone (i.e., EMU-HICP). Empirical studies (e.g., Kothari and Shanken, 2004) have confirmed the merits of ILBs in terms of hedging against inflation, low volatility and low correlation with other asset classes.

The world's first ILB was issued by the UK government back in 1981, known as the inflation-linked Gilts. In 1997, the US government issued its first ILB named Treasury Inflation Protected Securities (TIPS). Other prominent ILB issuers include Australia (1985), Canada (1991), Sweden (1994), New Zealand (1995), France (1998), Greece (2003), Italy (2003), Japan (2004), and Germany (2006). As shown in Panel A of Figure 5, the world ILB market has grown dramatically from US$145 billion in December of 1997 to US$1.12 trillion in June 2007. Panel B of Figure 5 shows that, as of June 2007, the US TIPS (38%) represent the largest share of the world ILB market, followed by the UK (24%), France (15%), Italy (9%) and Japan (5%). In terms of relative size as a percentage of the issuing country's entire government bond market, the UK ILB market has the largest size and best liquidity.

Table 7 presents the comparative return and yield performance of the Barclays Capital's regular government bond indices and government ILB indices. Since ILB pays a yield on inflation-adjusted principal, its yield is lower than the yield on regular government bonds.

Table 7. Comparative Performance of All Government Bonds and Government Inflation-Linked Bonds (ILBs)

Year	Panel A1 Total Return on All Government Bonds				Panel A2 Yield on All Government Bonds			
	US	UK	France	Sweden	US	UK	France	Sweden
1999	-2.58	-1.32	-2.93	-2.72	6.74	5.40	5.26	5.61
2000	13.55	8.91	7.17	10.01	5.50	4.75	4.94	4.70
2001	6.74	3.19	5.45	2.67	5.22	5.00	4.86	5.19
2002	11.74	9.13	9.60	8.89	4.02	4.46	4.04	4.39
2003	2.27	2.28	3.94	4.94	4.20	4.76	4.09	4.31
2004	3.53	6.33	7.38	8.59	4.27	4.56	3.56	3.50
2005	2.94	8.21	5.33	4.81	4.53	4.09	3.31	3.17
2006	3.02	0.59	-0.25	0.76	4.86	4.50	3.99	3.78
2007	1.65	-1.87	-0.95	-0.52	5.04	4.99	4.53	4.36
	Panel B1 Total Return on Government ILBs				Panel B2 Yield on Government ILBs			
1999	2.24	4.35	0.12	0.64	4.33	1.96	3.52	4.18
2000	13.19	4.24	5.63	11.46	3.76	2.04	3.51	3.59
2001	7.98	-0.88	5.18	4.98	3.52	2.41	3.38	3.73
2002	16.98	8.38	13.11	14.62	2.40	2.12	2.63	2.96
2003	8.19	6.80	8.30	6.42	1.99	1.93	2.20	2.77
2004	8.66	8.27	11.21	11.17	1.64	1.67	1.52	2.08
2005	2.73	9.86	6.21	7.60	2.05	1.16	1.25	1.60
2006	0.49	2.56	-2.11	2.45	2.42	1.32	1.83	1.65
2007	2.29	-0.55	-1.40	-1.51	2.66	1.66	2.33	2.06

(*Continued*)

Table 7. (Continued)

Year	US	UK	France	Sweden	US	UK	France	Sweden
	Panel C1 Return Difference between Government ILBs and All Government Bonds				Panel C2 Yield Difference between Government ILBs and All Government Bonds			
1999	4.81	5.67	3.05	3.36	-2.40	-3.44	-1.74	-1.43
2000	-0.36	-4.67	-1.54	1.45	-1.74	-2.72	-1.43	-1.11
2001	1.23	-4.07	-0.26	2.31	-1.70	-2.59	-1.48	-1.46
2002	5.24	-0.75	3.51	5.73	-1.62	-2.34	-1.41	-1.44
2003	5.92	4.51	4.36	1.48	-2.21	-2.83	-1.89	-1.54
2004	5.13	1.94	3.83	2.58	-2.63	-2.89	-2.04	-1.42
2005	-0.21	1.65	0.88	2.79	-2.48	-2.94	-2.06	-1.57
2006	-2.53	1.97	-1.86	1.69	-2.44	-3.18	-2.16	-2.13
2007	0.64	1.32	-0.44	-0.99	-2.38	-3.33	-2.20	-2.30
Mean	2.21	0.84	1.28	2.27	-2.18	-2.92	-1.82	-1.60
Stdev	3.10	3.49	2.44	1.80	0.38	0.35	0.32	0.38

Note: All figures are percentages based on local return and yield. 2007 figures are as of June 30, 2007. All other annual figures are based on year-end data.

Source: Barclays Capital All Government Bond Indices and Government Inflation-Linked Bond Indices.

Between 1999 and 2007, government ILB yields averaged 2.18%, 2.92%, 1.82% and 1.60% below regular government bond yields in the US, the UK, France, and Sweden, respectively. However, the more relevant measure of investment performance on an asset class should be total return, which measures what investors can earn from a security over a specified holding period and includes both price return and coupon return. During the same period, total returns on government ILBs are averaged 2.21%, 0.84%, 1.28% and 2.27% above those on all government bonds in the US, the UK, France, and Sweden, respectively. This outperformance has fueled worldwide investor interest in ILBs. However, it should be interpreted with caution since the performance of ILBs relative to regular government bonds largely depends on the expected and unexpected inflation. There is no guarantee that ILBs will outperform regular government bonds in the future.

5. Emerging Market Bonds

Emerging market bonds include Brady bonds, Eurobonds, global bonds and domestic bonds issued by developing countries in Latin America (e.g., Mexico, Brazil, Venezula, Argentina, Ecuador), Asia (e.g., China, India, Pakistan, Phillipines, Vietnam, Thailand), Russia, Eastern Europe (e.g., Poland, Romania, Bulgaria), Africa (e.g., Nigeria, Ivory Coast), and Middle East (e.g., Egypt, Lebanon). According to the Lehman Brothers Emerging Market Index, the market value of emerging market bonds outstanding is US$418 billion as of June 2007, which is only a small fraction of the total global bond market. Panel A of Figure 6 illustrates the composition of emerging market bonds outstanding as of year-end 2006, with Mexico, Brazil and Russia accounting for over half of the total. Ninety percent of emerging market bonds are issued by governments, while the remaining 10% are issued by corporations. The US dollar is still the dominant currency in emerging market bonds (81% of the investable emerging market bonds are denominated in the US dollar).

The Brady bonds, named after former US Treasury Secretary Nicholas F. Brady, were issued by governments of developing countries to address the Latin America debt crisis of the 1980s. These bonds

Panel A. Composition by Issuing Country

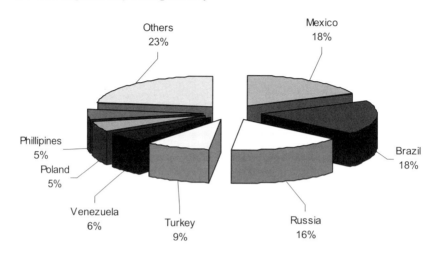

Panel B. Composition by Credit Quality

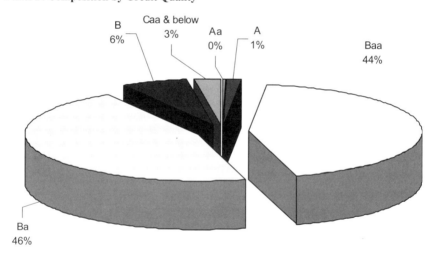

Figure 6. Composition of Global Emerging Market Bonds (as of December 2006).

Source: Lehman Brothers Emerging Market Index.

were issued as par bonds (original face value, reduced interest rate) or discount bonds (reduced face value, competitive interest rate) in exchange for the defaulted bank loans. In 1989, Mexico was the first country to restructure its defaulted bank loans under the Brady Plan, followed by 17 other nations, including Argentina, Brazil, Bulgaria, Costa Rica, Dominican Republic, Ecuador, Ivory Coast, Jordan, Nigeria, Panama, Peru, Philippines, Poland, Russia, Uruguay, Venezuela and Vietnam. At their peak in 1996, Brady bonds outstanding hit US$150 billion, representing 80% of the emerging market bonds outstanding and 60% of the emerging market bond trading volume. Panel A of Figure 7 illustrates the composition of the Brady debt in 1996, with Brazil, Argentina, Mexico and Venezuela accounting for 40%, 18%, 16%, and 12% of the market share, respectively. The Brady plan was quite successful in reducing the debt burden of many developing countries, allowing them to pursue aggressive economic reform, unloading LDC bank loans from commercial banks' balance sheet, and creating liquidity for emerging market debt. Originated from the late 1980s with the crisis-related stigma, the Brady bonds were traded at substantial discount to their non-Brady peers. Starting in the late 1990s, many countries restructured their Brady debt into more liquid and lower interest non-Brady instruments such as Eurobonds and global bonds (e.g., Argentina, Uruguay and Ecuador), or bought back their Brady debt at market value or by exercising the embedded call options to reduce their debt burden (e.g., Mexico in 2003, Brazil and Venezuela in 2006). As a result, by the end of 2006 only US$9.5 billion in Brady bonds were left on the market (see Panel B of Figure 7). The Brady bonds have gradually disappeared, replaced by more market-friendly external debt instruments, such as Eurobonds, global bonds and by internal debt instruments (i.e., domestic bonds).

For the past 10 years, there has been a dramatic change in the structure of emerging market debt. In terms of the external debt structure, the focus has been changed from Brady bonds to Eurobonds and global bonds. In terms of the overall debt structure, the focus has turned from external debt to internal debt due to the success of

Panel A. Distribution of Major Brady Debtors in 1996
(Total market size: US$150 billions)

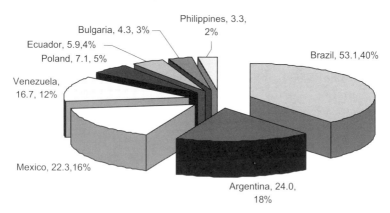

Panel B. Distribution of Major Brady Debtors in 2006
(Total market size: US$9.5 billions)

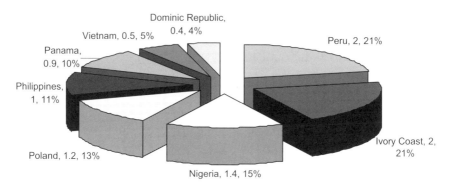

Figure 7. The Retirement of Brady Debt.

Note: Figures in USD billions.
Source: Merrill Lynch, *The Wall Street Journal*, *Financial Times*.

economic reforms and development of domestic capital markets. In terms of market frictions, ownership restrictions and capital barriers have been substantially reduced. In terms of credit quality, there has been a rise in credit quality among emerging countries, with 45% of the emerging market bonds currently rated as investment grade (see Panel B of Figure 6). However, emerging market bonds are still traded at a substantial discount to their peers in developed countries to compensate investors for undertaking credit risk (resulting from political, economic and social uncertainty in the emerging markets) and liquidity risk. Sovereign debt crises have frequently hit the emerging markets (see Pescatori and Sy, 2004). Examples include most of Latin America (1980s), Venezula (1994), Mexico (1995), Russia (1998), Ecuador (1999), Argentina (2001), and Uruguay (2003). Thus, while emerging market debt provides both attractive yield enhancement opportunities, it also carries significant credit and liquidity risks to global investors.

6. Risk Management of Global Fixed Income Portfolios

Since business cycles in different countries around the world are not perfectly synchronized, and investing internationally provides opportunities to reduce systematic interest rate risk through diversification and to introduce currency risk to enhance return, institutional portfolio managers are increasingly taking a global approach to fixed income investments. Global fixed income portfolios are often allocated according to currency (US Dollar, Euro, Yen, Pound, etc) or country/region, in addition to other parameters such as duration, credit quality, and type of issuer (government, financial institution, corporation, securitized pool). Global fixed income portfolio asset allocation can be done tactically to take advantage of higher yield opportunities or appreciated foreign currency potentials. It can also be done strategically to achieve better portfolio optimization through risk diversification across a wider selection of fixed income instruments in different countries.

In terms of multi-currency global fixed income portfolios, managers can choose to either hedge or unhedge their currency exposure. The currency hedging decision is an important decision parameter in foreign bond portfolio management. Global fixed income indices (such as those developed by Lehman Brothers, JP Morgan and Merrill Lynch, Barclays Capital) all provide both hedged and unhedged return benchmarks.

Unhedged foreign bond portfolios are exposed to exchange rate risk, but they provide better risk diversification across various currencies. The number of foreign currencies available for diversification, however, has been substantially reduced since the introduction of the Euro as the common currency for 11 European nations in 1999. As more European nations join the Eurozone and as the global market becomes more integrated, the efficacy of foreign diversification will be reduced further.

Hedged portfolios eliminated the exchange rate risk embedded in foreign bonds through the use of currency derivatives, such as futures, options and swaps. The benefits of hedging, however, are associated with the transaction costs of hedging and opportunity costs of appreciated foreign currencies. Some bond managers use selective hedging to remove unwanted exchange rate risk on certain currencies while taking an active strategy to capture potential gains on other currencies.

As for the interest rate risk embedded in global fixed income portfolios, active managers can customize the duration and interest rate exposure in each market to take advantage of their expectations in yield changes in different markets. The development of expectations in bond yield changes in each market typically involves the modeling and forecasting of key economic fundamentals, such as inflation, GDP growth, trade gap, government fiscal deficits, and monetary policy decisions. The performance of an active portfolio strategy highly depends on the success of interest rate forecasting and modeling.

In summary, expanding the investment universe to include international bonds will bring more risk diversification and yield enhancement opportunities. The exposure to interest rate and exchange rate risks inherent in global fixed income portfolios, however, requires more sophisticated risk management.

References

Amira, K. and W. C. Handorf, 2004, Global debt market growth, security structure, and bond pricing, *Journal of Investing*, Spring, 79–90.

Casey, J.-P. and L. Karel, 2005, Europe's Hidden Capital Markets, Center for European Policy Studies, Brussels.

Kothari, S. P. and J. Shanken, 2004, Asset allocation with inflation-protected bonds, *Financial Analysts Journal*, Jan/Feb 54–70.

Irish Association of Pension Funds (IAPF): Summer 2004 Newsletter, www.iapf.ie/IrishPensionsMag/Summer2004/file,702,en.pdf

Lehman Brothers, 2007, *A Guide to the Lehman Global Family of Fixed Income Indices.*

Merrill Lynch Global Fixed Income Research Team, 2002, *Size and Structure of the World Bond Market*.

Pescatori, A. and A. N. R. Sy, 2004, Debt crises and the development of international capital markets, International Monetary Funds (IMF) Working Paper.

Part III: Alternative Investments

Chapter 6

Hedge Funds*

Jot Yau[†] and Grace K. Yeung[‡]

The hedge fund industry has grown phenomenally in terms of assets under management and number of hedge funds in the past 15 years. Hedge funds invest in all capital markets, including emerging markets, and have started to raise capital from the world stock markets. We believe the hedge fund industry has reached another phase in its life cycle.

In this chapter, we focus on the performance of hedge funds and the replication of it. We begin with a review of the extant literature on the analysis of the historical performance of hedge funds. Earlier test results on the performance of hedge funds are in general favorable, suggesting excess returns for hedge funds and positive alphas to hedge fund managers. However, studies show that performance persistence was found only in underperformed hedge funds and not in over-performed hedge funds. This suggests that hedge fund performance and hence alpha determination need to be re-evaluated given the hefty performance fees charged by hedge funds. We therefore discuss the survivor, stale-price, and backfill biases that may have caused the measurement error in hedge fund performance and alpha determination. Moreover, we discuss another area of concern in hedge fund performance evaluation — benchmarking. We introduce a

* The opinions expressed here are those of the authors and do not necessarily reflect the opinions of PricewaterhouseCoopers.

[†] Albers School of Business and Economics, Seattle University, 901 12th Ave, Seattle, WA 98122, USA. Email: jyau@seattleu.edu.
[‡] PricewaterhouseCoopers, Hong Kong, 33/F, Cheung Kong Center, 2 Queen's Road Central, Hong Kong. Email: grace.k.yeung@hk.pwc.com.

sample of non-investable and investable hedge fund indices and discuss their use as benchmarks as the paradigm of performance evaluation has gradually shifted from an absolute-return basis to a relative-return basis. Finally, we introduce several approaches to replicating hedge fund returns.

Keywords: Absolute returns; alpha; alternative betas; hedge fund replication; performance persistence.

1. Introduction

The long/short equity fund that Alfred Winslow Jones established as a private partnership in the late 1940s is believed to be the first hedge fund.[1] The fund was constructed in such a way that it was "hedged" at all times and hence the name. The basic premise of Jones's strategy was that hedge fund managers had the stock-selection but not the market-timing ability.[2] Today, hedge funds are referred to those private, lightly regulated investment pools that employ dynamic trading strategies which may require short-selling and trading in both the cash and derivatives markets, often on a leveraged basis, in search of a maximum absolute return on behalf of their clients for an asymmetric performance fee.[3]

1.1 *Size and Growth*

The hedge fund industry has grown phenomenally since 1990. It is estimated that the hedge fund assets under management (AUM) have grown from less than US$50 billion in 1990 to about US$1.76 trillion in 2007, and the number of hedge funds has doubled from about 5,000 in 1990 to over 10,000 in 2007.[4]

Several factors have spurred the recent growth of the hedge fund industry. Such factors include the maturation of the industry's infrastructure, the growth length of track records for performance and

---

[1] Lhabitant (2007).

[2] Using a recent sample of global hedge funds, Fung *et al.* (2004) report the same result that hedge fund managers have the stock-selection but not the market-timing ability.

[3] Schneeweis (1998a).

[4] HFR at www.hedgefundresearch.com and Dyment *et al.* (2006).

volatility, historical instability in traditional asset classes, a wider range of hedge strategies to choose from than a decade ago, a growing cadre of highly talented managers with whom to invest, the creation of investable indices, and low barriers to entry (Dorsey, 2004). These factors have provided institutional investors the impetus to adopt hedge funds as viable investment options. Besides high-net-worth individuals, institutional investors such as corporate and public pension funds, endowments and trusts, and bank trust departments have included hedge funds as a separate asset class of a well-diversified portfolio.[5]

A recent survey indicates that investors have hedge fund exposures in four geographic markets, the US, Europe, Japan and Asian emerging markets.[6] Exposure in the US has been leading historically, but the gap is closing. The exposures to the US and Europe are now essentially the same. China, European emerging markets, Latin America, and Africa are newer markets where investors are still gaining exposure.

According to *2006 Alternative Investment Survey* (Dyment *et al.*, 2006), investors from Americas make the largest initial investments into hedge funds with an average size of US$32 million. Initial hedge fund investments from Asia and Europe are smaller, with an average size of US$24 million and US$25 million, respectively. The *Survey* also shows that long/short equity is the most popular strategy with 89% of those surveyed currently investing in the strategy. This is followed by event driven (68%), multi-strategy (65%) and macro (63%) strategies.[7]

The *Survey* also reports that in the US, the 100 largest hedge funds (by AUM) controls about two-third of the money in the hedge fund space in 2006, up from 49% at the end of 2003. Moreover, the 300 hedge funds with over US$1 billion AUM control about 85% of all the money in the business.[8] It is evident that bigger funds have attracted much more money than smaller funds. The large, long-established funds are increasingly capturing capital — squeezing the small funds

---

[5] Almost one-quarter of the US largest 1,800 pension funds, endowments and foundations held hedge fund investments in 2003, up from 12% in 2000. (Source: *Forbes*, May 24, 2004)

[6] Dyment *et al.* (2006).

[7] See Yau *et al.* (2007) for a description of hedge fund strategies.

[8] Zuckerman, G. "Big Hedge Funds Get Bigger." *The Wall Street Journal*, April 19, 2007.

and making it more difficult for new start-ups to raise capital.[9] This is consistent with the results from previous studies that large funds tend to produce a greater return than small funds.

1.2 *Private Equity and IPO*

An impetus for the growth of hedge funds in recent years is the involvement of private equity in the hedge fund space and vice-versa. Hedge funds have been investing in private equity or making loans to public companies. This trend seems to be more prevalent in Asia since the Asian markets are less liquid and thus new hedge funds look into opportunities outside publicly traded equities.[10] Likewise, private equity funds have been investing in hedge funds. Although there have been involvements from both sides of alternative investing, practitioners have a divergent view in terms of whether this is a sound investment strategy. According to *2006 Alternative Investment Survey*, 39% of investors surveyed felt that it was a bad idea for hedge funds to make private equity investments while 15% felt that it was a good idea.[11]

As hedge funds grow in size, their appetites for capital get bigger. Recently, several hedge funds raised permanent capital through the initial public offering (IPO) of their funds (as opposed to an IPO of the management company). They have gone public internationally in Switzerland, London, and New York, to name a few.[12] It appears that

---

[9] The *Alternative Investment Survey 2006* reports that three-quarters of respondents were willing to make investments on day one (seed-funding a hedge fund), and one-quarter of respondents would consider seeding start-up hedge funds for equity stakes, discount fees, a participation in the economics of the fund, etc. Among the 25% who were seed investors, 53% came from the Americas (mostly funds of funds), 30% from Europe and 17% from Asia.

[10] For example, Asian funds such as Balyasny Asset Management and Helios Capital Management, have arranged private deals with several companies in Asia (see Santini, L. "Asian Funds Adopt US Model," *The Wall Street Journal*, May 29, 2007).

[11] 34% of those survey held a neutral opinion and 12% were not sure.

[12] For example, Switzerland-based Partners Group went public on March 23, 2006, and Fortress Investment Group started trading on the NYSE in February 2007 (*Business Week*, December 11, 2006). The MW Tops Ltd. IPO from London began trading on Euronext Amsterdam on December 8, 2006. It is the first to be designed around the performance of a single hedge fund and it raised € 1.5 billion in its IPO (Patrick, M. "Hedge-Fund IPO is the latest test for Nascent Sector." *The Wall Street Journal*, December 8, 2006).

there is a strong interest in the publicly-traded shares of hedge funds.[13] These IPOs have been well received by investors who would like to participate in the up-markets, since unlike private equity, hedge funds can invest immediately with the invested capital.

1.3 *From Alpha to Hedge Fund Replication*

As the hedge fund industry continues to grow and mature, hedge fund managers who continue to market various hedge fund vehicles emphasizing absolute returns or value added (i.e., alpha) by the hedge fund managers via their unique skill and strategy, find it difficult to convince investors to pay fat performance fees in falling markets. Moreover, hedge fund investors have become more concerned about the declining performance of hedge funds and started to look for "alphas" which are net of all fees including the hefty performance fees. More important, as institutional investors have become the pre-dominant investors in the hedge fund space, evaluation of hedge fund performance has shifted from an absolute-return basis to a relative-return basis that requires benchmarking. This shift in paradigm in performance evaluation, coupled with a declining market, has forced the hedge fund industry to start searching for the "true alpha" which is defined as the excess return obtained by the hedge fund managers after accounting for the return that comes from the fund's exposure to all risk factors (systematic as well as unique to the fund and strategy). One approach to searching for the "true alpha" is replicating the hedge fund returns. In this chapter, we will discuss previous research findings that lead to this approach and some replication methods.

The rest of the chapter is organized as follows. In Section 2, we first review the recent evidence on the performance of hedge funds. We discuss several concerns by academics and practitioners over the evaluation of hedge fund performance given a shift in paradigm from an absolute-return to a relative-return basis. We then relate the research findings from these areas, which provide the theoretical

---

[13] According to *2006 Alternative Investment Survey*, more than half of the investors surveyed said that they were interested in hedge fund IPOs and hedge funds with side pockets.

underpinnings, to hedge fund replication in Section 3. We conclude the chapter in the final section.

2. Performance of Hedge Funds

Although there is a lack of reliable hedge fund data before 1994, some progress has been made on the research of understanding the performance of various hedge fund strategies in the last decade.[14] Previous research has studied the determination of alpha, sources of return, and impact of fund characteristics on the performance of various strategies (e.g., Schneeweis *et al.*, 2002 & 2003). In addition, issues that have been addressed include the absolute return versus relative return performance evaluation, benchmarking, creation of investable indices, and replication of hedge funds.[15] We present some of these research findings below.

Hedge funds have generated tremendous interest in the investment community because they are perceived to yield better returns than traditional investments in all market conditions (see Table 1). It is said that hedge funds attract the best talent, and that they can exploit market opportunities more quickly than traditional money managers who are required to track a stock or bond index. In contrast, many hedge fund managers do not explicitly attempt to track a particular stock or bond index. Since hedge funds are lightly regulated, hedge fund managers have greater flexibility in selecting securities and implementing trading strategies that offer a greater probability of obtaining returns which can often be attributed to their unique skills as compared with traditional fund managers. As Grossman (2005) puts it, "an investment in a hedge fund is really an investment in a manager and the specialized talent that he possesses to capture profits

---

[14] There are still myths and misperceptions about hedge funds. Schneeweis (1998b) has tried to debunk the myths in hedge funds as early as 1998, but until recently he laments that academics and practitioners still don't get it (Schneeweis, 2006).

[15] At the portfolio level, studies have looked at the roles of hedge funds in a traditional portfolio, and the optimization of hedge funds with other asset classes. Recent advances on how to optimally incorporate hedge funds into a traditional investment portfolio can be found in Popova *et al.* (2007).

Table 1. Performance of Hedge Fund Global and Strategy Indices (Annual Returns in Percentages)

Index	1998	1999	2000	2001	2002	2003	2004	2005	2006
HFRX Global Hedge Fund Index	12.94	26.66	14.29	8.67	4.72	13.39	2.69	2.72	9.26
HFRX Equal Weighted Strategies Index	5.97	17.16	13.14	9.58	5.61	11.32	2.72	1.28	8.83
HFRX Absolute Return Index	4.46	8.12	11.06	9.15	5.49	11.95	3.2	-0.03	7.43
HFRX Market Directional Index	8.91	29.48	17.26	2.71	1.8	25.22	4.85	4.2	10.45
HFRX Convertible Arbitrage Index	4.22	8.43	12.22	13.96	11.46	8.85	-0.14	-5.69	9.57
HFRX Distressed Securities Index	4.64	16.8	-1.57	21.33	9.75	20.9	8.95	1.21	9.56
HFRX Equity Hedge Index	17.14	41.03	16.97	8.96	2.12	14.47	2.18	4.19	9.23
HFRX Equity Market Neutral Index	3.81	-3.27	11.83	5.27	2.83	-2.38	0.32	0.21	4.76
HFRX Event Driven Index	-3.32	23.2	17.95	5.87	-1.5	18.74	6.93	2.81	10.32
HFRX Macro Index	14.76	25.82	12.5	8.32	14.04	14.61	-0.32	6.67	5.61
HFRX Merger Arbitrage Index	6.7	14.9	18.9	1.47	0.99	4.26	2.8	3.72	10.73
HFRX Relative Value Arbitrage Index	0.16	13.58	16.24	11.78	5.45	9.15	1.98	-0.97	10.65

Source: www.hedgefundresearch.com.
Note: Description of the indices can be found at the website.

from a unique strategy." Hence, hedge funds have often been marketed as "absolute return" vehicles, and in this sense, performance of hedge funds can be directly attributable to manager skill.

Problems in alpha determination have been discussed widely in the literature.[16] Earlier evidence on significant excess returns to hedge funds is mixed, and results on performance persistence are inconclusive.[17] Most of the persistence found in the literature was related to losers continuing to lose, rather than winners continuing to win — a result similar to that of the mutual fund managers. In addition, persistence was found to be short-lived and dependent on the method used to measure it as well as on the time frame under consideration (Rouah, 2005). For example, Barès *et al.* (2003) found short-term persistence in 1–3 month holding periods but not in longer holding periods.

The contradictory results from earlier hedge fund research may be attributable to the use of different databases and the inherent biases therein (discussed in Section 2.2 below). To properly measure the hedge fund excess return, adjustment for biases inherent in the databases that may have affected the performance of a particular hedge fund strategy is typically required.

A number of empirical studies have directly assessed the sources of returns (e.g., return drivers) of traditional and alternative investments. For instance, for traditional stock and bonds, a common set of (linear) factors has been used to explain stock and bond return.[18] Similarly, academic research indicates that for hedge funds, as for traditional stock and bond mutual funds, a common set of return drivers based on the trading strategy factors (e.g., option-like payoffs) and location factors (e.g., payoffs from buy and hold policy) helps to explain returns of each strategy (Fung and Hsieh, 1997; Schneeweis and Spurgin, 1998; Agarwal and Naik, 2000b).

---

[16] See Schneeweis and Spurgin (1999).

[17] Liang (1999), Edwards and Caglayan (2001), and Fung *et al.* (2002) found excess returns for the hedge funds, while Ackermann *et al.* (1999) and Asness *et al.* (2001) did not. Edwards and Caglayan (2001) found more persistence in hedge fund performance than Brown *et al.* (1999), and Agarwal and Naik (2000a).

[18] See Fama and French (1996).

As the measure of performance has moved from an absolute return basis to a relative return basis with a benchmark,[19] the choice of benchmarks and indices (investable vs. non-investable) and differences in fund/strategy attributes have been considered in the linear models. Various risk factors that affect the hedge fund returns have been included in the multifactor models.

Recently, the focus of research on hedge fund performance has moved from a linear model specification to a non-linear model specification that takes into account the non-linearities in hedge fund returns caused by the use of derivatives, dynamic trading strategies, and asymmetric performance fee structure. As the hedge fund returns and performance fees have been declining, non-linear/multifactor models have been applied to replicate hedge fund returns.

2.1 *Alpha Determination*

Absolute return vehicles are investments that have no direct benchmark. As institutional investors have started investing in hedge funds, measuring the hedge fund performance on a relative, risk-adjusted basis (i.e., against a benchmark) is usually mandated. When the return is measured on an absolute basis, the excess return, which is used to determine the performance fee received by the hedge fund manager is typically calculated as the return above the risk-free rate (e.g., LIBOR). With a shift in paradigm in which performance is measured on a relative basis (whether it is against an index that represents the general market movement or a set of risk factors that represent the markets as well as the strategy), correct computation of the "true alpha" has become a concern for academics, investors, and practitioners. To the academics, the factor risks to which the fund has been exposed should be accounted for in the measurement of the "excess return", i.e., the alpha that indicates the manager's skill or value-added. To the practitioners, alpha represents the compensation for their skill, regardless of how the alpha is computed and whether the

---

[19] Anson (2003) discusses the importance of hedge fund indices as benchmarks in the light of the demand of institutional investors for a relative return-based performance evaluation.

practitioners are accepting the new paradigm willingly or unwill-ingly. To the investors, alpha determination is important because it determines how much compensation they have to pay the hedge fund managers.

In addition to the market factors that affect a broad array of investment vehicles, previous studies have shown that individual fund factors may likewise affect the expected performance. Evidence from Schneeweis *et al.* (2002) is in support of results from previous stud-ies that: 1) young funds outperform old funds (Howell, 2001; Liang, 1999); 2) large outperforms small (e.g., Liang, 1999); 3) offshore and onshore may have some impact on performance due to differ-ences in holdings as well as liquidity; and 4) fund of funds may pro-vide closer approximation to return estimation than indices (Fung and Hsieh, 2000). There is little evidence of the impact of perform-ance fees on the equity hedge sector, but there is a small effect of lockup affecting the overall performance for the US opportunity hedge funds. Specifically, funds with quarterly lockups have higher returns than similar strategy funds with monthly lockups. Fung *et al.* (2002) found that management fees, fund size, fund age, and leverage are important micro factors in explaining excess returns using the appro-priate target market benchmarks, after adjusting for illiquidity and higher moments.

2.2 *Performance Measurement Biases*[20]

2.2.1 *Survivor Bias*

Survivor bias results when managers with poor track records exit the business, while managers with good records remain. If the survivor bias is large, then the historical record of the average return of sur-viving managers is higher than the average return of all managers over the test period. Since a diversified portfolio would likely consist of funds that are destined to fail as well as funds destined to succeed,

---

[20] Other biases discussed in the literature but not here are those found to have little impact on performance. For example, Fung and Hsieh (2000) found the self-selection and multi-period sampling biases small and negligible.

studying only survivors results in overestimation of the historical return. The extant literature reports the estimate of this bias to range from 0.16% (Ackerman *et al.*, 1999) to 3.0% (Brown *et al.*, 1999; Fung and Hsieh, 2000).

Schneeweis, *et al.* (2002) point out that different market factors produce different rates of survival for different styles. Their results show that survivor bias is minor for event-driven strategies but is higher for hedged equity, and is considerable for currency funds. Moreover, they show that survivor bias varies by style, time period, and economic conditions. They argue that the problem of survivor bias may be exaggerated if one assumes that current conditions do not evoke a market factor leading to increased probability of funds being driven out of business. Furthermore, they argue that the problem of survivor bias may be reduced by conducting superior due diligence or simply focusing on funds for which survivor bias may be reduced.

2.2.2 *Stale Price Bias*

Hedge fund managers have considerable flexibility both in valuing portfolios at month-end to determine the fund's net asset value and in delaying reporting because of lax regulation by the authorities. It is not unreasonable to presume that hedge fund managers have an incentive to smooth income such that the fund asset value does not necessarily reflect the true market value. In addition, when securities held by hedge funds are thinly or infrequently traded, stale prices will induce an autocorrelated portfolio return pattern similar to patterns observed in the case of income smoothing (e.g., Campbell *et al.*, 1997; Chalmers *et al.*, 2001; Lo, 2001). Thus, for securities with stale prices, whether induced by the manager or naturally arising from illiquidity (or thin trading), measured correlation may be lower than expected, and depending on the time period chosen, measured standard deviation may be higher or lower than would exist if actual prices existed.

Asness *et al.* (2001) argue that stale price bias can artificially reduce estimates of beta, volatility, and correlation with traditional indices. They present evidence of significant lagged relations between monthly market returns (based on S&P 500) and reported hedge fund returns.

Kazemi and Schneeweis (2004) disagree and question the empirical validity of Asness *et al.*'s argument. They argue that there is no significant stale price bias effect on hedge fund returns for two reasons. First, many hedge funds do not contain equity issues such that evidence of a correlation with lagged equity returns is not necessarily indicative of stale prices. Second, unlike tests of stale prices in traditional markets, most research in hedge funds used monthly data. It is unlikely that monthly data would capture stale price effects over lengthy time period especially since for many hedge fund strategies, the underlying holdings are relatively liquid compared to many traditional assets (e.g., real estate) or traditional alternatives such as private equity for which appraisal values are used. By replicating Asness *et al.*'s tests, Kazemi and Schneeweis (2004) empirically show that stale price bias was not significant and Asness *et al.*'s results were just a reflection of the historical anomaly due to the LTCM crisis in 1998.

2.2.3 *Backfill Bias*

Backfill (or instant history) bias happens when hedge funds choose to enter the database after achieving good performance with earlier good returns being backfilled between the fund's inception date and the date of fund's entry into the database. In other words, instant history of past good performance of a hedge fund will become part of the history of the hedge fund database. This tends to introduce an upward bias in the reported returns. Previous studies estimate this bias to be about 1.2–1.4% per year (Fung and Hsieh, 2000; Edward and Caglayan, 2001).

In summary, these biases overstate the return and understate the risk estimates of hedge funds. Thus, biases should be taken into consideration when the performance of hedge funds is being evaluated. Also, because these biases are inherent in the databases, their effect will be escalated to the indices which are sometimes used as benchmarks. Hence, caution is called for when indices are used as benchmarks. Fung and Hsieh (2004) show that using funds of funds (FOF) as a benchmark for hedge fund performance mitigates some of the problems resulting from the biases mentioned above. However, it still suffers from the problem of heterogeneity because the FOF indices are basically multi-strategy and they do not represent a specific strategy (Amenc and Martellini, 2002). It is thus not possible to use these FOF indices as benchmarks for individual hedge fund performance.

2.3 *Hedge Fund Indices and Benchmarks*

Many performance indices can be used as benchmarks for hedge fund performance. An appropriate benchmark shall reflect the particular style of an investment manager and serve as a surrogate for the manager in the studies of risk and return performance and asset allocation.

Earlier studies on the performance of hedge funds were often based on the use of various existing active manager-based hedge fund indices and subindices (Table 2).[21] The use of manager-based hedge fund indices in performance and asset allocation is based on the premise that the indices adequately reflect the underlying performance

Table 2. Sample of Major Non-Investable Hedge Fund Indices

Index Provider	Launch Date	Base Date	Index Weighting	Rebalancing Frequency
Barclay Group	2003	1997	EW	Monthly
CISDM	1994	1990	Median	Monthly
CS/Tremont	1999	1994	Value wt.	Quarterly
Dow Jones	2004	2002	EW	Quarterly
EACM	1996	1990	EW	Annual
Edhec	2003	1997	PCA	Quarterly
HedgeFund.net	1998	1976–1995♣	EW	Continual
HFR	1994	1990	EW	Monthly
MSCI	2002	2002	EW/VW*	Quarterly**

Note: EW — Equal-weighted; VW — Value-weighted; PCA — Principal component analysis.
♣Depends on strategy.
*For the global indices.
**For inclusion and monthly for the reranking of funds.
Source: Géhin and Vaissié (2004), Yau *et al.* (2007).

---

[21] See Yau *et al.* (2007) for a description of the major hedge fund indices.

of the strategy used by investors for actual investment. It is also assumed that investors have access to these managers whose performance is represented in the indices, i.e., funds managed by these managers are still open to new investors.

One of the primary concerns over the use of hedge fund indices is that since most databases are self-reported, indices may not reflect the performance of many individual managers because of its lack of representation. In addition, indices themselves may not be directly comparable in terms of expected return and risk.[22] For example, Schneeweis *et al.* (2002) show that the actual historical returns for various well-known hedge fund indices vary widely over a five-year period as well as across "similar strategy" indices. They suggest that the fund size and the fund age restrictions on the membership of a hedge fund index are one of the causes of such variations.

Previous studies have also analyzed the actual tracking error between various hedge fund indices as well as various weighting schemes (e.g., value-weighted versus equal-weighted).[23] Fung and Hsieh (2002) point out that indices that are value-weighted reflect the weights of popular bets by investors since the asset value of the various funds change due to asset purchases as well as price. As such, the ability of an investor to track such an index based on a market momentum strategy is problematic. Equal-weighted indices may better reflect potential diversification of hedge funds and funds designed to track such indices. However, the cost of rebalancing may make these indices likewise difficult to create in an investable form. Investable hedge fund indices have been created recently, which are themselves investable or created with the express goal of tracking a comparative non-investable index.

2.3.1   *Investable Hedge Fund Indices*

Many investable indices are based on either managed account platforms or direct investment in fund-based products. Examples of investable indices are presented in Table 3.

---

[22] Previous studies find that heterogeneity among hedge funds renders low correlation among different indices for the same universe (e.g., Amenc and Martellini, 2002).
[23] For example, McCarthy and Spurgin (1998) and Fung and Hsieh (2002).

Table 3. Sample of Major Investable Hedge Fund Indices

Index	Launch Date	Base Date	Strategy/Fund Weighting	Rebalancing Frequency
CS/Tremont Investable	2003	2000	VW / VW	Semi-annual
DJ BPI	2003	2002	NA/EW	Quarterly
FTSE	2004	2004	IW/IW	Annual
HFRX	2003	2003	VW/*	Quarterly
MSCI Hedge Invest	2003	2003	Adj. median asset weighted/EW	Quarterly
RBC Hedge 250	2006	2005	TW/VW	Monthly

Note: EW — Equal-weighted; VW — Value-weighted; TW — Target-weighted; NA — Not mentioned; IW — Investability-weighted.
*Fund-weighted optimizing correlation within group.

Conceptually, the investable indices are passively managed funds of hedge funds. Géhin and Vassié (2004) have identified three common attributes of investable indices: 1) full transparency; 2) initial and ongoing due diligence; and 3) investability in terms of low capital entry level and high redemption frequency. The index providers basically furnish investors with a low-cost approach to selecting hedge fund managers and strategy, allocating assets (by fixing the index weighting), and eliminating funds that are prone to operational risks in the future. They do not, however, attempt to allocate funds dynamically. Both management and incentive fees tend to be significantly lower for investable hedge fund indices than the funds of hedge funds (Géhin and Vassié, 2004).

Given that indices differ in a number of characteristics (e.g., strategy, availability, construction etc.), the common concern is that the number of managers/funds within the representative index is too small to represent the performance of the overall hedge fund universe or strategy. In brief, if the investable indices are not representative of the strategies, they are no more than funds of funds. Schneeweis and Remillard (2007) examine the Royal Bank of Canada (RBC) Hedge 250 Index which comprised approximately 250 funds,[24] and its

---

[24] For details on the characteristics of the RBC 250 Hedge Index, see www.rbchedge250.com.

constituent strategy-based sub-indices relative to other investable indices and non-investable and strategy-based indices in terms of risk and return to determine whether the investable index created based on a larger sample size is a better representation of the performance of hedge funds.[25] Their results show that for many hedge fund strategies, the RBC indices perform either markedly superior or inferior to other comparable indices. In addition, the RBC indices generally have higher volatility at the sub-index level and higher equity betas. However, the index history is still too short for a definitive conclusion.

Although the proliferation of investable indices is one step closer to benchmarking the hedge fund performance precisely, Schneeweis *et al.* (2003) note that one should not expect any one single hedge fund index to track the performance of hedge fund managers even within the same strategy. However, as for traditional securities, for a strategy-pure index of hedge funds, a portfolio of similar funds should have performance similar to that of the representative hedge fund index. The lack of a clear hedge fund benchmark, however, is not indicative of an inability to determine a comparable return for a hedge fund strategy. Hedge fund strategies within a particular style often trade similar assets with similar methodologies and are sensitive to similar market factors. Thus, replication of hedge fund returns is feasible.

3. Replication of Hedge Fund Returns

Since 2002, the average alpha extracted by hedge fund managers has been declining (Jaeger, 2007; Fung *et al.*, 2007). Pundits have suggested that this is an inevitable result of the capacity constraint for hedge fund strategies. For example, Jaeger and Wagner (2005) believe that alpha will decrease over time as the competitive advantage of hedge fund managers gets competed away in a crowded market. They

---

[25] Investable indices used in their study are Dow Jones BPI, Credit Suisse/Tremont, Morgan Stanley Capital International Hedge Investable and Hedge Fund Research (HFRX) indices, whereas the non-investable and strategy-based indices used are CISDM, HFR FOF Composite, and the Barclays Group.

also suggest that a declining alpha is indicative of the declining quality of the average hedge fund manager. Due to low entry barriers to the hedge fund industry, it has attracted numerous managers with a lower level of skill. The new managers tend to dilute the average performance and hence the average alpha of the entire industry. With a declining alpha, Wall Street investment houses and investors are interested in finding ways of replicating hedge fund returns that are not subject to the capacity constraint and high performance fees.

Others suggest that different hedge fund strategies exhibit different exposures to various systematic risk factors and alpha is not simply a function of manager skill (Schneeweis and Spurgin, 1998; Géhin and Vaissié, 2006). Put another way, hedge funds make bets on different market risk factors (or betas), traditional and alternative; the bet made on the manager skill is the alpha. Géhin and Vaissié (2006) show that alpha will be reduced if exposures to other risk factors (i.e., alternative betas) are accounted for. However, it does not mean that the opportunity for alpha has been reduced by the increasing number of hedge funds which are believed to have driven away the market inefficiencies and hence reducing the alpha for everybody. Géhin and Vaissié believe that alpha is generated more by successful bets on different exposures rather than by exploiting market opportunities, and thus alpha is not threatened by a problem of industry capacity constraint. In sum, previous research has shown that hedge fund returns can be replicated and so can alpha.

In subsequent sections, we discuss two principal means of establishing comparable portfolios which replicate hedge fund returns. One is using a single or multi-factor based methodology and the other is using optimization to create tracking portfolios with similar risk and return characteristics.

3.1 *Factor-Model Based Replication*

Previous academic studies have used both the single-factor and multi-factor models in identifying the sources of hedge fund returns (e.g., Fung and Hsieh, 1997; Schneeweis and Spurgin, 1998). The single-factor model suggests that returns of a hedge fund are a function of its exposure to the market risk. An example of a single-factor model is the market model in which the single factor is proxied by a market index (e.g., S&P 500) and measured by the "traditional beta." The multi-factor model suggests that hedge fund returns are a function of the fund's exposure to the market risk (traditional beta), other systematic risk factors (measured by the so called "alternative betas") and manager's skill (measured by the alpha). The systematic risk factors may include the volatility risk (specific to the hedge fund strategy), default risk, and liquidity risk (Fung and Hsieh, 1997, 2002; Schneeweis and Spurgin, 1998).[26] The multi-factor model can be linear or non-linear.

Based on these factor models, academic research has also focused on direct replication of the underlying strategies and uses location and volatility factors as well as trend-following momentum models to capture explicitly the implicit option payoff. In the non-linear multifactor models, the option-like payoff in the hedge funds is caused by the use of derivatives, leverage, and dynamic trading strategy, as well as the asymmetric performance fee (Mitchell and Pulvino, 2001; Fung and Hsieh, 2001; Agarwal and Naik, 2004). However, Schneeweis and Spurgin (2001) find that in previous studies, after taking market factors, changes in volatility and momentum factors into consideration, option-like payoff variables generally have little to add as explanatory variables. In other words, while the use of certain location and trading strategy factors is consistent with the return of the underlying strategy, such factors may not directly represent the underlying trading process.

Hasanhodzic and Lo (2007) provide some evidence that linear replication can be successful for certain strategies while offering certain advantages to hedge fund investing, such as more transparency, increased liquidity and fewer capacity constraints. However, they warn that the heterogeneous risk profile of hedge funds and the non-linear risk exposures greatly reduce the ability of these models to consistently replicate hedge fund returns. Likewise, Schneeweis and

---

[26] Non-directional hedge funds (e.g., convertible arbitrage, and market neutral long-short) are generally considered to be nonexposed to the market risk, but they are exposed to the volatility risk, default risk and liquidity risk.

Kazemi (2001a) note that each hedge fund strategy is designed to directly trade certain financial instruments in a pre-designed manner. For instance, a particular hedge fund strategy may be designed to capture returns in markets which are: 1) delta neutral/long gamma; 2) low volatility/high trend; 3) low volatility/high market convergence; 4) decreasing credit spreads; and 5) market-factor driven.

3.2 *Tracking Portfolio Based Replication*

Recently, research has also focused on developing passive indices (e.g., tracking portfolios) which are either based on active managers who trade similar to the strategy in question and/or on individual security holdings within a particular strategy designed to minimize the return differential between the hedge fund strategy and the passive index. For example, Schneeweis and Kazemi (2001a, 2001b) have created passive indices both from factors that underlie the strategy and financial instruments that are used in the strategy to track the return of the hedge fund strategy. Their results indicate that active hedge fund management gives evidence of positive alpha relative to the cited tracking portfolios.

3.3 *Other Approaches to Hedge Fund Replication*

In addition to the two approaches mentioned above, there are other approaches to hedge fund replication. Instead of identifying the return-generating betas, Amin and Kat (2003), and Kat and Palaro (2005) have attempted to replicate the distribution of hedge fund returns. The underlying idea is based on the notion that much of the trading activity undertaken by hedge funds is not creating value, but merely altering the timing of the returns available from traditional assets. In other words, many hedge funds are simply distorting readily available asset distributions. The authors attempt to find a better way to distort these distributions without actually investing in hedge funds.

Recently, Papageorgiou *et al.* (2007) use a multi-variate extension of Dybvig's (1988) payoff distribution model to replicate the marginal distribution of most hedge fund returns and their dependence on other asset classes. Their model attempts to improve the inefficiency and inconsistency in the Kat and Palaro (2005) model of replication. Papageorgiou, Rémillard, and Hocquard conclude that their model can replicate the hedge fund returns.[27] More importantly, they suggest that their results "reinforce the notion that on aggregate, hedge funds are simply repackaging beta returns."

4. Concluding Remarks

The hedge fund industry has grown phenomenally in terms of assets under management and the number of hedge funds in the past 15 years. Hedge funds invest in all capital markets, including emerging markets, and they have recently started to raise capital from the world stock markets. We believe the hedge fund industry has reached another phase in its life cycle.

As the hedge fund industry continues to grow, research on hedge funds has made good progress in many areas of hedge fund management. In this chapter, we have focused on the performance of hedge funds and the replication of it.

We begin with a review of the extant literature on the analysis of the historical performance of hedge funds. Earlier test results on the performance of hedge funds are in general favorable, suggesting the presence of excess returns to hedge funds and positive alphas to hedge fund managers. Studies on performance persistence, however, show that persistence was found only in under-performed hedge funds and not in over-performed hedge funds. Thus, previous studies suggest that hedge fund performance and hence alpha determination need to be re-evaluated given the hefty performance fees charged by hedge fund managers. We therefore discuss survivor, stale-price, and backfill biases that may have caused the measurement error in hedge fund performance and alpha determination.

In addition, we discuss another area of concern in hedge fund performance evaluation — benchmarking. We introduce a sample of

---

[27] Their results are based on non-investable indices, EDHEC and HFRI, which are known to be subject to significant biases.

non-investable and investable hedge fund indices and discuss their use as benchmarks as the paradigm of performance evaluation has started to shift from an absolute-return basis to a relative-return basis.

Finally, we introduce several approaches to replicating hedge fund returns. Replicating hedge fund returns is made feasible by advances in research on factor models, particularly non-linear multifactor models and the technology of tracking portfolios.

With the growing popularity of including hedge funds in traditional portfolios with stocks and bonds either as a risk diversifier or return enhancer, further research on hedge fund replications that are not subject to the industry capacity constraint and high performance fees could be very rewarding.

References

Ackermann, C., R. McEnally, and D. Ravenscraft, 1999, The performance of hedge funds: Risk, return and incentives, *Journal of Finance*, 54(3), 833–874.

Agarwal, V. and N. Y. Naik, 2000a, On taking the alternative route: Risks, rewards and performance persistence of hedge funds, *The Journal of Alternative Investments*, 2(4), 6–23.

Agarwal, V. and N. Y. Naik, 2000b, Performance evaluation of hedge funds with option-based and buy and hold strategies, Working paper, London Business School.

Agarwal, V. and N. Y. Naik, 2004, Risks and portfolio decisions involving hedge funds, *Review of Financial Studies*, 17(1), 63–98.

Amenc, N. and L. Martellini, 2002, The brave new world of hedge fund indices, Working paper, Edhec Business School.

Amin, G. S. and H. M. Kat, 2003, Hedge fund performance 1990–2000: Do the money machines really add value? *Journal of Financial and Quantitative Analysis*, 28(2), 251–274.

Anson, M. 2003, Benchmarking the hedge fund market place, *Journal of Indexes*, Third Quarter.

Asness, C., R. Krail, and J. Liew, 2001, Do hedge funds hedge? *Journal of Portfolio Management*, 28(1), 6–19.

Barès, P. A., R. Gibson and S. Gyger, 2003, Performance in the hedge fund industry: An analysis of short- and long-term persistence, *The Journal of Alternative Investments*, 6(3), 25–41.

Brown, S. J., W. N. Goetzmann, and R. G. Ibbotson, 1999, Offshore hedge funds: Survival and performance 1989–1995, *Journal of Business*, 72(1), 91–117.

Campbell, J., A. Lo, and C. MacKinlay, 1997, *The Econometrics of Financial Markets*, Princeton, NJ: Princeton University Press.

Chalmers, J., R. Edelen, and G. Kadlec, 2001, On the perils of financial intermediaries setting security prices: The mutual fund wild card option, *Journal of Finance*, 56(6), 2209–2236.

Dorsey, A. H., 2004, *How to Select a Hedge Fund of Funds: Picking Winners and Avoid Losers*. New York, NY: Institutional Investors Books.

Dybvig, P., 1988, Distributional analysis of portfolio choice, *Journal of Business*, 61(3), 369–393.

Dyment, J., J. Olstein, and A. Jones, 2006, 2006 Alternative investment survey, *Alternative Investment Quarterly*, Fourth Quarter, pp. 21–46.

Edwards, F. R. and M. O. Caglayan, 2001, Hedge fund performance and manager skill, *Journal of Futures Markets*, 21(11), 1003–1028.

Fama, E. F. and K. French, 1996, Multifactor explanations of asset pricing anomalies, *Journal of Finance*, 51, 55–84.

Fung, H. G., X. E. Xu, and J. Yau, 2004, Do hedge fund managers display skill? *The Journal of Alternative Investments*, 6(4), 22–31.

Fung, H. G., X. E. Xu, and J. Yau, 2002, Global hedge funds: Risk, return and market timing, *Financial Analysts Journal*, 58(6), November/December, 19–30.

Fung, W. and D. A. Hsieh, 1997, Empirical characteristics of dynamic trading strategies: The case of hedge funds, *Review of Financial Studies*, 10, 275–302.

Fung, W. and D. A. Hsieh, 2000, Performance characteristics of hedge funds and CTA funds: Natural and spurious biases, *Journal of Financial and Quantitative Analysis*, 35(3), 291–307.

Fung, W. and D. A. Hsieh, 2001, Risk in hedge fund strategies: Theory and evidence from trend-followers, *Review of Financial Studies*, 14(2), 313–341.

Fung, W. and D. A. Hsieh, 2002, Hedge fund benchmarks: Information content and biases, *Financial Analysts Journal*, 58(1), 22–34.

Fung, W. and D. A. Hsieh, 2004, Hedge fund benchmarks: A risk-based approach, *Financial Analysts Journal*, 60(5), 65–80.

Fung, W., D. A. Hsieh, N. Naik, and T Ramadorai, 2007, Hedge fund: Performance, risk and capital formation, Preprint.

Géhin, W. and M. Vaissié, 2006, The right place for alternative betas in hedge fund performance: An answer to the capacity effect fantasy, *The Journal of Alternative Investments*, 9(1), 9–27.

Géhin, W. and M. Vaissié, 2004, Hedge fund indices: Investable, non-investable and strategy benchmarks, Working paper, Edhec Business School, October.

Grossman, S. J., 2005, Talent required, *The Wall Street Journal*, September 29.

Hasanhodzic, J. and A. W. Lo, 2007, Can hedge-fund returns be replicated?: The linear case, *Journal of Investment Management*, 5(2), 5–45.

Howell, M. J., 2001, Fund age and performance, *The Journal of Alternative Investments*, 4(2), 57–60.

Jaeger, L., 2007, The new discussion: Replication of hedge funds, *AIMA Journal*, Summer, pp. 21–22.

Jaeger, L. and C. Wagner, 2005, Factor modeling and benchmarking of hedge funds: Can passive investments in hedge fund strategies deliver? *The Journal of Alternative Investments*, 8(3), 9–36.

Kat, H. and H. Palero, 2005, Who needs hedge funds? A copula-based approach to hedge fund replication, Technical report, Cass Business School, City University.

Kazemi, H. B. and T. Schneeweis, 2004, Hedge funds: Stale prices revisited (April 12, 2004). Available at SSRN: http://ssrn.com/abstract=530183.

Lhabitant, F.-S., 2007, *The Handbook of Hedge Funds*, Wiley, 2007.

Liang, B., 1999, On the performance of hedge funds, *Financial Analyst Journal*, 55(4), 72–85.

Lo, A. W., 2001, Risk management for hedge funds: Introduction and overview, *Financial Analysts Journal*, 57(6), 16–33.

McCarthy, D. and R. Spurgin, 1998, A review of hedge fund performance benchmarks, *The Journal of Alternative Investments*, 1(1), 18–28.

Mitchell, M. and T. Pulvino, 2001, Characteristics of risk in risk arbitrage, *Journal of Finance*, 56(6), 2135–2175.

Papageorgiou, N., B. Rémillard, and A. Hocquard, 2007, Replicating the properties of hedge fund returns, HEC Montréal, Paper presented at the SFA.

Popova, I., D. P. Morton, E. Popova, and J. Yau, 2007, Optimizing benchmark-based portfolios with hedge funds, *The Journal of Alternative Investments*, 10(1), Summer, 35–55.

Rouah, F., 2005, *Competing Risks in Hedge Fund Survival*. Ph.D. Dissertation, McGill University, Montreal, Canada.

Schneeweis, T., 1998a, The benefits of hedge funds, Working paper, CISDM/SOM, University of Massachusetts.

Schneeweis, T., 1998b, Dealing with myths of hedge funds, *The Journal of Alternative Investments*, 1(3), Winter, 11–15.

Schneeweis, T., 2006, Where academics and practitioners got it wrong, *Alternative Investment Quarterly*, Second Quarter, pp. 17–25.

Schneeweis, T. and H. Kazemi, 2001a, The creation of alternative tracking portfolios for hedge fund strategies, Working paper, CISDM, University of Massachusetts.

Schneeweis, T. and H. Kazemi, 2001b, Alternative means of replication hedge fund manager performance, Working paper, CISDM, University of Massachusetts.

Schneeweis, T., H. Kazemi, and G. Martin, 2003, Understanding hedge fund performance: Research issues revised — Part II, *The Journal of Alternative Investments*, 5(4), Spring, 8–30.

Schneeweis, T., H. Kazemi, and G. Martin, 2002, Understanding hedge fund performance: Research issues revised — Part I, *The Journal of Alternative Investments*, 5(3), Winter, 6–22.

Schneeweis, T. and J. Remillard, 2007, Comparison of RBC 250 Hedge Index using investible and non-investible hedge fund indices: A statistical analysis, Working Paper, CISDM, University of Massachusetts.

Schneeweis, T. and R. Spurgin, 1998, Multifactor analysis of hedge funds, managed futures and mutual fund return and risk characteristics, *The Journal of Alternative Investments*, 1(2), Summer, 1–24.

Schneeweis, T. and R. Spurgin, 1999, Alpha, alpha...Who's got the alpha? *The Journal of Alternative Investments*, 2(3), 83–87.

Schneeweis, T. and R. Spurgin, 2001, Trading factors and location factors in hedge fund return estimation, Working paper, CISDM/SOM, University of Massachusetts.

Yau, J., T. Schneeweis, T. Robinson, and L. Weiss, 2007, Alternative investments portfolio management. In *Managing Investment Portfolio: A Dynamic Process*, 3rd edition, The CFA Institute. New York: Wiley Finance.

Chapter 7

International Real Estate

*Gary A. Patterson**

Real estate represents a significant form of investment throughout the world that is sometimes overshadowed by the stock and bond markets. Investments in real estate once focused on direct investments in land and developed properties, and this chapter covers important aspects that vary across national borders that should be considered when making investment decisions. Investors interested in real estate now have more choices than in the past. The globalization of financial markets now makes it possible for investors to include real estate in their portfolios by trading in financial securities such as Real Estate Investment Trusts (REITs). This chapter examines the unique characteristics of these securitized real estate investments and focuses on their performance in the global financial markets.

Keywords: Real estate; international; real estates investment trusts (REITs); diversification, investments.

1. Overview

Real estate is the largest asset class owned by global businesses and represents around 15% of global gross domestic product (GDP). Additionally, investments in real estate account for more than 50% of global total assets (Bloomberg, 2004). While investments in other

*College of Business, University of South Florida, St. Petersburg, FL 33701, USA. E-mail: pattersg@stpt.usf.edu

asset categories, such as stocks and bonds, may get more publicity, real estate plays a significant role within international finance. In fact, capital flows to developing countries that target the real estate sector have been one of the more consistent drivers of economic development throughout the world. Such transfers of funds reflect financial commitments to a region that are more long-term and less likely to be transferred quickly to another location.

The globalization of financial markets has made it much easier for investors to consider the benefits of including real estate in their portfolios. The potential of diversifying a portfolio by including international real estate is of growing interest to portfolio managers. The goal of investors should be to look for new asset categories or securities that may improve their portfolio returns after adjusting for risk.

There are two common ways to invest in real estate. The standard approach has been for a firm to buy property directly and become the owner of the physical asset. An increasingly popular method of investing in international real estate is through securitized assets such as in the shares of a Real Estate Investment Trust (REITs) or stocks in property companies. These real estate firms are companies that invest directly in various property types and distribute their income to their shareholders. This indirect form of real estate investment is experiencing significant international growth. This chapter will focus on both forms of investments in international real estate.

2. Alternative Investments with International Real Estate

Significant developments and opportunities have increased the interest in real estate investments on an international scale, and some of the more common benefits are listed below (Worzala and Newell, 1995):

- Favorable interest rates and exchange rates for the investor
- Fewer restrictions on ownership and more tax incentives to attract foreign capital
- Fewer local investment opportunities in the home country

- Diversification across economic and political landscapes
- Changes in the investment policies of MNCs and in many countries
- Advances in global communication and information retrieval
- Significant economic growth in the foreign economy

Multinational corporations should attempt to maximize the benefits from their real estate acquisitions, regardless of the reason for investing in real estate.

While real estate comprises a significant portion of the assets for MNCs, the acquisition of properties has often been treated differently from other types of assets that are part of the firm's investment strategy. Some firms may have real estate at the center of their strategic plans, and properties may be assessed primarily as an investment vehicle. Conversely, a sizeable portion of MNCs have perceived real estate to be a necessary asset to help achieve the firm's primary mission, thus it represents a supporting role for the core business of the firm. This approach to property acquisition for support purposes may lead to a sub-optimal allocation of assets. As MNCs strive to increase efficiency and profitability, more firms are reassessing their property holdings and searching for ways to turn each of their asset groupings into profit centers (Hines, 1990).

3. Motives for Direct Real Estate Investments

A direct investment in real estate occurs when a firm acquires ownership of real property. The mechanism for this transaction may be the complete or partial ownership of the property. In some countries, long-term leases of 100 years or more would also represent a form of property ownership with the ability to transfer ownership of the lease to a third party.

Most investments in real estate are made with the idea of meeting the primary needs of the firm in which the real estate represents a supporting asset. Examples of such acquisitions include a production facility for a manufacturer or an office building for a firm in a service industry. The property may be obtained primarily for non-real estate purposes. Thus, the firm may not specifically consider or analyze the potential profits from the purchase of the real estate since the focus is on the core business.

Investments in real estate may be made with the expectation that the firm may profit from capital gains. MNCs have begun modifying the traditional approach to real estate acquisitions with an emphasis on developing a coordinated strategy to maximize the market value of international real estate holdings (Hines, 1990).

A decision should be made at the corporate level whether the firm's real estate department should be a profit center or a service center. The overall mission of the real estate department would differ considerably under the two scenarios. If the goal is to optimize profits for the real estate operation, then subsequent investment decisions focusing on the real estate may negatively impact the profits of the firm's primary business operations. The firm may consider implementing a strategy that attempts to balance the support of the core business practice while attempting to achieve healthy profits from the firm's properties.

Real estate investment and its subsequent management often begin when the firm's domestic operations have grown significantly with an accumulation of properties that support its activities. The firm, as it expands across national borders, introduces new complexities to the core business practice, including the acquisition and management of foreign real estate. The need to manage the firm's property holdings may assume greater importance as real estate becomes a more significant category among the firm's total assets.

When the company's operations expand to other countries, the need to manage foreign properties becomes more complicated and decisions should be made about the management of foreign real estate. If the domestic real estate department maintains direct oversight, then the use of technology becomes critical in this function. The firm may use a property manager in the host country who would be able to provide closer supervision of the property. Using an overseas property manager is more common among MNCs, and that person would be expected to understand the local regulations and laws that apply to property owners.

4. Investment Analysis of International Real Estate

The guideline for evaluation of a real estate investment is similar to those of other investments an MNC makes. Such a process should be made if the firm is making an overt investment in real estate, either directly or indirectly.

The firm should engage in an extensive risk analysis of the property that adds to the uncertainty of the potential returns. Some of the risks that may impact the returns of the real estate investment are listed below (Hines, 2001).

Financial risk originates from the use of debt to finance the firm's operations. The firm can expect greater volatility in its earnings when a relatively larger amount of assets, such as real estate, are financed by debt. This risk may assume greater significance if the MNC creates limited partnerships to engage in real estate development practices.

Business risk reflects the possible loss of value or cash flow from the property that occurs from economic fluctuations in the real estate market. The profitability of a real estate investment can be greatly impacted by the conditions of the real estate market, a highly cyclical industry. The difference between success or failure for a real estate development project may depend upon the state of the property market at the time of a project's completion.

Liquidity risk is often quite high in real estate investments. A highly liquid asset is one that can be bought or sold quickly with only a relatively small change in price. In real estate, the firm may not be able to sell the property in a timely manner at what it perceives to be a reasonable price. The transaction costs associated with real estate transactions are also quite high compared to entry and exit costs for investments in different asset classes.

Inflation risk represents the loss in value of the cash flow from the property if the inflation rate increases in the host country. The risk facing the investor is that the purchasing power of the initial investment declines significantly during the life of the investment. The

MNC also faces inflation risk in the home currency country. This risk is closely associated with interest and exchange rate risks.

Interest rate risk introduces volatility into the returns of an investment because of changes in interest rates. This risk can greatly impact the value of long-term investments such as real estate, and international real estate investments are made more complex with the interest rate fluctuations in the host and home countries.

Exchange rate risk focuses upon the loss in value to the MNC when the cash flow or sale proceeds from the real estate investment in the host currency are converted to the home currency. The magnitude of this risk would increase with the duration of the real estate investment.

Political or country risk is greater among countries where laws are more easily enacted that could diminish the value of the real estate to the MNC. The risk exposure may be heightened by the location of the property, particularly if the real estate increases in value within the context of the host country's national security or pride, e.g., sensitive waterway property or natural mineral deposits. The economic stability of the host country remains an underlying factor in assessing the exposure from this risk.

Environmental risks may have greater impact upon investments in real property if the environmental conditions deteriorate in the host country. Properties situated along the water front or in wetlands may be subject to environmental regulations that limit the flexibility of the MNC to manage or develop.

5. Return (Yield) Analysis

The firm should identify the holding period of the investment, which can vary considerably. The investment horizon may span many years if the property is raw land bought for speculative purposes or potential development. There may be some uncertainty about the length of the investment, particularly if the acquisition is commercial property that is expected to meet the needs of the MNC's operations in the host country. The firm should then measure the required return that would compensate the firm for the aggregate exposure to the various risks.

Present value analysis would be a method commonly used in other investment analysis. The Net Present Value (NPV) and Internal Rate of Return (IRR) approaches would provide the analysts or appraiser with information about the value of perceived cash flows with current valuation or appraisal.

The scheduling of anticipated cash flows should include financial commitments made throughout the life of the investment. These cash flows include the following:

Initial investment costs reflect the acquisition cost and other immediate outlays needed to secure the property for the MNC.

Development and construction costs would accrue if the property were to be developed to meet the needs of the MNC's primary business or as part of a general investment vehicle.

Cash flow from operations, including leases, would need to be estimated to assess ongoing revenue or expense streams.

Interest rate changes may prompt refinancing activities that would impact the MNC as lender and as financier.

The sale of the property would represent the ending cash flow for the investment. The capital gains and impact of depreciation of the property may be impacted by tax laws in the host and home countries.

6. Acquisition of Property

The appraisal process varies across countries, but the two dominant appraisal methods are represented by the US-based American Institute of Real Estate Appraisers and the London-based Royal Institute of Chartered Surveyors. These approaches are similar and are sometimes combined as part of a real estate acquisition project. The output of the appraisal will be affected by the simple demand and supply of the property. Thus, the economic conditions in the host country and region will blend in with the market conditions for real estate properties to determine the property's valuation.

MNCs often select a local branch of an international real estate appraisal firm to conduct the valuation process. The significant items that would be incorporated into this process are:

Location of property — The adage "location, location, location" applies to the valuation of real estate throughout the world. Regional and local factors influence desirability and the price of property, and the appraisal process should incorporate this type when valuing property.

Property ownership constraints — The appraisal process should identify constraints that may apply to foreign ownership of property. National and regional restrictions may prevent a MNC from acquiring property along specific waterways or near designated sites that are significant to the national or regional security within the host country. Such restrictions may not apply to domestic buyers, thus the appraisal process should quickly determine if the property of interest can be acquired by foreign investors.

Property development constraints — Many countries maintain code restrictions that categorize areas according to a range of use. The appraisal process should verify the existence of local restrictions so that the interested buyer can explore the potential impact of usefulness and the overall value of the property.

Data and methodology used in appraisal — The appraisal firm should clearly identify the data variables used in the valuation process. A common practice is to use "comparable" properties to establish a benchmark value for the desired property. The buyer can assess the appropriateness of the properties used in this process and examine other data that may be applied to the evaluation.

Other items that may be used in this valuation process include location to transportation hubs, the availability of telecommunications, water, energy and other essential services are important input into the appraisal methodology. The MNC should become fully informed of the presence and stability and the quality of the services provided within the regional infrastructure. Additionally, the MNC should consider the police, fire, and medical services that are available within the area of the property. Security concerns or safety requirements for personnel are important aspects for the MNCs to consider when evaluating a specific property.

Appraiser credentials — The MNC should verify the qualifications and experience of the appraisal firm conducting the assessment. The local firm should identify what methodology is used in the appraisal process, such as the US-based or London-based approaches or a different methodology that dominates the particular region.

7. Real Estate Management Decisions

A firm that decides to invest directly in real estate must make some early decisions about the ownership and use of the property. These initial decisions have long-term implications for the property's investment potential; cash flow requirements; legal implications; and political risks.

Acquisition or leasing of property is one of the earliest decisions that the firm should make when obtaining property. Leasing property will reduce the financial exposure and the cash flow requirements of the firm. Leasing the property will give the MNC greater operational flexibility over time, but the firm would then forego any potential capital gains that accrue to real estate owners. The purchase of property involves greater financial commitment from the firm with the benefits and costs of property ownership. The operational needs of the firm may not permit the real estate manager adequate time to find the best property at a reasonable price, so the various costs associated with the timing of the purchase should be part of the evaluation process.

Management of the real estate may be performed by the firm or by an outside firm. The corporate real estate department should explore the benefits of either relying upon internal management that involves hiring adequate staff or selecting external contractors who specialize in property management. A local manager would be responsible for overseeing the maintenance of the property and make sure the firm is in compliance with local laws on rents and price controls, tenant rights, taxes, and other legal rulings that affect property owners.

Usage of the property has an impact on the cash flows associated with the real estate, particularly if some rental activity is possible. The firm should evaluate the benefits of obtaining lease income if the corporate activities do not require the use of all the facilities.

Location is an extremely important variable in the cost and future appreciation of real estate. The site must meet the business needs of the firm, but consideration should also be given to the profit potential of the site.

8. Differences in Real Estate Ownership Across Countries

Property ownership varies across countries, and investors need to acquaint themselves with the specific conditions within each country or region. The general attitude toward property ownership that is grounded in Western economic principles is slowly expanding as global capital flows impact national economies. The Western concept of property ownership places strong emphasis on physical ownership of the real estate, the ability to generate cash flows from the use of the property, and the right to retain the proceeds of a sale or transfer of the property.

Ownership is available to foreign entities in most countries, but restrictions are fairly common and the range of property rights varies. While private ownership of property is available in most countries, a small group of countries maintain state ownership of land and property.

China passed legislation in 2007 that offered specific legal protection for private ownership of property. Land reform, beginning in the late 1970s, became an important part of China's economic reform as it attracted foreign capital and encouraged entrepreneurial activities within its borders. While the state continues to own all land in China, the rights of individual use will be renewed automatically within the time span of 30 to 70 years.

An important attribute that encourages international investment in real estate is access to clear, unambiguous ownership of the property. A variety of land ownership and tenure exists across countries. MNCs should understand the different types of land and property ownership traditions since historical ownership patterns may affect existing property laws. Specific types of land ownership include the following:

Fee simple ownership is one of the most complete forms of property ownership available. Some limitations to this form of property ownership exist through governmental authority, such as eminent domain. Fee simple ownership of property is typically found in countries grounded in common law, usually countries that were once part of the British Empire.

Leasehold is a type of ownership that provides right of access and use of a property for a specific time period. These leases can be purchased and sold on the open market since they convey all the rights and privileges offered to the original parties who signed the lease, which reflects contract and property laws. The time frame for such leases is usually long-term, with a 99-year lease being quite common, though much longer leaseholds exist.

Traditional land tenure represents a group or tribal-based ownership of land. Regions that possessed this form of ownership in the past may offer greater challenges to MNCs that wish to invest in real estate without possible challenges to ownership or use of the property.

9. Registration of Ownership

Land registration systems are an important element of real estate investment since they record the ownership and the transfer through time in ownership of the property. Developed economies typically have property registration systems that are reliably accurate and complete. Developing economies may have incomplete registration systems that pose greater risks to the real estate investor.

Title insurance has emerged in some countries as an effective way to reduce the financial risk exposure of real estate investments from inaccuracies within property registration systems. This form of insurance is a contract that protects the holder of the policy from losses that are due to defects in the property title. The distinctive feature of this insurance is that it offers protection for past mistakes or events but not for errors or events that occur in the future.

This form of insurance emerged in the US in the late 1800s to protect property owners from errors and omissions in the property records that were unknown at the time of the transfer of property (Worm, 2006). Unlike many European countries, most jurisdictions within the US implement a property recording system that does not require a governmental official to make a determination of whether there is valid title ownership or a proper transfer.

The use of title insurance expanded significantly in the late 1900s to provide financial protection for the lending industry. The use of title insurance has expanded to other countries, but this event has been driven primarily by US firms as a method to reduce their financial risk. Part of the demand for US-style title insurance by US MNCs appear to be motivated by unfamiliarity with the property record systems of host countries (Arrunada, 2001). The country-specific policies are governed by the local legal system where the property transfer is filed. Importantly, international policies often provide less protection than the standard policies in the US.

Title insurance is now an established means of reducing financial risk throughout the world. The primary areas include Australia, Asia, the Caribbean, Canada, and Latin America. It exists in limited form in the UK while interest is increasing in Central and Eastern Europe. There have been recent attempts to introduce title insurance in Western Europe, which has an established land registry system. Historically, a need for financial protection in real estate transactions has not appeared to be critical and in need of such insurance (Wurm, 2006).

10. Impact of Corporate Real Estate on MNCs

MNCs often possess significant holdings of real estate that support their global operations, and this pattern of ownership is found throughout the world. The presence of vast real estate holdings of US MNCs is well known, and many non-real estate UK firms own properties that rival the holdings of firms specializing in real estate. Asian firms also fit this trend where real estate comprises roughly 40% of total corporate assets for the average firm in Singapore.

Despite the significant allocation of resources into real estate, there has been little empirical research about the impact that real estate holdings have upon the general performance of a firm. Some early findings indicate a need to improve the investment performance of corporate real estate. These observations acknowledge that that management of real estate varies across firms, with a significant portion focusing on the support function of the real estate and not actively incorporating an investment approach to the properties.

Empirical studies have not found strong evidence suggesting that corporate real estate ownership provides diversification benefits to the firms (Seiler *et al.*, 2001; Cheong and Kim, 1997; Liow, 1999). A later study by Liow (2004) examines the impact that real estate holdings have upon the stock market performance of non-real estate firms that are also property-intensive. The findings suggest that the real estate component of the corporate portfolio has a detrimental impact to the risk-return characteristics of the firm's stock: lower returns and lower abnormal return performance; higher total risk; and higher systematic risk. One interpretation of the results is that the property-intensive firms own or manage their properties for non-investment reasons.

It may be that MNCs should re-orient their approach to their real estate holdings to create an asset base that is more responsive to the needs of shareholders. There are possible reasons by non-property firms to accumulate large real estate holdings instead of leasing their properties. The overall corporate strategy may focus on property ownership, since the firm may perceive a positive benefit to the presence of real estate within its asset base that enables it to achieve operational efficiency.

The reassessment about owning instead of leasing real estate to meet the operational needs of the firm appears to have begun in the 1980s after a period of heightened merger and acquisition activity. Bruggeman *et al.* (1990) notes that corporate restructuring among US firms in the 1980s generated a shift toward leasing more real estate while European firms maintained higher ownership of their properties. Glascock *et al.* (2002) suggests Asian firms prefer to own properties since the combination of population density and land scarcity makes the ownership of real estate potentially profitable beyond its operational use. The impact that a firm's real estate has upon the measures of financial performance suggests that real estate will be increasingly integrated into the corporation's financial management and strategic planning.

11. Diversification Benefits

An important goal of investors is to maintain adequate returns while controlling the risk exposure. An appeal for real estate as an investment vehicle is the potential for diversification across geographical regions and property types. The reduction of risk through a careful asset selection process would reduce the impact of the downturn within any specific market or asset class. The diversification benefits that international real estate would add to a portfolio are dependent upon the level of integration or segmentation that exists between the portfolio's broader components.

An integrated property market would imply that an investor would derive little, if any, risk reduction by acquiring properties in different national markets. If property markets were highly segmented, then risk reduction should occur when a portfolio contains properties spanning different markets. Investors would be able to manage their risk exposure by reallocating their property holdings based upon changing market conditions. It seems reasonable that investors would expect properties that span national borders to be subject to different economic and currency cycles that would diversify risks while contributing to the portfolio's returns.

Yet research suggests that property valuation across national markets may be somewhat integrated and may not always offer substantial diversification benefits. Several studies have identified market segmentation across national borders, particularly across continents (Liu and Mei, 1998; Ziobrowski and Curcio, 1991). But the evidence suggests that property markets within the same continent are more integrated than those in different continents. Thus, investors wanting to achieve the greatest amount of diversification through real properties would need to explore investment options outside their continent (Eichholtz *et al.*, 1998).

In addition to geographic diversification, some studies such as Barry *et al.* (1996) examined the property valuation in developed versus emerging markets. The study observes potential benefits of diversification for real estate investments in developing economies. Despite the greater risk associated with investments, they found support for diversification in a relatively low correlation between the returns from property investments in developed and developing economies. Another study by Addae-Dapaah *et al.* (2005) found that portfolios of real estate investments targeted at emerging economies outperformed comparable investments in developed economies at any level of risk. This study used real estate data from the 1990–1999 in five emerging economies (Thailand, Indonesia, Malaysia, China, and the Philippines) and seven developed economies (Singapore, Japan, Hong Kong, France, UK, Ireland, and New Zealand). Adjustments were made to control for currency risk.

12. The Asian-Pacific Financial Crisis of 1997

The Asian financial crisis of 1997 provides a good test case about the diversification benefits in property markets across the continent. Among the nations that experienced the financial crisis, a common feature was the over-extension of bank credit to the real estate markets. The collapse of this bank credit coincided with the precipitous drop in currency values and in the national stock markets. A contagion effect would exist if the crisis spread from one country to another with the subsequent devaluation of the property markets, thus lowering the potential for diversification within property markets throughout the region. Yet the potential for diversification exists if there is not a consistent pattern of property devaluation across national markets.

Studies of the Asian property markets before the 1997 financial crisis have found mixed results about the potential for diversification within the region. Some observe substantial potential for diversification

176 G. A. Patterson

across the national real estate markets, particularly when compared to the equity markets (Bond *et al.*, 2006). The authors note that there were differences between the property and equity markets in how the transmission of bad economic events and subsequent devaluations occurred across national boundaries. This difference provides some risk reduction for investors who have real estate within the asset mix of their portfolios.

Other studies, such as Gerlach *et al.* (2006), find that the property markets in Asia were integrated and that the 1997 Asian financial crisis did not significantly alter the integration across property markets in the region. This means that what happens to property values in one country may be replicated in property markets in other countries within the region. This spill-over effect has implications for international real estate investors since it highlights the effects of globalization upon the performance of international real estate portfolios.

The integration among property markets in the Asia-Pacific region does not imply that the transmission of economic shocks is uniformly distributed. They found that Japan and Singapore were the two most influential markets that impacted other Asian/Pacific markets at that time.

For example, the devaluation in property values in a large, important country such as Japan would more greatly impact the property markets in smaller regional markets than the reverse order with Japan's property markets reacting to events in smaller regional economies.

13. Indirect Real Estate Investment

Investment advisors often recommend that real estate be included as one of the components of a broadly diversified portfolio. An indirect investment in real estate focuses on the purchase of securities in entities that represent the ownership of real properties or mortgage backed securities. A primary advantage to this form of real estate investment is that it avoids many of the complications associated with direct ownership of real estate. Investors also benefit from the enhanced liquidity associated with ownership of equity in real estate firms.

14. Securitized International Real Estate Investment

Institutional investors have long considered real estate to be a necessary component to a portfolio, but most individual investors emphasize the standard financial securities within the bond or equity markets. Individual investors as a group have not emphasized real estate except for the family residence, but indirect investments now offer greater opportunities. Investors now have access to real estate securities that offer convenient access to global real estate investments through the financial markets.

The international market for real estate securities has grown significantly over the past few decades. The financial markets now provide investors with easy access to international real estate investments without inheriting the obligations to search, acquire, manage, and sell the properties. They also avoid being directly subject to various legal and political obligations that come with direct ownership of real estate.

Indirect ownership of real estate is most commonly obtained through the purchase of stock in property firms such as Real Estate Operating Companies (REOCs) and Real Estate Investment Trusts (REITs). While REOCs are formed with the typical corporate structure, the REITs are more similar to mutual funds for preferential tax treatment. Both types of firms provide investors with real estate exposure without incurring the responsibilities of direct property ownership. These firms enable investors to incorporate real estate into their overall portfolio while maintaining the benefits of liquidity from financial securities that would not exist with real properties.

15. Real Estate Investment Trusts (REITs)

REITs have been well established in the US, Canada and Australia and offer investors a range of investment options by property type and asset classification. REITs are broadly categorized as equity, mortgage, or hybrid. Equity REITs focus their efforts in the acquisition, management, and sale of specific types of real estate. Their lease cash flow represents a major portion of their operating income. Mortgage REITs emphasize the ownership of property mortgages with the interest income representing most of their operating earnings. These firms may either originate or purchase the mortgages. The investment activities of Hybrid REITs reflect their name — they engage in buying properties and property mortgages.

Equity REITs usually specialize in specific property types, which often have different cash flow patterns and different sensitivities to economic cycles. Some of the larger property groupings are presented below.

Office and Industrial REITs span different forms of properties that have distinct subsets. Office REITs own office properties, including office buildings, complexes, and centers. The cash flows for these REITs are sensitive to vacancy rates, rental rates, and the demand for office space. The industrial sector includes manufacturing plants, warehouse and distribution facilities, and research and development facilities. Demand for this sector is closely linked to the economy, though office properties may generate more cyclical cash flows, given the duration of lease contracts. These earnings flows impact the distribution patterns of these equity REITs.

Retail REITs include malls and shopping centers. There are often high barriers to entry for regional malls, and this situation gives firms which own established businesses a strong competitive advantage.

Lodging and resorts REITs generate cash flows that are highly correlated to the economic cycles since much of their business comes from discretionary income from commercial and individual customers.

Health care REITs emphasize facilities like hospitals, nursing homes, assisted living facilities and other medically oriented properties. This property group generates relatively stable revenue streams. Analysts observe an increase in mergers and acquisitions within this property type and suggest long-term trends are at work: a means for cost effective expansion, an attempt to diversify holdings within the field, and competitive positioning in preparation for aging baby boomers that will generate an extraordinary demand for health care services.

Residential REITs specialize in apartments and other residential properties that are leased. This property type is often counter-cyclical to the housing market. Significant increases in affordable home costs often encourage greater demand for rental properties.

Self-storage REITs attract significant corporate clients, in addition to individuals, to rent their properties. This sector has witnessed an expansion encouraged by consumer storage needs as well as the increased cost of housing that has directed more households into apartments.

Diversified REITs have not assembled properties in any specific niche. A mix of properties makes it more difficult for REIT management to gain expertise in any specific property sector.

The different property types that exist among REITs provide investors with a convenient method to focus on desired sectors within the real estate industry. Additionally, investors should be mindful that other real estate firms exist that do not have the corporate structure of REITs. These real estate firms may focus upon real estate investments, but the operating cash flows may contain sizable portions of non-rental activities.

16. Governance Structure of REITs

A strict set of rules establishes the structural requirements of REITs to benefit from favorable tax treatments by the US government. The US tax laws permit such funds to avoid paying federal income taxes when they meet specific operational and cash disbursement standards. Legislation now exists in many countries that replicate the US-based corporate and tax structures. Thus, investors should decide whether the resulting cash flow is optimal from a risk-return and after-tax perspective. These investment firms are supposed to target their sector, so real estate must make up at least 75% of their assets and their income. The funds must also pay dividends to their shareholders so that they distribute 90% of their annual taxable income.

The management and investment structure of REITs also has implications for agency costs within the firms. REITs have either internal management or external advisors that make the investment decisions of the firms. REITs with internal management teams typically have fewer agency problems since the managers are employed by the firm and often own sizable amounts of shares in their firms. Such incentive-based compensation structures encourage investment decisions are that are beneficial to shareholders. REITs with external advisors usually establish a compensation structure that rewards the investment team for the size of the asset base and not for the earnings stream. The compensation package for such REITs may lead to a large, but sub-optimal portfolio of real estate assets.

17. Expansion of International REITs

Expanding the breadth of a portfolio to include international real estate is no longer limited to institutional investors now that such asset categories are available on the global financial markets. Real estate investment securities, structured like US REITs, have been publicly traded for decades, but were initially limited to relatively few countries such as the US, Canada, Australia, and the Netherlands. The number of countries with REITs may have been limited, but a variety of firms within these national markets offered investors a fairly broad selection. The maturity of the US REIT market, with its breadth and depth throughout the real estate sectors, has also offered opportunities for non-US investors. The international investment community was able to expand the asset base of their portfolios by investing in US-based REITs. Additionally, some of the REITs in these initial countries developed international portfolios, so shareholders were able to select from a limited variety of international real estate portfolios.

The need to offer investors easy access to the global real estate market began to expand significantly in the 1990s in the developed and emerging markets. While the international REIT market is still in the early stages of its development, the expansion of firms throughout the world should increase the diversification benefits for investors. Many additional governments are either in the process of adopting or considering REIT-like investment structures. The anticipated growth in this securities market is expected to improve diversification for investors (Jacobius, 2006).

The first Asian REIT was formed in Japan in 2001, and there has been a rapid expansion throughout the region. Investors can now select from a large number of REITs that focus on different real estate markets throughout Asia. In addition to Japan, Hong Kong, Taiwan, South Korea, Singapore, Malaysia, and New Zealand have introduced REIT-like structures in their financial markets. Additionally, innovations in the types of funds offered suggest that the investor pool will continue to expand, and in 2006, a Malaysian Islamic REIT was the first to be structurally and operationally Shariah compliant.

The growth in European REITs began more slowly than it did in Asia, but such firms now operate throughout the region. Investors can select from a variety of REITs that trade on European markets and operate in countries such as the UK, France, Germany, Italy, and other Western European countries. Investors may also select from a growing list of firms investing in East European countries such as the Czech Republic, Hungary, and Romania. The pending legislation throughout the continent suggests that investors will soon have access to an even broader group of real estate markets.

18. International Diversification

International diversification became significantly easier to obtain when portfolio managers could invest in the shares of real estate companies operating overseas. Many of the structural hurdles associated with direct investment of real estate were mitigated by the liquidity of the financial markets and the ability of foreign companies to invest outside their home regions. The global financial markets make it possible for investors to construct diversified portfolios that include real estate throughout the world.

An investor may assemble a diversified portfolio by selecting securities from different asset categories that are also expected to have a positive impact on the risk-return characteristics of the portfolio. An early study that examined international diversification of real estate securities compared the relative benefits for real estate, stock and bond investors. This study by Eichholtz (1996) observed that there were significantly lower correlations in returns for real estate than for stocks and bonds. The study, using data from seven developed economies, suggested that international diversification offered greater benefits for investors of real estate securities than for common stocks or corporate bonds. Yet other studies have found less stark results. Many empirical studies of stock returns in the general equities markets and those of US REITs have consistently observed high correlations which usually reduce the diversification benefits (see Gyourko and Keim, 1992). While the REITs offer investors the opportunity to invest in real estate in a highly liquid format, the REIT returns behave very similarly to returns in other industries. The question of diversification benefits arises and has been extended to investors outside the US who invest in US REITs.

Portfolio managers should understand the scope of geographic diversification for real estate markets. International diversification may not be achieved if real estate securities are concentrated in two neighboring countries with highly integrated economies. Eichholtz *et al.* (1998) broadened the analysis of geographical diversification and observed the presence of continental factors that affected real estate returns throughout the region, particularly in Europe and North America. The national real estate markets within the Asia-Pacific region were more independent of continental factors, but a trend toward greater integration was also noted. Given the patterns of integration, a portfolio manager would be able to construct a diversified real estate portfolio by focusing upon one country within each continent. Such an approach would also make it easier for a portfolio manager to monitor the performances of the real estate investments. The study also noted that European investors would obtain greater opportunities for diversification in the Asia-Pacific region, though North America would also have potential. The test results suggested that North American investors of real estate should focus on Europe for more opportunities with diversification but could also expand into the Asia-Pacific region. The investors in Asia-Pacific would be able to look to other continents and to countries within the region since those markets were more independent and less affected by continental factors.

Ling and Naranjo (2002) examined commercial real estate returns across many countries to see if there were potential benefits for geographic diversification. The study identified a significant world-wide factor that explained the returns of international real estate securities. Despite the presence of the common risk factor, the study identified significant differences across country real estate returns. Thus, opportunities exist for international diversification by investing in international real estate securities. Their position is supported by Hamelink *et al.* (2004) who also find that country factors are dominant risk factors in explaining about one-third of the returns of real estate securities. Their study of real estate securities in ten countries from 1990–2003 found that other variables, in addition to country, impacted the returns: size of the property firm, growth, and property type emphasized by the real estate company. Yet the country risk factor dominates other factors in explaining the returns of the real estate securities. Portfolio managers may wish to integrate the results of these studies, for there are significant implications to the way an investor would incorporate international real estate into a portfolio. For example, the investor should understand that an emphasis on Japanese real estate securities would be subject to risk factors specific to that country, but the security returns would also be affected by other characteristics such as the value/growth risk factor for the real estate firm. These additional risk factors may affect the overall diversification benefits of a geographically distributed portfolio.

The common factor affecting international real estate securities in Ling and Naranjo (2002) is also identified in a study by Wilson *et al.* (2007). Their study identifies the common trend affecting international returns, but the sensitivity differs across countries. The US market was least affected by this global real estate factor, yet movement in the US market also impacted other countries' real estate markets. This cointegration between the US real estate market and the rest of the world has implications for international diversification.

While some investors may consolidate all real estate securities into one industry, studies such as Downs *et al.* (2003) and Hamelink *et al.* (2004) note that there are differences in return behavior among real estate securities from different property or REIT types. Such differences may be incorporated into the construction of a portfolio.

Other studies have focused on the ability of international real estate markets to provide improvements in diversification benefits over foreign stocks. Liu and Mei (1998) found that minor diversification benefits were found but were limited to the unexpected portion of portfolio returns. They also observed that changes in exchange rate risk partially explained the benefits that real estate securities offered.

19. Property Firms

There have been few studies on property firms even though this form of corporate structure has a longer history than those of REITs. A recent study by Boer *et al.* (2005) examined the stock performance between property firms that focused their investments geographically and those that diversified their holdings across regions.

Boer *et al.* (2005) examined real estate firms and the intensity of their focus in real estate investments. Those firms that targeted specific real estate sectors or geographic regions generated higher risk-adjusted returns than those firms that diversified across regions or real estate sectors. A firm with a focused investment strategy had higher firm-specific risk, but there was no significant difference in systematic risk with the diversified firms.

References

Addae-Dapaah, K. and H. L. Loh, 2005, Exchange rate volatility and international real estate diversification: A comparison of emerging and developed economies, *Journal of Real Estate Portfolio Management*, 11(3), 225–240.

Arrunada, B., 2001, A global perspective on title insurance, *Housing Finance International*, 16(2), 3–11.

Bloomberg, 2004, Global capital flows surging into property, *The Business Times*, June 15.

Barry, C. B., M. Rodriguez, and J. B. Lipscomb, 1996, Diversification potential from real estate companies in emerging capital markets, *Journal of Real Estate Portfolio Management*, 2(2), 107–118.

Boer, D., D. Brounen, and H. Op't Veld, 2005, Corporate focus and stock performance: International evidence from listed property markets, *Journal of Real Estate Finance and Economics*, 31(3), 263–281.

Bond, S. A., M. Dungey, and R. Fry, 2006, A web of shocks: Crisis across Asian real estate markets, *The Journal of Real Estate Finance and Economics*, 32, 253–274.

Brueggman, W. G., J. D. Fisher, and D. M. Porter, 1990, Rethinking corporate real estate, *Journal of Applied Corporate Finance*, 3(1), 39–50.

Cheong, K. and C. S. Kim, 1997, Corporate real estate holdings and the value of the firm in Korea, *Journal of Real Estate Research*, 13(3), 273–295.

Downs, D. H., H.-G. Fung, G. A. Patterson, and J. Yau, 2003, The linkage of REIT income- and price-returns with fundamental economic variables, *The Journal of Alternative Investments*, 6(1), 39–50.

Eichholtz, P. M. A., R. Huisman, K. Koedijk, and L. Schuin, 1998, Continental factors in international real estate returns, *Real Estate Economics*, 26(3), 493–509.

Eichholtz, P. M. A., 1996, Does international diversification work better for real estate than for stocks and bonds? *Financial Analysts Journal*, 52(1), 56–62.

Gerlach, R., P. Wilson, and R. Zurbruegg, 2006, Structural breaks and diversification: The impact of the 1997 Asian financial crisis on the integration of Asia-Pacific real estate markets, *Journal of International Money and Finance*, 25, 974–991.

Glascock, L., C. Lu, and R. W. So, 2002, REIT returns and inflation: Perverse or Reverse Causality Effects? *Journal of Real Estate Finance and Economics*, 24(3), 301–317.

Gyourko, J. and D. B. Keim, 1992, What does the stock market tell us about real estate returns? *Journal of the American Real Estate and Urban Economics Association*, 20(3), 457–485.

Hamelink, F. and M. Hoesli, 2004, What factors determine international real estate security returns? *Real Estate Economics*, 23(3), 437–462.

Jacobius, A., 2006, International REITs provide little diversification benefit, *Pensions and Investments*, 32(15), 21–22.

Ling, D. C. and A. Naranjo, 2002, Commercial real estate return performance: A cross-country analysis, *Journal of Real Estate Finance and Economics*, 24(1/2), 119–142.

Liow, K. H., 1999, Corporate investment and ownership in real estate in Singapore: Some empirical evidence, *Journal of Corporate Real Estate*, 1(4), 329–342.

Liow, K. H., 2004, Corporate real estate and stock market performance, *The Journal of Real Estate Finance and Economics*, 29(1), 119–140.

Liu, C. H. and J. Mei, 1998, The predictability of international real estate markets, exchange rate risks and diversification consequences, *Real Estate Economics*, 26(1), 3–39.

Seiler, M. J., A. Chathrath, and J. R. Webb, 2001, Real asset ownership and the risk and return to stockholders, *Journal of Real Estate Research*, 22(1/2), 199–212.

Wilson, P. J., S. Stevenson, and R. Zurbruegg, 2007, Foreign property shocks and the impact on domestic securitized real estate markets: An unobserved components approach, *Journal of Real Estate Finance and Economics*, 34, 407–424.

Worzala, E. and G. Newell, 1995, International real estate: A review of strategic investment issues, *Journal of Real Estate Portfolio Management*, 3(2), 87–96.

Wurm, J.-B, 2006, How US-style title insurance is transforming risk management in European real estate markets, *Housing Finance International*, 20(4), 16–19.

Ziobrowski, A. and R. J. Curcio, 1991, Diversification benefits of US real estate to foreign investors, *Journal of Real Estate Research*, 6(2), 119–142.

Books

Hines, M. A., 1990, *Global Corporate Real Estate Management: A Handbook for Multinational Businesses and Organizations*, New York: Quorum Books.

Hines, M. A., 2001. *Investing in International Real Estate*, New York: Quorum Books.

Chapter 8

Global Perspectives on Venture Capital and Private Equity

Xiaoqing Eleanor Xu*,†

Private equity encompasses all types of equity investments in non-publicly traded companies, such as venture capital and buyout investing. Venture capital funds specialize in long-term private equity investments in startup and super-growth companies that offer high potential returns and substantial risks, while buyout funds invest in established businesses that need financing capital for the change of ownership. Global venture capital and buyout funds provide investors with the opportunity to capture innovations and growth around the world while enjoying the enhanced return potential and risk diversification. Major private equity hotbeds include the established markets of Europe, Israel, Canada, and the emerging markets of China, India, and Russia. While PE investments provide superior return relative to public equity, they are also associated with illiquidity and various other risks. As an alternative investment asset class, investors need to assess its risk and return profile carefully before making the asset allocation decision.

Keywords: Venture capital; private equity; fundraising; investments; divestments.

---

* The author thanks Emily Mendell of National Venture Capital Association, Sandy Anglin of Thomson Financial, Jennifer Vandermosten of European Private Equity & Venture Capital Association, Vincent Pun of Asian Venture Capital Association, and Michael Kang, Robin Zhu, and Wonnie Wang of Zero2IPO for data assistance.
† Stillman School of Business, Seton Hall University, 400 South Orange Avenue, South Orange, NJ 07079, USA. Email: xuxe@shu.edu.

1. Introduction

As part of alternative investments, private equity (PE) encompasses all types of equity investments in non-publicly traded companies, such as venture capital (VC) and buyout investing. Companies that issue private equity are generally unable or unwilling to obtain financing via public equity or debt. Investors of private equity typically participate in PE investing through private equity funds that are organized as limited partnerships in which the private equity firm serves as the general partner and the investors serve as limited partners.

Venture capital funds specialize in long-term private equity investments in startup and super-growth companies that offer high potential returns and substantial risks. Since venture capital investments are made in non-publicly traded companies that are characterized by a high level of information asymmetry between entrepreneurs and investors, venture capitalists are actively involved in monitoring, strategic management, planning and decision-making of the portfolio companies they fund. Venture capitalists usually provide capital infusion in well-defined stages tied to significant development of the company's products, market, and profitability. In addition, venture capitalists typically take an active role in guiding an exit decision, such as IPOs or M&As. Venture capital funds are illiquid investments with a typical investment horizon of 7–10 years. Successful venture capital exits through IPOs and M&As bring returns and liquidity to a venture capital fund, but it is still much more illiquid relative to public equity portfolio with securities traded in the secondary market. Buyout funds invest in established businesses that need financing capital for the change of ownership. Leveraged Buyouts (LBOs) involve the acquisition of products or businesses, either public or private companies, using a significant amount of senior debt (typically 90% debt and 10% equity). Similar to venture capital funds, buyout funds take concentrated private equity positions, but they are often associated with acquisitions of products and companies using a high degree of leverage.

According to the 2007 Global Trends in Venture Capital Survey conducted by Deloitte & Touche LLP in conjunction with the National Association of Venture Capital (NVCA), emergence of entrepreneurial environment, high-quality deal flow, access to quality entrepreneurs, access to foreign markets, diversification of industry and geographic risk, lower cost locations, and extensive competition for deal flow in the domestic market were cited as the primary drivers for global VC investing. On the other hand, VC investing abroad is associated with various possible risks and challenges, including lack of intellectual property protection, lack of experienced local investors, lack of quality deals that fit investment profile, lack of talented portfolio management teams, lack of skilled workers, difficulty in achieving successful exits, weak regulatory environment, unstable political environment, unstable economy, and exchange rate risk. The survey results indicate that over half of the US venture capitalists intend to implement a global investment strategy, mainly by investing in domestic companies with global operations, or by partnering with firms and investors who have track records in target countries. For those investing directly in international markets, expertise in those markets (cultural background, regulations, personal connections, etc.) and close contact with local entrepreneurs are critical to success in foreign VC investing. As shown in Figure 1, the survey indicated that China, India, UK and Ireland, and Israel are the primary foreign locations where US venture capitalists would like to expand their investment focus.

2. Global VC and PE Landscape

Globalization occurs in every corner of the financial sector, including private equity. As estimated by Ernst & Young (see *Acceleration — Global Venture Capital Insight Report*, 2007), the global pool of private venture-backed companies approaches 10,000 as of January 2007, with US$173 billion invested in them. While the mature markets of US, Europe, Israel and Canada continue to dominate the global PE industry in terms of fundraising, investments and exits, the emerging markets of China, India, Russia and Brazil have the most significant impact on the current global VC landscape and show the most promise for future strategic growth.

The US has long been a venture capital hotbed that nurtured and financed innovative enterprises. For the past 50 years in the US, VC

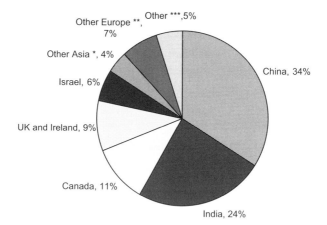

Figure 1. Primary Location Where US Venture Capital Investors Would Like to Expand Investment Focus

* Australia/New Zealand, Other Asia, South Korea
** Austria, Germany, Liechtenstein, Switzerland, Central & Eastern Europe, Nordic Countries
*** Africa, Latin America, Middle East (excl. Israel)
Source: Global Trends in Venture Capital 2007 Survey, by Deloitte & Touche and the National Venture Capital Association (NVCA).

has provided initial funding to companies such as Microsoft, Apple, Genentech, Home Depot, Compaq, Intel, Lotus, Sun Microsystems, Federal Express, and has established itself as the "engine" for innovative entrepreneurial enterprises. Table 1 provides a summary of the US venture capital and buyout fundraising, investing, and exiting from 1990 to 2006. During this 17 year period, US$389/$745 billions were raised by 3,753/1,935 US VC/buyout funds, and US$466/$357 billions were invested in 62,975/22,173 VC/buyout investment rounds. In addition, exits through 2,336/628 VC/buyout-backed IPOs and 3,432/626 VC/buyout-backed M&As provided the return and liquidity to US private equity investors. A recent survey demonstrated the paramount importance of US VC in contributing to jobs (9% of private sector employment), sales revenue (16.6% of US GDP), economic growth, and technological advancement (see *Global Insight Venture Impact Study*, 2007). However, with the creation of one unified currency in the Eurozone, the emergence of developing markets such as China and India, the globalization of

Table 1. Private Equity Fundraising, Investments and Exits in the US

Panel A. Venture Capital

	VC Investments		VC Fundraising		VC IPO Exits		VC M&A Exits		
Year	Number of Investments	Total Investment ($bil)	Funds	Funds Raised ($bil)	Number of IPOs	Amount ($bil)	Number of M&A Exits	Number of Disclosed M&A Exits	Disclosed Offer Amount
1990	1,860	3.74	89	3.46	70	1.40	19	9	0.21
1991	1,586	2.84	42	2.00	157	4.92	17	4	0.20
1992	1,971	5.79	82	5.32	196	7.28	75	46	2.54
1993	1,675	4.77	91	4.13	221	6.69	75	44	1.70
1994	1,744	6.35	138	8.93	167	4.67	100	64	3.41
1995	2,315	9.56	172	10.13	205	8.15	97	60	3.79
1996	3,272	14.73	162	11.84	272	11.48	118	77	8.53
1997	3,977	18.17	243	19.74	138	4.83	166	116	7.44
1998	4,953	27.28	290	30.31	78	3.78	211	133	9.55
1999	6,127	63.24	451	56.24	270	20.87	239	162	37.51
2000	8,782	116.31	647	106.08	264	25.50	318	203	68.49
2001	5,309	46.12	317	38.79	41	3.49	353	165	16.80
2002	3,670	27.31	203	3.82	22	2.11	318	152	7.92
2003	3,563	26.83	162	10.64	29	2.02	291	123	7.73
2004	3,771	28.98	212	19.00	93	11.01	339	186	15.44
2005	3,895	29.41	224	28.15	56	4.46	347	168	16.09
2006	4,505	34.39	228	30.98	57	5.12	349	151	16.77

Source: Thomson Financial/National Venture Capital Association (NVCA).

Panel B. Buyouts

	Buyouts Investments		Buyouts Fundraising		Buyouts IPO Exits		Buyouts M&A Exits		
Year	Number of Investments	Total Investment ($bil)	Funds	Funds Raised ($bil)	Number of IPOs	Total Offer Amount ($bil)	Number of M&A Exits	Number of Disclosed M&A Exits	Disclosed Offer Amount ($bil)
1990	640	5.43	63	7.91	23	0.60	3	1	0.12
1991	391	2.62	28	6.19	40	3.00	9	5	0.57
1992	569	5.49	58	11.03	62	4.21	10	9	0.31
1993	531	3.76	79	16.13	56	2.88	22	11	0.46
1994	657	5.25	99	20.45	35	1.46	11	2	0.18
1995	804	7.18	105	26.48	31	1.98	31	17	4.43
1996	1,378	14.57	99	29.28	16	1.32	30	24	7.63
1997	1,592	15.59	133	41.89	36	3.38	55	37	10.61
1998	1,743	26.48	161	61.60	24	3.19	53	40	20.53
1999	2,120	39.39	150	54.18	34	6.79	34	19	8.37
2000	3,412	51.54	156	75.87	22	4.99	33	18	9.06
2001	2,028	24.74	121	46.21	15	2.76	35	22	6.58
2002	1,089	23.43	89	24.24	21	4.37	27	21	6.67
2003	1,048	42.43	98	30.70	22	5.04	34	22	6.12
2004	1,113	30.43	144	53.03	58	11.41	31	20	7.90
2005	1,344	27.59	182	96.61	67	15.76	91	52	19.85
2006	1,714	31.12	170	147.08	66	17.45	117	53	25.59

Source: Thomson Financial.

consumer markets, the globalization of industry competition, and the advancements of technology, the PE industry has become more and more global as investors try to put their risk capital to the most productive use.

Table 2 shows the comparative statistics on VC and buyout investments in US, Europe and Asia Pacific from 1990 to 2006. As of 2006, annual VC investments in the US are still 1.55 times the total VC investments in Europe and 2.03 times the VC investments in Asia

Table 2. Venture Capital vs. Buyout Investments: US, Europe and Asia-Pacific

Location	US			Europe			Asia-Pacific		
Year	VC	Buyout	VC/ Buyout	VC	Buyout	VC/ Buyout	VC	Buyout	VC/ Buyout
1990	3.74	5.43	0.69	3.01	1.96	1.54			
1991	2.84	2.62	1.08	3.55	2.07	1.72			
1992	5.79	5.49	1.05	3.13	2.41	1.30			
1993	4.77	3.76	1.27	2.69	2.17	1.24			
1994	6.35	5.25	1.21	3.36	3.09	1.08			
1995	9.56	7.18	1.33	3.38	3.31	1.02			
1996	14.73	14.57	1.01	4.07	4.06	1.00			
1997	18.17	15.59	1.16	5.27	6.23	0.85	3.54	0.78	4.54
1998	27.28	26.48	1.03	7.70	9.55	0.81	2.06	1.83	1.13
1999	63.24	39.39	1.61	13.75	17.08	0.80	4.38	3.94	1.11
2000	116.31	51.54	2.26	25.32	18.56	1.36	6.32	5.42	1.17
2001	46.12	24.74	1.86	15.71	14.10	1.11	5.69	5.23	1.09
2002	27.31	23.43	1.17	12.62	21.80	0.58	2.82	6.11	0.46
2003	26.83	42.43	0.63	10.78	23.76	0.45	2.80	13.62	0.21
2004	28.98	30.43	0.95	13.24	33.18	0.40	2.74	13.66	0.20
2005	29.41	27.59	1.07	16.35	41.36	0.40	7.55	18.69	0.40
2006	34.39	31.12	1.11	22.24	64.87	0.34	16.98	29.62	0.57
CAGR* (1997– 2006)	6.6	7.2		15.5	26.4		17.0	43.9	

Notes: * CAGR refers to Compound Annual Growth Rate.
All figures of PE investment amounts are in billion US dollars. VC/Buyout refers to the ratio of VC investment amount relative to buyout investment amount.
Source: Thomson Financial, NVCA, EVCA, and AVCJ.

Pacific, indicating the dominating role of the US in the global venture capital industry. However, worthy PE investment opportunities in the developed market of the US have been limited, and so investors have been exploring productive investment opportunities in the other established markets (such as Europe, Israel and Canada) and emerging markets (such as China, India and Russia). As seen from Table 2, during the past 10 years from 1997 to 2006, the compound annual growth rates in

VC and buyout investments for Europe (15.5% and 26.4%) and Asia (17.0% and 43.9%) are dramatically higher than those in the US (6.6% and 7.2%). Buyout investments in Europe have exceeded those in the US from 2004 to 2006, and buyout investments in Asia Pacific have risen to a total size close to those in the US in 2006, indicating the growing importance of European and Asian buyouts in the global private equity arena. Table 2 also shows that while VC and buyout investments are about the same total amount in the US, VC investment amounts are only 34% and 57% of buyout investment amounts in Europe and Asia Pacific, respectively.

3. Private Equity Investments in Europe

For the past 50 years in the US, venture capital has provided initial funding to innovative entrepreneurial enterprises, while the European venture capital industry has only really emerged over the past decade. A decade ago, Europe had substantially lagged behind the US in providing a nurturing environment for innovative entrepreneurial activities, with small and medium enterprises often finding it difficult to get started and grow due to the lack of "risk capital". The amounts of VC and buyout investments in Europe were both less than 30% of those in the US in 1996. In contrast, the amounts of VC and buyout investments in Europe rose to 67% and 208% of those in the US in 2006. As shown in Table 2, the European VC/PE has experienced dramatic growth for the past two decades, especially since the creation of the Euro in 1999. The creation of the Euro eliminated the thirteen member national currencies across country borders within the Eurozone, encouraged the development of venture capital and buyout investments across Europe, and resulted in a much more active and integrated European PE market.

As shown in Table 3, the average annual PE investment in Europe between 1999 and 2006 is 5.6 times the average annual investment between 1990 and 1998. Buyout investment in Europe registered the most impressive growth due to a surge in mergers and acquisitions across country borders after 1999. Cross-border investments within

Table 3. European Private Equity Fundraising and Investments

Year	Total Funds Raised (in thousand Euros)	Distribution by Location of Private Equity Source (in %)		No. of Investments	Total Investments (in thousand Euros)	Distribution by Location of Investments (in %)		
		Within Europe	Outside Europe			Domestic	Other European Countries	Non-European Countries
1990	4,578,580	85.0	14.0	5,362	4,125,718	86.59	10.75	2.66
1991	4,187,801	90.0	10.0	6,907	4,631,900	90.60	6.55	2.86
1992	4,213,775	91.2	8.8	6,197	4,701,243	88.96	7.93	3.11
1993	3,425,013	88.3	11.7	5,436	4,115,083	89.42	7.27	3.31
1994	6,693,077	80.1	19.9	5,683	5,439,626	86.51	11.35	2.15
1995	4,398,223	88.8	11.2	4,955	5,546,060	87.87	9.27	2.86
1996	7,960,403	83.2	16.7	5,686	6,787,646	83.74	12.48	3.79
1997	20,001,510	66.5	33.5	6,252	9,654,942	80.49	17.01	2.50
1998	20,342,696	68.9	31.1	7,628	14,460,781	76.80	16.76	6.44
1999	25,401,452	78.4	21.1	11,253	25,115,694	77.28	17.74	4.97
2000	48,023,389	73.1	26.9	13,107	34,985,752	72.71	20.07	7.21
2001	40,011,974	65.4	34.6	10,672	24,331,362	71.31	23.32	5.36
2002	27,532,526	71.1	28.9	10,229	27,648,381	75.67	21.54	2.79
2003	27,019,756	71.7	28.3	10,375	29,095,918	71.17	25.08	3.75

(Continued)

Table 3. (*Continued*)

Year	Total Funds Raised (in thousand Euros)	Distribution by Location of Private Equity Source (in %)		No. of Investments	Total Investments (in thousand Euros)	Distribution by Location of Investments (in %)		
		Within Europe	Outside Europe			Domestic	Other European Countries	Non-European Countries
2004	27,451,215	76.0	24.0	10,236	36,919,765	65.44	31.21	3.35
2005	71,823,422	65.5	34.5	10,912	47,057,275	61.91	34.47	3.63
2006	112,337,269	60.8	39.2	10,760	71,164,505	67.06	28.13	4.81
Mean:								
(1990–1998)	*8,422,342*	*82.44*	*17.44*	*6,012*	6,607,000	85.66	11.04	3.30
(1999–2006)	*47,450,125*	*70.26*	*29.68*	*10,943*	37,039,832	70.32	25.20	4.48
(1990–2006)	*26,788,358*	*76.71*	*23.20*	*8,332*	20,928,332	78.44	17.70	3.86

Source: European Private Equity & Venture Capital Association (EVCA).

Europe account for over 25% of the PE investments in Europe, compared to only 11% before 1999 (see Table 3). A country by country composition analysis of European PE investments in Table 4 and Figure 2 shows that the UK is still the dominant European PE investment destination across all investment stages and all investment sizes. Among the 71 billion Euros of private equity investments in 2006, 57.5% was disbursed to UK companies, followed by France (14.2%), Sweden (6.0%), Germany (4.9%), Italy (4.8%), Spain (3.96%), and Netherlands (3.36%).

Exit or divestment can be accomplished by a number of means, such as IPOs or M&As. Studies of the US market (Barry *et al.*, 1990; Lerner, 1994; Gompers, 1996; Brav *et al.*, 1997; Xu, 2004a) suggest that the most profitable venture capital exit has, on average, been disproportionately by way of an IPO. Between 2000 and 2006, 562 US venture-backed companies exited through IPOs, accounting for 46% of the number of US IPOs during the same period. Private equity exits European investments by public offerings, repayment of reference shares/loans, trade sale, write-off, management buybacks, sale to another venture capitalist, sale to financial institution, etc. Table 5 documents the distribution of these various exiting channels for European PE from 1999 to 2006. Although only an average 9% of the European PE-backed portfolio companies were divested through public offering, an IPO brings liquidity and return to private equity funds. According to Dow Jones Venture One, 69 and 91 European VC-backed IPOs raised 2.2 billion and 1.75 billion Euros in 2005 and 2006, respectively.

Using quarterly data from 1993 to 2003, Xu (2004b) examines and compares the return and risk performance of venture capital funds in the US and Europe. Several results are noteworthy. First, pooled venture capital returns in the US and Europe are 3.273% and 0.765% (on a quarterly basis) above the CAPM market risk-adjusted returns, respectively. Second, US venture capital fund performance dominates that of Europe in all measures: mean return, total-risk adjusted return, and market-risk adjusted return. Third, the linkage between US VC fund performance and the US stock market is much stronger than the co-movement between the European VC and

Table 4. Private Equity Investments in Europe by Country (as of 2006)

	Europe Total (in thousand €)	Distribution of PE Investments by Country (%)							
		UK	France	Sweden	Germany	Italy	Spain	Netherlands	Other Countries
By Investment Stage									
Venture Capital	17,254,396	54.68	11.06	4.03	5.45	5.76	5.36	2.82	10.84
Seed	197,704	34.83	0.00	7.16	15.76	1.96	16.32	7.74	16.24
Start-up	5,666,756	73.61	9.46	2.88	4.11	0.44	4.13	0.87	4.50
Expansion	11,389,936	45.60	12.04	4.55	5.93	8.48	5.78	3.71	13.90
Replacement Capital	3,573,674	69.81	3.29	6.77	2.74	4.62	8.85	1.61	2.31
Buyout	50,336,435	57.55	16.04	6.60	4.93	4.48	3.13	3.67	3.60
By Investment Size									
Small	4,785,382	32.51	29.34	3.41	7.12	8.29	2.70	4.64	11.99
Mid-market	18,584,754	49.87	17.80	6.03	1.51	7.20	5.98	5.80	5.82
Large	7,500,497	65.99	14.34	5.95	4.66	0.00	4.46	2.48	2.12
Mega	19,465,802	67.79	11.75	8.17	7.76	2.67	0.00	1.86	0.00
Total PE Investments	**71,164,505**	57.47	14.19	5.98	4.94	4.80	3.96	3.36	5.29

Source: European Private Equity & Venture Capital Association (EVCA).

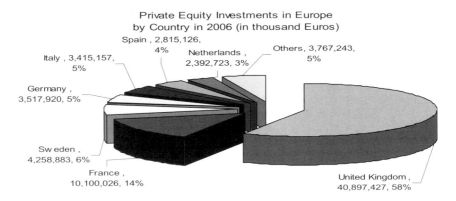

Figure 2. Private Equity Investments in Europe by Country in 2006

Source: European Private Equity & Venture Capital Association (EVCA).

European stock market. Finally, the introduction of Euro.NM in 1997 has substantially enhanced the relationship between the venture capital and stock market performance in Europe. Table 6 presents a more updated comparison between the US and Europe using longer annual time series (between 1990 and 2006) of private equity performance indices created by Venture Economics. Consistent with Xu (2004b), Table 6 shows that European VC funds (11.1% average annual return) underperform US VC funds (24.64% average annual return). However, the average annual returns on buyout funds are about the same for the US (15.89%) and Europe (15.38%). This partly explains the popularity of European buyout investments relative to VC investments.

4. Private Equity Investments in the Asia-Pacific Region

The Asia-Pacific (APAC) region includes established markets, such as Australia and Japan and emerging markets, such as China and India. Table 7 presents a 10-year time series of private equity commitments and investments in APAC. The 10-year cumulative annual growth rates (CAGR) are both at 44% for APAC PE investments and PE commitments, much higher than the growth rates in the US and Europe. As of

Table 5. Private Equity Divestments in Europe (1999–2006)

Year	Divestment by Trade Sale	Divestment by Public Offering	Divestment by Write-off	Repayment of Reference Shares/Loans	Sale to Another Venture Capitalist	Sale to Financial Institution	Sale to Management (Buy-Back)	Divestment by Other Means	Total Divestments in Year
				Percentage for Each Channel of Divestment					
Panel A. Amount of Divestments									
1999	36.6	20.7	6.6	17.1	5.0	4.6	—	9.5	8,616,056
2000	33.0	14.0	7.6	19.6	11.6	3.9	—	10.3	9,102,568
2001	33.9	11.1	22.8	14.5	3.8	4.3	—	9.5	12,474,403
2002	30.9	11.8	30.0	8.4	3.9	3.9	—	11.0	10,674,685
2003	20.4	11.8	11.6	15.9	20.2	6.0	5.5	8.6	13,553,691
2004	23.7	11.8	9.7	21.3	13.1	2.9	4.8	12.7	19,550,298
2005	22.6	9.0	4.7	23.3	18.4	4.0	5.3	12.7	29,832,728
2006	22.7	16.2	3.8	17.1	16.6	5.4	6.1	12.1	33,106,730
Mean	**28.0**	**13.3**	**12.1**	**17.2**	**11.6**	**4.4**	**5.4**	**10.8**	**17,113,895**
Panel B. Number of Divestments									
1999	26.4	17.9	15.9	15.7	3.5	2.0	—	18.6	5,706
2000	27.3	17.7	15.8	15.2	3.3	2.3	—	18.4	5,654
2001	24.4	12.8	26.3	10.8	2.2	1.4	—	22.1	6,293
2002	17.1	11.2	29.3	16.2	1.8	1.3	—	23.1	5,524

(*Continued*)

Table 5. (*Continued*)

Year	Divestment by Trade Sale	Divestment by Public Offering	Divestment by Write-off	Repayment of Reference Shares/Loans	Sale to Another Venture Capitalist	Sale to Financial Institution	Sale to Management (Buy-Back)	Divestment by Other Means	Total Divestments in Year
				Percentage for Each Channel of Divestment					
2003	14.2	8.3	18.0	27.2	3.6	2.2	10.2	16.3	5,605
2004	16.1	9.3	17.1	22.7	4.9	1.8	15.5	12.5	5,917
2005	18.2	12.4	11.9	22.2	5.4	1.6	12.4	15.9	7,241
2006	16.7	11.8	9.0	17.9	6.5	3.4	17.6	17.1	6,670
Mean	**20.1**	**12.7**	**17.9**	**18.5**	**3.9**	**2.0**	**13.9**	**18.0**	**6,076**
Panel C. Number of Companies									
1999	26.8	14.9	16.0	15.9	3.8	2.2	—	20.3	4,628
2000	27.7	15.3	15.3	16.4	3.6	2.1	—	19.6	4,726
2001	25.1	12.5	26.7	11.4	2.3	1.6	—	20.4	4,913
2002	16.7	9.8	31.1	15.2	1.8	1.2	—	24.0	4,911
2003	15.6	6.7	18.6	26.7	3.5	2.3	10.1	16.7	4,019
2004	16.3	8.0	16.7	22.2	5.3	1.9	16.8	12.6	4,195
2005	18.5	10.2	13.0	19.7	6.2	1.9	13.3	17.2	4,830
2006	18.2	9.9	11.1	17.7	7.5	3.4	19.3	12.9	4,448
Mean	**17.3**	**9.1**	**16.4**	**20.1**	**5.4**	**2.2**	**15.6**	**15.8**	**4,485**

Source: European Private Equity & Venture Capital Association (EVCA).

Table 6. Comparative Performance of US and Europe Private Equity Funds

Period	US			Europe			US-Europe		
	Venture Capital	Buyouts	All Priv Equity Funds	Venture Capital	Buyouts	All Priv Equity Funds	Venture Capital	Buyouts	All Priv Equity Funds
1990	3.00	(11.90)	(4.20)	1.60	21.30	5.10	1.40	(33.20)	(9.30)
1991	22.80	23.20	22.20	6.60	(38.70)	(5.10)	16.20	61.90	27.30
1992	14.90	8.50	11.50	(7.40)	(3.80)	(6.50)	22.30	12.30	18.00
1993	19.10	16.90	18.60	18.20	6.20	13.90	0.90	10.70	4.70
1994	15.30	26.60	20.80	6.30	14.60	9.50	9.00	12.00	11.30
1995	49.20	22.30	32.00	12.70	7.90	10.50	36.50	14.40	21.50
1996	42.70	32.20	34.90	32.50	40.70	36.30	10.20	(8.50)	(1.40)
1997	33.00	24.50	26.80	37.10	21.60	26.80	(4.10)	2.90	—
1998	19.00	15.20	15.60	29.10	22.80	24.60	(10.10)	(7.60)	(9.00)
1999	185.70	27.40	71.40	32.70	70.80	55.90	153.00	(43.40)	15.50
2000	24.00	1.70	10.50	36.80	24.80	26.80	(12.80)	(23.10)	(16.30)
2001	(34.20)	(15.00)	(20.70)	(28.90)	4.00	(7.00)	(5.30)	(19.00)	(13.70)
2002	(29.40)	(5.50)	(12.70)	(29.50)	(4.10)	(10.20)	0.10	(1.40)	(2.50)
2003	6.50	25.00	18.00	(13.60)	0.20	(2.90)	20.10	24.80	20.90
2004	15.30	18.10	16.60	7.80	22.70	19.70	7.50	(4.60)	(3.10)
2005	12.90	28.10	20.60	28.80	29.60	30.70	(15.90)	(1.50)	(10.10)
2006	19.00	24.20	22.50	17.20	29.60	36.10	1.80	(5.40)	(13.60)
Mean	24.64	15.38	17.91	11.06	15.89	15.54	13.58	(0.51)	2.36
Median	19.00	22.30	18.60	12.70	21.30	13.90	1.80	(1.50)	(1.40)
Stdev	46.52	14.63	20.16	21.41	23.13	18.81	38.39	23.89	14.12

Note: Performance is expressed in a pooled time weighted internal rate of return (in %).
Source: Thomson Financial/Venture Economics.

Table 7. Private Equity Fundraising and Investments in the Asia-Pacific Region

	1997	1998	1999	2000	2001	2002	2003	2004	2005	2006
Investments (m)	$ 4,611	$ 4,914	$ 9,071	$ 12,329	$ 11,224	$ 9,781	$ 17,884	$ 18,649	$ 31,623	$ 60,644
VC	26.8%	6.9%	22.6%	21.4%	12.7%	7.0%	1.0%	2.0%	1.6%	3.5%
Growth Capital	50.0%	35.0%	25.7%	29.8%	38.0%	21.9%	14.7%	12.7%	22.3%	24.5%
Buyout	16.9%	37.1%	43.4%	44.0%	46.6%	62.5%	76.2%	73.2%	59.1%	48.8%
*Others	6.2%	21.0%	8.3%	4.8%	2.8%	8.6%	8.2%	12.1%	17.0%	23.2%
CAGR (2002–2006)	44.0%									
CAGR (1997–2006)	29.4%									
Funds raised (m)	$ 9,259	$ 5,725	$ 22,422	$ 18,375	$ 13,277	$ 6,536	$ 7,313	$ 14,856	$ 25,593	$ 35,471
VC & Growth Capital	40.6%	65.3%	51.7%	72.5%	44.6%	48.8%	34.0%	30.0%	40.9%	29.5%
Buyout	0.3%	11.1%	13.0%	23.5%	8.0%	28.7%	26.5%	46.7%	43.7%	36.2%
**Others	59.1%	23.6%	35.3%	4.0%	47.4%	22.5%	39.5%	23.3%	15.4%	34.3
CAGR (2002–2006)	40.3%									
CAGR (1997–2006)	14.4%									
Capital Under Management (m)	$ 32,137	$ 45,785	$ 69,132	$ 81,186	$ 85,554	$ 89,196	$ 97,598	$ 106,383	$ 122,039	$ 158,485
CAGR (2002–2006)	12.2%									
CAGR (1997–2006)	17.3%									

*Others include Bridge Loan, Franchise Funding, Mezzanine/Pre-IPO, and PIPE Financing.
**Others include Fund-of-Funds, Infrastructure Fund, Mezzanine/Pre-IPO Fund, NPL/Distressed Debt, Secondary Fund,
Special Situation Fund, and Venture Loan/Debt Financing.
Source: AVCJ Research/Asian Venture Capital Journal/Private Equity Asia.

year-end 2006, the Asian Venture Capital Journal (AVCJ) estimated that there are US$158 billion of private equity capital pools under management in the APAC region. Table 8 provides a country breakdown of APAC PE investments in 2006. Although Australia captures a larger share of PE investments (25.5%) than greater China (23.7%, including 15.6% in mainland China, 1.5% in Hong Kong SAR, and 6.6% in Taiwan), 40.36% of APAC new PE funds raised in 2006 are oriented toward greater China. China has become an increasingly important market and a strategic growth location for global VC firms that are looking for innovative enterprises to invest. As illustrated in Figure 1, China is the most desirable foreign VC investment destination, where 34% of US venture capital investors would like to expand the investment focus. Given the pivotal role of the China market, I will focus the remaining discussion on venture capital and private equity in China.

Table 8. Asia-Pacific Private Equity Investments by Country/Region (as of 2006)

Country/Region Total Amount (in mil US$)	Investments $ 60,644	Funds raised $ 35,943
Australia	25.51%	12.01%
China (PRC)	15.51%	12.53%
China (Hong Kong SAR)	1.48%	27.69%
India	11.99%	12.38%
Indonesia	1.18%	0.00%
Japan	18.27%	17.51%
Malaysia	0.08%	1.07%
New Zealand	4.73%	0.02%
Pakistan	0.02%	0.19%
Philippines	0.15%	0.00%
Papua New Guinea	0.00%	0.04%
Singapore	3.42%	3.90%
South Korea	4.04%	11.77%
Sri Lanka	0.02%	0.14%
Taiwan	6.55%	0.44%
Thailand	6.49%	0.14%
Vietnam	0.55%	0.17%

Source: AVCJ Research/Asian Venture Capital Journal/Private Equity Asia.

With the world's largest population, fastest economic growth engine, and an aggressive agenda of market transformation and global integration, China has been highly regarded as a promising "dream land" for venture capital investments. In the 1990s, foreign venture capital started to make slow inroads into China, attracted by the tremendous growth opportunity but pushed back by a difficult exit environment, the weak institutional/legal framework, and the Asian financial crisis.

Starting in 1999, venture capital activities in China began to show significant growth due to a more accommodating regulatory environment, the expected entry to WTO, the development of various feasible exiting channels for VC in China, and a decline in the number of worthy venture investment opportunities in developed countries. As shown in Figure 3, a record of US$1.78 billion of venture capital was disbursed to 324 Chinese companies in 2006, representing more than four times the VC investments in China five years ago. In addition, Figure 4 shows that China-oriented VC fund commitments were close to US$4 billion in each of the past two years, suggesting even greater growth capacity for VC investments in China.

Statistics from Zero2IPO, a leading research and advisory firm for venture capital in the greater China area, show that 70% of the number

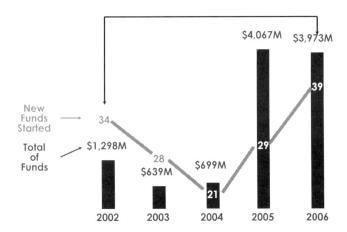

Figure 3. Venture Capital Fundraising in China (2002–2006)
Source: Zero2IPO — China Venture Capital Annual Report 2006.

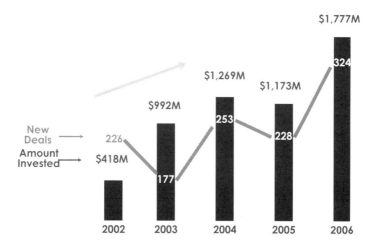

Figure 4. Venture Capital Investments in China (2002–2006)
Source: Zero2IPO — China Venture Capital Annual Report 2006.

of VC deals and 82% of the dollar amount of VC funding in China were from a foreign source. In addition, 17 and 28 China venture-backed companies launched their initial public offerings (IPOs) in local and overseas markets in 2005 and 2006, respectively. The effective exits of venture capital from Chinese portfolio companies to the public equity market further injects liquidity into the China VC industry and stimulates global interests in the emerging China market.

Major IPO listing places include the overseas markets of the New York Stock Exchange (NYSE), NASDAQ, Hong Kong Stock Exchange (HKSE), Hong Kong Growth Enterprise Market (HKGEM), Singapore Exchange (SGX), SESDAQ, and the local market of Shenzhen Small and Medium Enterprise (SME) Board (see Table 9 for the number of US and Hong Kong listed China VC-backed IPOs). On top of the list is the US public equity market, including the NAS-DAQ (the world's most visible high-tech stock market) and NYSE (the world's largest stock exchange). The advantages of a US listing include direct access to the vast pool of global capital (leading to a lower cost of capital), greater appeal to institutional investors due to the enhanced trading liquidity and rigorous disclosure mandated by a

Table 9. Overseas Venture-backed IPOs from Mainland China

Year	US		H-Shares		Red-Chips	
	NYSE	NASDAQ	Hong Kong Stock Exchange (HKSE) Main Board	Hong Kong Growth Enterprise Market (HKGEM)	Hong Kong Stock Exchange (HKSE) Main Board	Hong Kong Growth Enterprise Market (HKGEM)
2000	4	0	3	3	2	
2001	0	0	3	5	3	1
2002	0	0	4	12	1	
2003	1	0	10	8	1	1
2004	7	2	8	9	4	
2005	6	0	9	3	4	2
2006	4	2	17	6	2	
2000–2006	**22**	**4**	**54**	**46**	**17**	**4**

Notes: There are two types of mainland China shares listed in Hong Kong: those issued by companies incorporated in mainland China are called "H-Shares", while those issued by Hong Kong-incorporated mainland China enterprises are called "Red-Chips".
Source: Hong Kong Stock Exchange, Hong Kong Growth Enterprise Market; NYSE; NASDAQ; Venture Economics.

US listing, and increased visibility and marketing leverage for the listed firm due to broader international media coverage (by television, newspapers, online sources and financial data systems). However, an overseas listing on the US exchange also comes with many challenges. The disadvantages of a US listing include higher floatation costs (underwriting, legal, accounting, investor relations, etc.), rigorous initial listing requirements (with respect to size, shareholder base, and financial performance), extensive disclosures and reporting requirements mandated by the SEC, and costly compliance with the Sarbanes-Oxley (SOX) Act on corporate governance and internal control mechanisms.

Other popular overseas listing locations for Chinese VC-backed companies include stock markets in Hong Kong and Singapore, the two major Asian financial centers that have close cultural ties with China (see Xu, 2006). Both markets include main boards (HKSE and SGX) and NASDAQ-style high-tech boards (HKGEM and SES-DAQ). As a special administration region (SAR) of China, Hong Kong offers an established capital market with the closest location, language, cultural, and regulatory ties with mainland China. Similar to Hong Kong, Singapore offers a well-developed capital market with few cultural or language barriers (since the majority of the businesses in Singapore are conducted by ethnic Chinese) and low compliance costs. In 2006, Singapore hosted the largest number of China venture-backed IPOs among all overseas listing locations. In addition to overseas listings, China's domestic listing environment has also been substantially improved. The new trading board, called "Small and Medium Enterprises Board" (hereafter "SME Board"), is an important capital market for the listing of high-tech private enterprises that would otherwise have been excluded from the consideration of the domestic listing.

In addition to supporting venture capital exiting abroad and at home, China has also taken bold steps in building a stronger and more comprehensive legal foundation to ensure more flexibility and greater protection for foreign venture capital investments. As of January 2007, it is estimated that there are 406 private companies in the pool of venture-backed companies in China, with about US$5 billion invested in them.

5. Summary

Global venture capital and buyout funds provide investors with the opportunity to capture innovations and growth around the world while enjoying the enhanced return potential and risk diversification. Major private equity hotbeds include the established markets of the US, Europe, Israel, Canada, and the emerging markets of China, India and Russia. While PE investments provide superior returns relative to public equity (see Xu, 2004a, b), they are also associated with illiquidity and various other risks. For instance, according to the 2007 Global Trends in Venture Capital Survey, VC investors are most concerned about the protection of intellectual property when investing in China, the unfavorable tax environment when investing in Canada, and the weak regulatory environment when investing in India. As an alternative investment asset class, investors need to assess the risk and return profile carefully before making the asset allocation decision.

References

Acceleration — Global Venture Capital Insights Report 2007, Ernst & Young.

Asian Venture Capital Journal (AVCJ)/Private Equity Asia, http://www.asiaventure.com/

Barry, C. B., C. J. Muscarella, J. W. Peavy, and M. R. Vetsuypens, 1990, The Role of venture capital in the creation of public companies: Evidence from the going-public process, *Journal of Financial Economics*, 27, 447–471.

Brav, A. and P. A. Gompers, 1997, Myth or Reality? The long-run underperformance of initial public offerings: Evidence from venture and non-venture capital-backed companies, *Journal of Finance*, 52, 1791–1821.

China VC, PE, M&A, IPO Markets 2006, Zero2IPO.

European Private Equity & Venture Capital Association (EVCA), http://www.evca.com/

Global Trends in Venture Capital Survey, 2007, Deloitte & Touche.

Gompers, P. A. 1996, Grandstanding in the venture capital industry, *Journal of Financial Economics*, 42, 133–156.

Lerner, J., 1994, Venture capitalists and the decision to go public, *Journal of Financial Economics*, 35, 293–316.

National Venture Capital Association, http://www.nvca.com/

Venture Economics, http://ventureconomics.com/

Venture Impact: The Economic Importance of Venture Capital Backed Companies to the US Economy, 2007, Third Edition, Global Insight.

Xu, X. E., 2004a, Evaluating venture capital and buyout funds as alternative equity investment classes, *Journal of Investing,* 13(4), 74–82.

Xu, X. E., 2004b, A comparative study of venture capital performance in US and Europe, *Journal of Entrepreneurial Finance and Business Ventures,* 9(3), 61–76.

Xu, X. E., 2006, Venture-backed IPOs and the exiting of venture capital in China, *Journal of Entrepreneurial Finance and Business Venture,* 11(3), 39–55.

Chapter 9

Managed Futures

Aysegul Ates* and George H. K. Wang†

Managed futures refers to the trading of futures and forward contracts on commodities and financial instruments by professional money managers who are either commodity trading advisors (CTAs) or commodity pool operators (CPOs). In this chapter, we first describe the managed futures industry and explain the roles of CTAs and CPOs. Next, we explain three ways of investing in managed futures: investing in public managed futures funds (and funds of funds), private commodity pools, and separate managed accounts managed by CTAs. We then discuss how the managed futures industry is regulated by the Commodity Futures Trading Commission (CFTC), National Futures Association (NFA) and Securities and Exchange Commission (SEC). We explain the systematic and discretionary trading strategies used by CTAs. Finally, we present and discuss the results of previous studies on the performance of managed futures. In general, results on the usefulness of managed futures as a stand-alone investment are mixed. Results are in general more favorable when managed futures were evaluated as part of a well-diversified portfolio with stocks and bonds. Portfolios including managed futures had higher returns and lower volatility than portfolios which were comprised of either stocks, bonds, or stocks and bonds. The diversification benefit of managed futures to a portfolio combining with stocks and bonds comes from the low or negative correlation of managed futures with traditional assets.

Keywords: Managed futures; commodity trading advisors (CTAs); alternative investments.

* Department of Economics, Akdeniz University, Dumlupinar Bulvari Kampüs, 07058, Antalya, Turkey. Email: aates@akdeniz.edu.tr.
† School of Management, George Mason University, 4400 University Drive, MS 5F5, Fairfax, VA 22030, USA. Email: gwang2@gmu.edu.

1. Introduction

In the US, organized futures markets have been in existence since the mid-19th century. In 1848, with the official opening of the Chicago Board of Trade (CBOT), futures trading first started with grains as the underlying commodity. Grain producers and dealers used futures as a protection against adverse future price movements. Until the 1970s, the futures industry was dominated by agricultural commodities. The growth in futures trading increased substantially in the early 20th century when newly established exchanges introduced a variety of commodity contracts. The introduction of the world's first financial futures contracts (foreign currency futures) by the Chicago Mercantile Exchange (CME) in 1972 was an important landmark in futures trading. Other financial futures contracts, e.g., interest rate and stock index futures were introduced in the late 1970s and 1982, respectively.

The successful introduction of futures contracts to encompass equity indices, interest rates, currencies, options and conventional commodities as well as the globalization of futures trading have expanded the scope of investment possibilities and thus created new profit opportunities for a new type of market participants — the managed futures investors. These investors hire professionals and commodity trading advisors to manage their assets invested in the futures markets. Assets invested in futures markets and managed by these professionals are collectively known as managed futures.

The managed futures industry did not take off until the late 1970s. While there was less than US$500 million invested in managed futures in 1980, the total investment in managed futures had exceeded US$120 billion in 2005.[1] Allocation of funds to managed futures has increased tremendously over the years because of the investors' desire for higher returns and more effectively managed portfolio risk.

---

[1] Edwards and Park (1996) and Schneeweis *et al.* (2007).

In this chapter, we discuss the developments in the managed futures industry. In the following section, we first provide a general background of the managed futures industry. In Section 3, we explain the trading strategies used in managed futures. In Sections 4 and 5, we discuss the benefits and risks of managed futures investing, respectively. In Section 6, we present the research findings from previous studies regarding the performance of managed futures. We provide a summary in the last section.

2. General Background on Managed Futures

Managed futures refers to the trading of futures and forwards contracts on commodities and financial instruments by either institutions or trading advisors who manage assets in these markets on behalf of their clients. Hence, the managed futures industry comprises professional money managers known as commodity trading advisors and commodity pool operators who manage clients' assets on a systematic or discretionary basis, using global futures and options markets as investment media.

The Commodity Futures Trading Commission (CFTC) defines a commodity trading advisor (CTA) as any person, who, for compensation or profit, directly or indirectly advises others regarding the buying or selling of commodity futures and/or option contracts. It defines a commodity pool operator (CPO) as any individual or firm that operates or solicits funds for a commodity pool. CPOs operate public funds and/or private pools. Typically, a number of individuals contribute funds to form a commodity pool. In the US, a commodity pool is usually organized as a limited partnership. Most CPOs hire independent CTAs to make daily trading decisions. The CPO may distribute the investment directly or act as wholesaler to a broker/dealer.

Investing in managed futures can be made in three ways. First, investors can purchase shares of public commodity funds which are similar to equity or bond mutual funds, except that they invest in futures contracts.[2] Public funds provide a way for small (retail) investors to participate in an investment vehicle usually reserved for large investors because they typically have the lowest minimum investment requirements. Second, investors can place funds with a private CPO who pools all investors' funds together and retains one or more professional traders, i.e., CTAs, to manage the pooled funds.[3] Pools have higher minimum investment requirements than public funds. Third, investors can place their funds directly with one or more CTAs to manage their funds on an individual basis. The minimum investment required by CTAs typically is set higher than public commodity funds and private CPOs.

The total management fees vary significantly by the type of managed futures account. CTAs charge both a management fee based on assets under management (about 2–3% of the principal) and an incentive fee based on the profit made in the account (about 15–20% of the net annual profit) (Edwards and Liew, 1999a).

The managed futures industry is regulated by the CFTC under the Commodity Exchange Act. The Act subjects CTAs and CPOs, but not commodity pools, to regulation. Once registered, CPOs and CTAs must comply with the rules of the National Futures Association (NFA), avoid conflicts of interest and protect customer funds, provide written disclosure of the risks of commodity investing to prospective investors, adhere to restrictions on advertising, satisfy record-keeping and reporting requirements, and subject themselves to periodic inspections by the NFA. They must provide detailed disclosure documents to the public. Part 4 of the CFTC Regulations specifies the information that must be included in the disclosure documents, account statements, and annual reports, the time frames within which they must be provided, and the specific records that a CPO must maintain.

---

[2] Initially, CTAs were limited to trading commodity futures (which explains the terms like commodity funds, CTAs and CPOs). With the introduction of financial futures in the 1970s, the trading spectrum was widened substantially. Nowadays, CTAs trade not only commodity futures but also financial futures.

[3] CPOs generally manage more than one private pool and retains CTAs to trade the funds in each pool.

Part 4 also stipulates that for CTAs who manage accounts, they must distribute disclosure documents and maintain specified records relating to their activities and clients as well.

In general, registration is required unless the CPO qualifies for one of the exemptions from registration outlined in CFTC Regulations 4.5 or 4.13. Entities or individuals who may be exempt include:

- Entities otherwise regulated, such as a bank, an insurance company, or a registered investment company;
- Entities who operate one or more small pool(s) that has received less than US$400,000 in aggregate capital contributions and that have no more than 15 participants in any one pool;
- Entities whose pools are only open to persons meeting certain sophistication standards and that have limited futures activity; or
- Entities whose pools restrict participation to persons who demonstrate a certain level of sophistication or net worth.

Managed futures funds are subject to some government regulation and oversight. Public funds must register with the CFTC and the Securities and Exchange Commission (SEC). CPOs are also required to register with the SEC if they accept public funds. A CPO is not considered to have accepted "public funds" if it does not have more than 499 investors in the pool and does not have more than 35 "unaccredited" investors. An "accredited" investor is one with a net worth of at least US$1 million or an annual income of more than US$200,000 for at least two consecutive years.

3. Trading Strategies

CTAs are typically classified by their trading approaches: systematic, discretionary, or a combination of both. The dominant trading strategy is systematic trend following strategy. Discretionary trading is rare among the CTAs (Fung and Hsieh, 2006).

Managers who adopt a systematic trading approach typically use a proprietary trading model with a particular trading technique, such as the trend-following, counter trend, or spread-trading. Systematic managers normally have a well-diversified portfolio across different markets where they abandon their losing trades as soon as they materialize while allowing their winning trades to operate. In general, systematic trend followers maintain positions throughout the long-term trends that take place in markets. Active systematic futures strategies identify price trends, evaluate the momentum through the use of technical analysis, and try to capitalize on such opportunities using futures positions with stop losses in place.[4] Quantitative models are primarily relied upon and trading is mostly computerized.

In contrast, discretionary traders are non-systematic CTAs. The basis of trading decisions for discretionary traders is the CTA's personal experience. They tend to trade more concentrated portfolios, and use both the fundamental (economic) data to assess the markets and the technical analysis to improve market timing. For the discretionary managed futures strategy, CTAs exclusively make bets with futures by using fundamental forecasts and/or specific information. Specialization is common among discretionary CTAs. These managers often specialize in a particular sector (energy, metals, interest rates etc.) or focus exclusively on a narrow market. Familiarity with factors that can potentially move the markets is important for the discretionary trading strategy.

4 The Benefits of Managed Futures

The increasing investor demand for managed futures products over the years indicates that the general performance profile of the managed futures industry is deemed to be attractive by investors. Investing in managed futures can provide certain benefits.

One of the most important benefits of adding managed futures to traditional asset portfolios is diversification. Academic research indicates that a portfolio that combines managed futures with stocks and/or bonds exhibits more optimal mean/variance characteristics,

---

[4] Technical analysis is a method of analyzing markets that uses only market data such as prices, volume, open interest to predict direction of futures prices.

combining higher returns with lower volatility, than one composed entirely of stocks and bonds alone.[5]

Portfolio theory states that investors can improve portfolio performance by diversifying across unique asset classes. Allocating funds to asset classes with a low or negative correlation reduces portfolio risk without necessarily reducing expected returns. Diversification benefits of managed futures stem from the lack of observed correlation between managed futures returns and those of the traditional investment portfolios composed of bonds and equities. Due to this low correlation with the returns of traditional investment vehicles, managed futures are able to reduce the volatility risk of stock, bond or stock and bond portfolio.[6]

Adding managed futures to traditional investment portfolio may also enhance stock/bond portfolio returns. As reported by Schneeweis and Georgiev (2002), managed futures derive returns from different sources than stock/bond portfolios and hedge funds, and thus, adding managed futures to traditional stock and bond funds as well as hedge fund portfolios provide beneficial diversification.[7] Managed futures have historically been demonstrated to enhance portfolio returns with the ability to profit in up and down markets. Recent research on managed futures has shown that when returns are segmented according to whether the stock/bond market rise or fall, managed futures are shown to have a positive correlation with stocks/bonds in a bull

---

[5] There are numerous studies on the subject of managed futures with respect to the diversification effect they have on traditional stock and/or bond portfolios. (See Chance, 1994; McCarthy *et al.*, 1996; Schneeweis, 1996; Kat, 2002). Recent research suggests that diversification benefits of managed futures are not restricted to traditional bond/stock portfolios. Investors of a hedge fund portfolio or funds of funds portfolio can also benefit in a similar manner from the addition of managed futures. (See Schneeweis and Spurgin, 2002; Kat, 2002; Liang, 2003).

[6] Kat (2002), Jensen *et al.* (2003), and Cerrahoglu (2005) provide evidence of the risk reduction benefits of managed futures.

[7] In futures and options markets, the daily gains must equal daily losses for market participants (i.e., a zero sum game). However, academic research (Schneeweis, 1996; Chan *et al.* 1996; Schneeweis *et al.*, 1996) shows that this does not restrict commodity trading advisors from obtaining positive returns. The existence of arbitrage returns, convenience yields, and returns to providing liquidity as well as the existence of trending markets due to institutional and market trading characteristics may provide a source of positive return for CTAs.

market and a negative correlation in a bear market. As a result, managed futures investments offer the potential to reduce the downside risk of a traditional portfolio and improve overall performance of the portfolio. The ability of managed futures to offer a potential protection when the stock/bond markets are not performing well is one of its main strengths.

Several academic studies (Chance, 1994; Schneeweis, 1996; Fung and Hsieh, 1996) have noted that commodity trading advisors have different investment styles and market opportunities than traditional stock and bond managers. These alternative investment styles and market opportunities, which stem from the use of futures instrument and the ability to trade in multiple markets, take long and short positions, and use varying degrees of leverage in varying market conditions, may permit trading advisors to capture risk-return opportunities uniquely different from traditional stock/bond portfolio returns.

Most traditional investment managers are restricted by regulation or convention to holding primarily long investment positions and from using actively traded futures and options contracts. On the other hand, the trading advisors have the ability to go long (buy in anticipation of rising prices) or short (sell in anticipation of declining prices). The flexibility to go long or short permits CTAs to take advantage of price trends and gives managed futures the potential to profit in different market environments such as inflationary or deflationary periods. They can buy futures if they anticipate a rising market or sell if they anticipate a falling market and thus they have the ability to participate and profit in both bull and bear markets.

Managed futures enjoy the ease of global diversification due to the establishment of global futures exchanges around the world and the increasing number of actively traded contracts. Trading advisors have the ability to trade in over 150 different markets worldwide, including currency, metals, energy products, financial instruments, and agricultural products. Managed futures can also provide exposure to many of the world's largest economies through currency and interest rate derivatives. The ability to trade in such diverse markets give trading advisors opportunities for profit as well as risk reduction among a wide range of uncorrelated markets.

Managed futures benefit from the special opportunities that futures/options traders have in terms of lower transaction costs, lower market impact costs, use of leverage, and trading in liquid markets. The use of leverage, explicitly and implicitly (through futures contracts), gives trading advisors a chance to amplify profits from price movements. The structural efficiencies of futures markets also provide managed futures opportunities not available to traditional asset classes. High liquidity in the futures markets allows managers to adjust their risk profile almost continuously. Besides, liquid markets will have lower transaction costs as compared to illiquid markets. Transaction costs and market impact costs in futures markets are much lower than those for comparable positions in the cash markets (Frino *et al.*, 2007).

In addition to these benefits, managed futures offer investors market integrity and safety due to the government oversight, and self-regulation in the managed futures industry.

In summary, the real benefit to managed futures stems from their ability to provide risk and return characteristics that are uniquely different from traditional investment vehicles. Managed futures provide exposure to global financial and non-financial markets while offering (through their ability to take both long and short positions) returns not available to traditional investment vehicles as well as many alternative investments such as real estate, private equity, and commodities.

5. The Risks of Managed Futures

Investing in managed futures can incur substantial risks. Managed futures which employ trend-following trading strategy are subject to certain risks. The buy and sell signals generated by a trend-following trading strategy are based on an examination of price fluctuations, volume variations, and changes in open interest in the markets. The profitability of any trend-following trading strategy depends upon the occurrence of significant, sustained price moves in the markets traded. Therefore, in periods when markets are dominated by fundamental factors that are not reflected in the technical data or during prolonged periods without sustained moves in the markets traded, managed futures which employ trend-following strategy can incur substantial trading losses. Trading losses may also be realized when trends can suddenly reverse or the market environment changes (delta risk). In addition, erroneous identification of the market trends (model risk) can generate losses.

Another set of risks in investing in managed futures arise from trading in futures, a speculative activity per se. Futures prices are often highly volatile and influenced by many factors such as the economic policy changes, climate conditions, changing supply and demand relationships, national and international political and economic events, and thus they are difficult to predict. In addition, government intervention in particular markets, especially in financial instruments and currency markets both directly and indirectly by regulation, can cause such markets to move up or down rapidly. The factors that increase volatility in the market may also cause CTAs to incur losses.

Futures trading normally requires low margin deposits permitting a high degree of leverage. Leverage adds risk to managed futures trading and can potentially amplify even small losses in case of unfavorable price changes. The greater the leverage employed, the greater the change in the investment value should a substantial price change occur in either an up or down direction.

Illiquidity in the market also creates risk for managed futures. Trading advisors usually use similar money management and trading techniques. As they trade and take leverage at the same time, it would easily lead to excessive contemporaneous buy or sell orders which may ultimately create a liquidity problem. In illiquid markets, it will be difficult for managed futures traders to execute a buy or sell order at the desired price or to liquidate an open position, either due to the market condition or the daily price limit. Particularly, in times of crisis, it becomes very hard to liquidate quickly an unfavorable position due to price limits. Even when futures prices have not moved to the daily limit, the CTAs might not be able to execute trades at favorable prices due to a lack of liquidity in the markets they trade.

Another risk that trading advisors are exposed to is the counterparty risk arising from trading in the over-the-counter (OTC) derivatives markets. Counterparty risk arises when a party to an OTC derivatives contract fails to perform on its contractual obligations, causing severe losses to the other party.

6. Empirical Evidence on the Performance of Managed Futures

Previous studies have examined the performance of managed futures as a stand-alone investment and/or assets in diversified portfolios. Results vary with the type of managed futures investment and the time period examined.

Earlier studies by Lintner (1983) and Brorsen and Irwin (1985) found some evidence that commodity funds make good stand-alone investments, but those studies examine a relatively small number of funds for only a few years during the early 1980s. Lintner (1983) found a low correlation between the returns of 15 CTAs and stock, bond or combined stock/bond portfolios over a 3½-year period. In contrast, Elton *et al.* (1987, 1990) found that public commodity funds perform poorly relative to stocks and bonds and they are not attractive alone or as an addition to a stock and bond portfolio. Irwin *et al.* (1993) also found that adding public commodity funds to a diversified portfolio does not enhance performance.

Edwards and Park (1996) examined the performance of three types of managed futures investments from 1983 to 1992 as stand-alone investments and portfolio assets. Investments in randomly selected CTAs, private pools, and public funds as well as equally weighted market portfolios of CTAs, pools, and funds were examined by using the data consisted of 596 registered CTAs, 292 private commodity pools and 361 public commodity funds. They found that managed futures generally performed poorly in the 1989 to 1992 period and public futures funds were the poorest stand-alone investment with the lowest return and Sharpe ratio.[8]

Schneeweis and Spurgin (1996) reviewed the risk/return performance of the various commodity indices and indices used to track

---

[8] Sharpe ratios are used to compare different investments on the basis of risk-adjusted returns. An asset with a higher Sharpe ratio is considered to have a higher risk-adjusted return.

managed futures performance. Since their results indicate that managed futures benchmark indices have sources of risk and return that are distinct from traditional assets, the authors conclude that these indices offer investors an important means of diversification.

Fung and Hsieh (1997) presented evidence that some CTAs trading styles can generate option-like returns and concluded that this type of performance makes commodity funds valuable as an alternative investment to the standard asset classes.

Schneeweis and Spurgin (1998) examined various multi-factor models in describing the return performance of an array of mutual funds, hedge funds, and CTAs. Their results indicate that hedge funds and managed futures may provide unique access to certain return opportunities under various market environments that cannot be obtained from traditional stock and bond investments.

Edwards and Liew (1999b) examined the performance of managed futures investments, both as stand-alone investments and as assets in diversified stock and bond portfolios for the period 1982 through 1996.[9] Nine stylized managed futures investments were examined: randomly-selected, single-CTAs, pool, and fund portfolios; equally weighted (EW) market portfolios of CTAs, pools, and funds; and value-weighted (VW) portfolios of CTAs, pools, and funds. Based on an analysis using Sharpe ratios as the performance criterion, the EW portfolio of CTAs and VW portfolio of pools received the highest ranking among the alternative managed futures investments.[10] The result of VW market portfolios of pools stood out as an attractive stand-alone investment, with respect to both traditional asset classes and other managed commodity funds indicating that pool managers add value by generating higher returns and higher Sharpe ratios than most traditional asset classes. These results suggest that single CTA, pool, or fund portfolio or any type of public commodity fund

---

[9] The data set comes from Managed Account Reports (MAR) database and consists of monthly returns of 1,150 CTAs, 439 commodity pools, and 619 public funds that existed at some time during the period 1980–1996.

[10] The authors argue that the strong performance of an EW portfolio of CTAs during 1982–1988 should probably be given less credibility due to severe survivorship bias during this period.

investment do not make attractive stand-alone investments due to their high return volatility. In addition, with the exception of public funds, including managed futures in a diversified stock and bond portfolio can significantly enhance the performance of those portfolios.

Jensen *et al.* (2000) examined commodity futures as a standalone investment and as a portfolio component over the period 1973–1997 by using Goldman Sachs Commodity Index (GSCI). They found that commodity futures were a poor stand-alone investment in the study period. However, in a portfolio context, the use of commodity futures in portfolios comprised of stocks, bonds, T-bills and real estate was supported by the empirical evidence. The results indicate that commodity futures could be a valuable addition to portfolios due to their low correlation with other asset classes during the study period. In their study, the influence of monetary policy in the performance of commodity futures and their role on efficient portfolio construction was also examined.[11] Their results suggest that under restrictive monetary periods, commodity futures exhibited strong risk/return performance as a standalone investment and in the optimal portfolios containing large commodity futures position. In contrast, commodity futures offered no benefit as a portfolio component during expansive periods.

Schneeweis *et al.* (2002) examined alternative investments in institutional portfolios and analysed the risk and return benefits of various hedge funds and managed futures investments along with other principal alternative investment assets (e.g., real estate, private equity, commodities) as stand-alone investments or as part of an investor's diversified stock/bond portfolio. Their results show the benefits of adding managed futures, hedge funds, and traditional alternative investments to stock and bond portfolios as well as to mixed portfolios (stock, bond, commodity, real estate, private equity and private debt). They suggest that alternative investment vehicles

---

[11] GSCI approximates a passive buy and hold strategy. Extant literature has established that active managed futures strategies exhibited superior performance to passive buy and hold strategies (See Edwards and Park, 1996; Irwin *et al.*, 1993). However, the use of GSCI avoids the biases associated with the managed futures databases. (See Edwards and Park [1996] for a discussion of managed futures database biases.)

such as managed funds and hedge funds must be included with traditional stock and bond investment to obtain the maximum risk and return benefits.

Kat (2002) studied the role of managed futures in portfolios of stocks, bonds and hedge funds for the period from June 1994 to May 2001. In his study, managed futures were represented by the Stark 300 index which contained 248 systematic and 52 discretionary traders. He found that managed futures were better diversifiers than hedge funds. Adding managed futures to a portfolio of stocks and bonds would reduce that portfolio's standard deviation more and quicker than hedge funds but without the undesirable side-effects on skewness and kurtosis.

Soueissy and Sidani (2003) examined managed futures returns during four crises: The 1994 US bond market turbulance, 1997 Asian currency crisis, 1998 Russian ruble and the LTCM crisis, and the TMT Crash.[12] They found that managed futures had positive returns over a 20-year period. It showed significant positive returns during most of all four major crises (or all four according to CSFB/Tremont Index). They concluded that managed futures benefited from the volatility in the markets and negative correlations in declining equity markets.[13]

Kidd and Brorsen (2004) provided evidence that returns to managed futures had decreased dramatically after 1990. Their results suggest that the structural change in futures price movements could explain the reduced fund returns. They found that the volatility of futures prices decreased and concluded that the decrease in volatility translated into less trading opportunities and hence decrease in return prospects for quantitative funds.

Gorton and Rouwenhorst (2004) examined the commodity futures as an asset class by constructing an equally weighted index of commodity futures from July 1959 to March 2004. They found that commodity

---

[12] The 2000 Internet Stock Washout called the one-month period from March 14 to April 14, 2000, the Technology, Media, and Telecommunications (TMT) crash when the NASDAQ market plummeted down 35% and the S&P 500 fell 5%.

[13] Soueissy and Sidani (2003) argue that this result is mainly due to the long call option profile in managed futures, i.e., it can potentially achieve upside returns while limiting downside losses.

futures had been effective in providing diversification to stock and bond portfolios.

In summary, evidence from previous studies indicates that there may be a case for managed futures investment, especially as part of an investor's diversified stock/bond portfolio.

7. Summary

Managed futures refer to the trading of futures and forward contracts on commodities and financial instruments by professional money managers who are either commodity trading advisors (CTAs) or commodity pool operators (CPOs). Investors can invest in managed futures in three ways: 1) Investors can purchase shares of public managed futures funds (and funds of funds); 2) investors can place funds with a private CPO who pools all investors' funds together and retains one or more CTAs to manage the pooled funds; and 3) investors can place their funds directly with one or more CTAs who would manage their funds on an individual basis. Both CTAs and CPOs are required to register with the Commodity Futures Trading Commission (CFTC) and become members of the National Futures Association (NFA). Public managed futures funds are subject to regulation and oversight by the CFTC and the Securities and Exchange Commission (SEC).

Typically, CTAs can be classified by their approach to trading: 1) the systematic approach; 2) the discretionary approach; and 3) a combination of both. CTAs who use a systematic trading approach employ a proprietary trading model with a particular trading technique, such as trend-following, counter trend and spread-trading. For CTAs who adopt a discretionary trading approach, their trading decisions are often based on fundamental economic data and personal experience. They often specialize in a particular sector or focus exclusively on a narrow market.

Previous studies on the performance of managed futures have examined the effectiveness of managed futures either as a stand-alone investment and/or as an addition to diversified portfolios with bonds and stocks. In general, results on the usefulness of managed futures as a stand-alone investment are mixed. Results are in general more favorable when managed futures were evaluated as part of a well-diversified portfolio with stocks and bonds. Portfolios including managed futures had higher return and lower volatility than portfolio funds which were comprised of either stocks, bonds, or stocks and bonds. The diversification benefit of managed futures to a portfolio combining with stocks and bonds comes from the low or negative correlation of managed futures with traditional assets.

References

Brorsen, B. W. and S. Irwin, 1985, Examination of commodity funds performance, *Review of Futures Markets* **4**, 84–94.

Cerrahoglu, B., 2005, The benefits of managed futures 2005 update, Working paper, Center for International Securities and Derivatives Markets, Isenberg School of Management, Amherst, Massachusetts.

Chan, L., N. Jedadeesh, and J. Lakoniskok, 1996, Momentum strategies, *Journal of Finance* LI(5), 1681–1713.

Chance, D., 1994, *Managed Futures and Their Role in Investment Portfolios* Institute of Chartered Financial Analysts.

Edwards, F. R. and J. M. Park, 1996, Do managed futures make a good investment, *Journal of Futures Markets*, 16(5), 475–517.

Edwards, F. and J. Liew, 1999a, Managed commodity funds, *Journal of Futures Markets*, 19(4), 377–411.

Edwards, F. and J. Liew, 1999b, Hedge funds versus managed futures as asset classes," *Journal of Derivatives*, 6(4), 45–64.

Elton, E. J., M. J. Gruber, and J. Rentzler, 1987, Professionally managed, publicly traded commodity funds, *Journal of Business*, 60(2), 177–199.

Elton, E. J., M. J. Gruber, and J. Rentzler, 1990, The performance of publicly offered commodity funds, *Financial Analysts Journal*, 46, 23–30.

Frino, A., J. Bjursell, G. H. K. Wang, and A. Lepone, 2007, Large trades and intraday futures price behavior, Paper presented at Financial Management Association International Annual Meeting, Orlando, Florida.

Fung, W. and D. A. Hsieh, 1996, Performance attribution and style analysis: From mutual funds to hedge funds, Working Paper # 9609 Duke University.

Fung, W. and D. A. Hsieh, 1997, Investment style and survivorship bias of commodity trading advisors: The information content of performance track records, *Journal of Portfolio Management*, 24(1), 30–42.

Fung, W. and D. A. Hsieh, 2006, Hedge fund: An industry in its adolesence, Working Paper, Duke University.

Gorton, G. and K. G. Rouwenhorst, 2004, Facts and fantasies about commodity futures, Yale ICF Working Paper No. 04–20.

Irwin, S., T. Krukemyer, C. R. Zulauf, 1993, The investment performance of public commodity pools over 1979–1990, *Journal of Futures Markets*, 13, 799–820.

Jensen, G. R., R. R. Johnson, and J. M. Mercer, 2000, Efficient use of commodity futures in diversified portfolios, *Journal of Futures Markets*, 20(5), 489–506.

Jensen, G. R., R. R. Johnson, and J. M. Mercer, 2003, The time variation in the benefits of managed futures, *Journal of Alternative Investments*, 5(4), 41–50.

Kat, H. M., 2002, Managed futures and hedge funds: A match made in heaven, Working paper, Alternative Investment Research Centre, London, UK.

Kidd W. V. and W. B. Brorsen, 2004, Why have the returns to technical analysis decreased, *Journal of Economics and Business*, 56(3), 159–176

Lintner, J., 1983, The potential role of managed commodity-financial futures accounts in portfolios of stocks and bonds, *Annual Conference of the Financial Analysts Federation*, Toronto, Canada.

Liang, B., 2003, On the performance of alternative investments: CTAs, hedge funds, and funds of funds, Working Paper, Isenberg School of Management, University of Massachusetts.

McCarthy D., T. Schneeweis, and R. Spurgin, 1996, Investment through CTAs: An alternative to public commodity funds, *Journal of Derivatives*, 3(4), 36–47.

Schneeweis, T., R. Spurgin, and M. Potter, 1996, Managed futures and hedge fund investment for downside equity risk management, *Derivatives Quarterly*, 3(1), 62–72.

Schneeweis, T., 1996, *The Benefits of Managed Futures*. European Managed Futures Association.

Schneeweis, T. and R. Spurgin, 1996, Comparisons of commodity and managed futures benchmark indices, CISDM Working Paper, University of Massachusetts.

Schneeweis, T. and R. Spurgin, 1998, Multi-factor models in managed futures, hedge fund and mutual fund return estimation, *Journal of Alternative Investment*, 1–25.

Schneeweis, T. and R. Spurgin, 2002, Managed futures, hedge fund and mutual fund return estimation: A multi-factor approach, Working Paper Series, University of Massachusetts.

Schneeweis, T., V. N. Karavas, and G. Georgiev, 2002, Alternative investments in institutional portfolio, CISDM Working Paper, University of Massachusetts.

Schneeweis, T. and G. Georgiev, 2002, Benefits of managed futures, Working Paper AIMA.

Schneeweis, T., R. Gupta, and J. Remilland, 2007, CTA/managed futures strategy benchmark performance and review, CISDM Working Paper, University of Massachusetts.

Soueissy, M. and R. Sidani, 2003, The risk underlying hedge fund strategies, Working Paper, Universite de Lausanne.

Part IV: Derivatives

Chapter 10

Credit Derivatives: Trends, Challenges and Opportunities

*Gaiyan Zhang**

The explosively-growing credit derivatives market provides international investors a new and complementary platform to trade and hedge credit risk and sovereign risk, alone or combined with other positions. Understanding the products and functions, participants, risk and opportunities in the credit derivative market is essential for international investors to maximize investment returns and minimize risk in this market, as well as in traditional bond and loan markets. This is particularly important in an increasingly integrated global financial market. This chapter provides an overview of the global credit derivatives market, including the history, new trends, products, participants, and risk, and then discusses the alternative investment and hedging opportunities provided by this market to international investors.

Keywords: Credit derivatives; credit default swaps; liquidity risk; operational risk; material risk; market opportunities.

1. Introduction

Credit derivatives are financial instruments that offer protection against credit risk on a variety of corporate and sovereign names with a wide range of maturity. The credit derivatives market primarily

* College of Business Administration, University of Missouri-St. Louis, One University Blvd, St. Louis, MO 63121, USA. Email: zhangga@umsl.edu.

231

comprises two sectors: the corporate sector, accounting for 80% of the market, and the sovereign sector (20%), mostly composed of credit derivatives on emerging sovereign bonds. A diversity of products are traded in the credit derivatives market, such as Credit Default Swaps (CDS), Collateral Debt Obligations (CDO), Credit-linked Notes (CLN), CDS indices, and portfolio swaps.

CDS are the simplest type of credit derivatives and the building block of the credit derivatives market. A CDS resembles an insurance contract, in that the protection buyer makes periodic payments (CDS premium/spread) over the life of the swap contract, in exchange for protection against default or other credit events specified in the contract. Essentially, the purchase of a CDS is equivalent to shorting credit risk on the credit market. Selling a CDS is equivalent to having a long exposure on the credit market. The market price of the CDS reflects the riskiness of the underlying credit. The CDS market allows credit risk transfer from lenders and big bondholders to insurers, reinsurers and hedge funds who often take one-way bets by selling protection.

A second important credit derivative instrument is the synthetic CDO, in which the credit risk of a portfolio of exposures is tranched and transferred with credit default swaps. Specifically, the credit losses associated with the portfolio of exposures are allocated separately to individual tranches, depending on priority rules established at the inception of the CDO. The riskiest tranche, which is the first to absorb any losses, is the "equity" ("first-loss") tranche. At the other extreme are the "senior" and "super-senior" tranches, which will only absorb losses after all of the tranches that are subordinate to them have absorbed their maximum loss. In between are the "mezzanine" tranches.

Since 1996, the credit derivatives market has experienced a phenomenal growth. This is partly explained by heightened interest in credit risk, among financial institutions, hedge funds and insurance companies, due to deteriorating corporate credit qualities (record bankruptcies of investment-grade firms, correlated downgrades and defaults, etc.) in the recent economic downturns. Increasingly diverse and complex products have also fueled the evolution of the credit derivative markets. According to the June 2006 survey by the International Swaps and Derivatives Association (ISDA), the notional

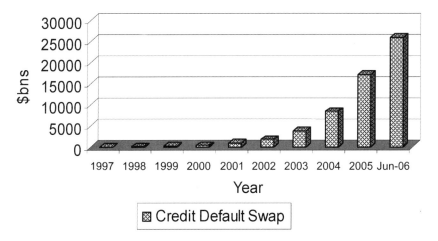

Figure 1. Growth of Global Credit Default Swap Market (Notional Amount of Contracts).

Sources: Bank for International Settlements; International Swaps and Derivatives Association; British Bankers' Association.

amount of the credit derivatives market has exceeded US$26 trillion. Figure 1 presents the development of the global derivatives markets based on surveys from various sources.

Despite the significant growth, several issues remain in this market. The absence of a liquid secondary market is mitigating potential gains from credit derivatives. The operational risk are major concerns to the market participants and regulatory institutions. Investors also face considerable market risk, which is partly brought about by the entry of hedge funds in the credit derivatives market.

The credit derivatives market provides international investors with a new and complementary platform to trade and hedge credit risk and/or sovereign risk, alone or combined with other positions. Understanding the products and functions, participants, risk and opportunities in this market is essential for international investors to maximize investment returns and minimize risk in the credit derivatives market, as well as in traditional bond and loan markets. This is particularly important in an increasingly integrated global financial market. For example, local banks can diversify their geographic credit exposures by selling the CDSs of foreign companies.

The rest of the chapter is organized as follows. Section 2 describes the history, general structure, and new trends of the credit derivatives market. Section 3 introduces market participants. Section 4 focuses on products. Section 5 evaluates the liquidity risk, operation risk, and market risk. Section 6 discusses the alternative investment and hedging opportunities provided by this market to international investors. The conclusions are summarized in Section 7. Data, quotes and other background elements used in this chapter come from various sources, including the ISDA, the Joint Forum special report by the Bank for International Settlements (BIS) (2005), the IMF Global Financial Stability Report (2006), and the Markit Group, a major participant bank active in credit derivatives.

2. Market Developments and New Trends

2.1 *History of Credit Derivatives*

As an indicator of the move away from relationship banking toward credit trading, the first credit derivative transaction was created by a handful of banks in 1995. The goal was to shift credit risk off the banks' balance sheets by pooling credits and remarketing portfolios, and buying default protection after syndicating loans for clients. Since 1996, the single name CDS market took hold and started to grow. Basket portfolio trading began in 1998. At the same time, the coverage of the CDS contracts extended from the investment-grade entities to below-investment grade obligors.

The increasingly standardized CDS contract and increasing emphasis on quantitative approaches to credit risk management by many market participants, together with the Internet revolution, helped spur continued growth in the market. The ISDA published its first documentation related to credit derivatives in 1998 and followed up with a set of Credit Derivative Definitions in 1999 to reflect market needs. ISDA definitions have become the market standard since 2003. The burst of the dotcom bubble in 2000 led to waves of bankruptcies, defaults, and deterioration of credit qualities. Investors had increasingly realized the importance of credit protection. The CLN market in Europe grew rapidly since 2001, paving the way for rapid growth of the credit derivatives market. The CDO market expanded in 2003 when banks packaged company loans or bonds and sold off tranches to investors.[1]

Credit derivative markets have grown rapidly in size and complexity in recent years. Credit derivative volume has expanded exponentially to roughly US$26 trillion, according to ISDA. Notional value of single-name CDS outstanding is now about US$20 trillion versus US$40 trillion in bonds.[2] Globally, trading in the CDS market occurs with some regularity in approximately 1,200 reference entities. Table 1 lists the top 25 reference entities by the end of 2005 in terms of gross protection sold and bought by volume, respectively.[3] Investment-grade corporate obligations comprise most of the underlying credit transferred in the CDS and CDO markets, particularly in the synthetic form. Banks using credit derivatives to hedge will largely be hedging exposures to investment grade credits. According to Fitch Ratings (2006), 62% of gross protection sold is related to non-financial corporate obligations. CDS contracts with five-year maturities are the most liquid compared to other maturities (1-, 3-, 7-, 10-, 30-year) in the market. While the CDS contract is largely an over-the-counter product, Chicago Mercantile Exchange (CME) is now considering listing standardized single name CDS contracts to create the first retail market.[4]

There is growing interest in emerging market (EM) obligations, but activity in EM structured credit products has developed more slowly. This is primarily because of a relative scarcity of liquid underlying obligations and related default and recovery rate data, as well as a perception that EM credits are relatively highly correlated (Dages *et al.*, 2005). To date, almost all EM credit derivatives activity has involved sovereign and sovereign-backed obligations. However, there appears to be a growing demand for structured credit products in Asia and the Middle East. Therefore, investment banks have begun to apply synthetic risk-transfer techniques to package the EM credit risk more effectively.[5]

---

[1] The source for the history of the credit derivative market is www.financial-edu.com/history-of-credit-derivatives.php.

[2] Source: www.isda.org/statistics/recent.html.

[3] Source: Fitch Ratings (2006).

[4] Source: www.financial-edu.com/history-of-credit-derivatives.php.

[5] Source: IMF (2006).

Table 1. Top References Entities Year-End 2005: Gross Sold and Bought Protection by Volume

	Protection Sold	Protection Bought
1	General Motors/GMAC	General Motors/GMAC
2	Ford Motor Corp./Ford Motor Credit Co.	Ford Motor Corp./Ford Motor Credit Co.
3	Brazil	Brazil
4	DaimlerChrysler	DaimlerChrysler
5	Italy	Italy
6	France Telecom	General Elcetric/GECC
7	Russia	Russia
8	General Electric/GECC	France Telecom
9	Turkey	Telecom Italia
10	United Mexican States	Turkey
11	Telecom Italia	United Mexican States
12	Volkswagen	Volkswagen
13	Deutsche Telekom	Gazprom
14	AT&T Corp	AIG
15	Gazprom	AT&T Corp.
16	France	Deutsche Telekim
17	Fannie Mae	France
18	Hutchison Whampoa	Hutchison Whampoa
19	Japan	Japan
20	AIG	Fannie Mae
21	Spain	Goldman Sachs
22	British American Tobacco	Boots Group
23	Portugal	Philippines
24	Boots Group	JP Morgan Chase
25	Countrywide	PCCW-HKT Telephone

Source: Fitch Ratings, 2006.

2.2 *New Trends*

There has been significant innovation in products in recent years. The growth of CDS indices and index-related products and the growth of "single-tranche" synthetic CDOs are two recent innovations in the market (*BIS Report*, 2005).

The CDS indices are calculated by averaging the CDS spreads associated with a pool of reference entities. The development of CDS indices is extremely helpful to the growth and liquidity of the credit derivatives markets. The indices provide a standard benchmark against which other more customized pools of exposures can be assessed. They also provide a mechanism with which broad-based credit risk can be traded and hedged. In addition, the indices can be used as the building blocks for constructing other products.[6] According to Fitch Ratings (2006), indices and index-related products which have grown 900% significantly drive the growth in the CDS market. With a notional market value at US$3.7 trillion, this segment of the CDS market now accounts for 31% of the gross sold positions.

The second main product innovation is the growth of single-tranche CDO structures. The first generation of synthetic CDOs involved the issuance of tranches representing the full capital structure of the securitization. However, synthetic CDO issuers often had difficulty placing certain parts of the capital structure, for example the high-risk equity tranche or a large super-senior tranche. In recent years, it became increasingly common to structure the CDO such that only a single tranche is issued. The investor can select all aspects of the reference portfolio as well as the specific portion of the loss distribution to which they wish to be exposed. This product becomes popular because it better tailors credit exposures to meet investors' demands.

3. Major Market Participants

The most active participants in the credit derivatives market include banks, insurance companies, pension funds, hedge funds and other asset managers. According to Fitch Ratings (2006), banks and broker-dealers accounted for the vast majority of the outstanding credit derivative protection purchased at year-end 2004. Fitch estimates hedge funds account for up to 30% of the credit derivative trading volume. Protection buying is dominated by large sophisticated banks, while smaller regional banks typically sell protection to realize more diversified credit exposure (i.e., outside their local market). In addition, insurers and financial guarantors account for 13% of protection sales.

---

[6] Source: The Joint Forum (2005).

3.1 *Banks*

Banks use credit derivatives primarily to manage exposure concentrations to investment-grade corporate customers. Further, there is also a growing amount of geographically motivated risk transfer within the banking sector (Joint Forum, 2005). Table 2 reports all US banks that made use of CDS at the end of 2005. The total notional amount of credit risk protection bought and sold by banks was US$7,958 billion at year-end 2005. Consistent with the findings in Hirtle (2007), usage is clustered among the largest banks, with nearly all banks with US$100 billion or more in assets using credit derivatives. Some of these large banks are dealers who manage large portfolios of customer-related positions, as well as positions held for their own internal credit risk management purposes. Table 2 indicates that JP Morgan was the largest protection buyer, with the total amount at US$1,114 billion. Bank of America had the largest protection sold at the amount of US$1,218 billion at the end of 2005. Among the 39 banks that used credit derivatives, 15 are net protection buyers, and 24 are net protection sellers.

Minton *et al.* (2006) find that while few banks use credit derivatives, those that do own two thirds of the assets of all banks in their sample. With the development of bank internal risk systems and the evolution of bank accounting and regulatory standards, major banks are expected to become more significant users of credit derivatives.

The major US securities firms, as top counterparties in the global credit derivatives market, participate primarily as intermediaries and underwriters, although they also use these products to hedge their own proprietary credit risks. Top 10 counterparties in the credit derivatives market in 2005 were Morgan Stanley, Deutsche Bank, Goldman Sachs, JP Morgan Chase, UBS, Lehman Brothers, Barclays, Citigroup, Credit Suisse First Boston, and BNP Paribas (Fitch Rating, 2006). In the emerging credit derivatives market, broker dealers are mainly the major investment banks involved in the emerging bond market (Deutsche Bank, JP Morgan Chase, Salomon-CitiBank, etc.).[7]

---

[7] Ranciere (2002).

Table 2. The US Banks' Use of Credit Derivatives (Year-End 2005, in Thousands)

Entity	Protection Bought	Protection Sold	Total Notional of Protection Bought and Sold	Net Protection Bought
JP morgan Chase & Co.	1,114,192,000	1,127,255,000	2,241,447,000	−13,063,000
NB Holdings Corporation	800,040,033	1,220,639,011	2,020,679,044	−420,598,978
Bank of America Corporation	799,941,733	1,217,954,351	2,017,896,084	−418,012,618
Citigroup Inc	499,323,000	531,422,000	1,030,745,000	−32,099,000
HSBC Investments (North America) Inc	220,231,346	167,476,753	387,708,099	52,754,593
Wachovia Corporation	96,293,000	113,610,000	209,903,000	−17,317,000
Keycorp	3,395,706	3,378,166	6,773,872	17,540
Wells Fargo & Company	2,688,000	2,766,000	5,454,000	−78,000
Suntrust Bank Holding Company	664,267	902,947	1,567,214	−238,680
Metlife, Inc	593,044	5,563,930	6,156,974	−4,970,886
PNC Bancorp, Inc	500,668	995,425	1,496,093	−494,757
National City Corporation	492,913	1,420,684	1,913,597	−927,771
Barclays Group US Inc	422,000	0	422,000	422,000
Bank of New York Company, Inc	386,000	1,099,000	1,485,000	−713,000
Deutsche Bank Trust Corporation	298,000	6,135,000	6,433,000	−5,837,000
John Hancock Holdings (Delaware) LLC	185,000	201,000	386,000	−16,000
U.S. Bancorp	169,000	143,000	312,000	26,000
Fifth Third Bancorp	129,145	56,293	185,438	72,852

(*Continued*)

Table 2. (*Continued*)

Entity	Protection Bought	Protection Sold	Total Notional of Protection Bought and Sold	Net Protection Bought
Harris Bankcorp, Inc	81,901	14,075	95,976	67,826
Bank Leumi Le-Israel Corporation	60,000	0	60,000	60,000
SNBNY Holdings Limited	22,000	0	22,000	22,000
Texas Regional Bancshares, Inc	10,138	0	10,138	10,138
First South Bancorp, Inc	3,175	0	3,175	3,175
Citizens Financial Group, Inc	1,640	401	2,041	1,239
Eastern Virginia Bankshares, Inc	45	0	45	45
ABN Amro North America Holding Company	0	7,848,915	7,848,915	-7,848,915
Lasalle Bank Corporation	0	7,848,915	7,848,915	-7,848,915
Mellon Financial Corporation	0	598,484	598,484	-598,484
Sky Financial Group, Inc	0	551,638	551,638	-551,638
Regions Financial Corporation	0	133,650	133,650	-133,650
Northern Trust Corporation	0	116,250	116,250	-116,250
Oriental Financial Group Inc	0	87,524	87,524	-87,524
Community Bancshares of Mississippi, Inc	0	25,000	25,000	-25,000
Countrywide Financial Corporation	0	24,500	24,500	-24,500
Community Banks, Inc	0	7,500	7,500	-7,500
Amsouth Bancorporation	0	6,000	6,000	-6,000
First State Banking Corp	0	54	54	-54
Total	3,540,123,754	4,418,281,466	7,958,405,220	-878,157,712

3.2 *Insurance Firms*

The insurance sector (including reinsurance firms) has been a significant source of credit protection. Traditional life and P&C insurers have taken the form of purchasing highly rated CDO tranches. On the other hand, North America insurance companies are among the largest sellers of credit protection.

3.3 *Hedge Funds*

Increasingly, hedge funds are viewed as significant contributors to the liquidity of the CDS market. The number of funds increased from 4,000 in 2002 managing US$2 trillion to over 8,000 in 2005 managing US$4 trillion (Fitch Ratings, 2006). This has created intense demand for new structured products with higher yields.

The activity of hedge funds has largely switched from macro-directional strategies to relative values strategies, including cash versus credit derivatives basis trade, arbitrage trades on differentials in price movements across different markets or instruments (e.g., across equity and credit markets), as well as arbitrage trades on the slope of the default swap curve. Hedge funds are increasingly buyers of highly risky "first-loss" tranches of synthetic CDOs. They have also been a driving force behind the growth of the standardized CDS index market, as well as the emergence of correlation trading. The growth of credit-oriented hedge funds has accelerated credit derivatives market development and credit risk dispersion (IMF, 2006). The arbitrage behavior of hedge funds provides important price discovery and market liquidity benefits to the market.

3.4 *Insider Information and Adverse Selection*

In the early days of the credit derivatives market, investors and analysts expressed concern about insider information and adverse selection possibilities because market participants in this market are assumed to have information advantages. Indeed, there is a handful of anecdotal evidence that improper inside information was leaked in the CDS market.[8] In some of the early CDOs, banks were required by investors to retain some of the equity tranches due to the adverse selection problem.

Using news reflected in the stock market as a benchmark for public information, Acharya and Johnson (2007) report evidence of significant incremental information revelation in the CDS market for negative credit news consistent with the use of non-public information by informed banks. However, they find no evidence that insider information adversely affects prices or liquidity in either the equity or credit markets.

The adverse selection problem is mitigated due to two reasons. First, with increasing market depth and price transparency, as well as rating agency involvement and increased experience, investors are able to better price and monitor the corporate credits included in CDO portfolios independently. Second, the banks most active in these risk transfer markets must preserve their reputation for a continued market presence. Therefore, they are unlikely to seek a short-term gain at the expense of greater long-term costs.

4. Major Products

4.1 *Credit Default Swaps*

CDS represents about 50% of the global credit derivatives markets, and it is the dominant product in the emerging market. CDS contracts are offered on a maturity ranging from 1 to 30 years. The five-year CDS contract is the most liquid contract in the market. The underlying obligation category is generally "bonds" and sometimes

---

[8] For example, the CDS market seemingly anticipated the deterioration in the credit condition of automobile manufacturer GM weeks before GM's debt was downgraded to junk bond status on May 5, 2005. More recently, trading in Harrah's CDS contracts surged dramatically before news of a leveraged-buyout was disclosed, while the stock market lagged behind the derivatives markets (*The Wall Street Journal*, "Trading in Harrah's Contracts Surges Before LBO Disclosure," October 4, 2006.)

"bonds or loans". The pay-offs of CDS are summarized by the following figure:

Periodic Payment

    Protection Buyer → *default swap spread* → Protection Seller

Following a credit event:

    If cash settlement:
    Protection → *100-Recovery Value of underlying securities* → Protection
    Buyer   Seller

    If physical settlement:
    Protection Buyer ←100 ← Protection Seller
    Protection Buyer → underlying securities→ Protection Seller

---

The protection buyer makes periodic payment (premium, or CDS spread) to the protection seller in exchange for the full value of underlying bonds/loans if the underlying reference entity experiences a credit event (default, restructuring, failure to pay, etc.) The protection seller agrees to compensate the difference between the par value and the market value of the reference bond should such an event occur. Following a credit event, contracts are settled either physically (i.e., through the delivery to the protection buyer of defaulting bonds and/or loans for an amount equivalent to the notional value of the swap) or in cash, with the net amount owed by the protection seller determined by the market value of defaulting bonds and/or loans and recovery rate after the credit event. Essentially, the single-name CDS contract allows credit risk transfer from the protection buyer to the protection seller.

4.2 *First Default Basket Products*

The design of this product is similar to the design of a default swap or credit link notes, but the protection is not against the default of a single name, but rather against the first default of a basket of names. The pricing depends on individual default risks as well as on default correlations. These products are tailor-made for clients and account for a marginal but growing share of the market.

4.3 *CDOs*

CDOs are a type of asset-backed security or structured finance product. CDOs emerged as the fastest growing sector of the asset-backed securities market. According to the Securities Industry and Financial Markets Association, aggregate global CDO issuance totaled US$157 billion in 2004, US$249 billion in 2005, and US$489 billion in 2006.[9] The term CDO is often used as a generic term that includes Collateralized Bond Obligations (CBOs), which is backed primarily by bonds and Collateralized Loan Obligations (CLOs), which is backed primarily by leveraged loans.

CDOs can be classified into Cash CDOs and Synthetic CDOs by funding. "Cash CDOs" involve a pool of physical assets, such as loan contracts, corporate bonds, whose ownership is transferred to the legal entity issuing the CDO (known as a special purpose vehicle or SPV).

"Synthetic CDOs" tranche a pool of underlying default swaps into different classes of credit risk. The credit risk of assets is transferred from balance sheets to CDOs without the sale or transfer of the assets themselves. In Europe, over 90% of CDO deals are synthetic. Synthetic CDOs allow more flexible structure than cash CDOs. For example, they have enabled the development of portfolio swap products based on customized stand-alone reference portfolios (i.e., single-tranche CDOs), and standardized CDS indices. Globally, in 2005, about US$205 billion of cash CDOs were issued, versus synthetic issuance of US$65 billion (see Lehman Brothers, 2005).

A typical capital structure comprises an "equity" tranche that absorbs default-related losses (often representing idiosyncratic risks) on the underlying portfolio up to the 3% "detachment point," one or more "mezzanine" tranches that absorb losses that exceed the 3% "attachment point" up to a 10% "detachment point," one or more "senior" tranches (10–30%), and a "super-senior" tranche (the final 30–100%), with the senior tranches viewed as reflecting systemic risk (Figure 2).

---

[9] Source: en.wikipedia.org/wiki/Collateralized_debt_obligation.

Reference Portfolio   Typical CDO Tranching

Individual bonds/loans
Notional size: $100 million
Average rating: BBB

Type	Amount	Rating
Super-senior	70	AAA
Senior	20	AA
Mezzanine	7	BBB
Equity	3	n.a.

Figure 2. CDO Structure.

4.4 *CDS Indices*

The development of synthetic structures fosters the growth of CDS indices. CDS indices and related sub-indices track the performance of baskets of the most actively traded single-name CDSs. The standardized features of indices (i.e., maturities and risk tranches, credit ratings, and sector delineations) have increased the liquidity of credit derivatives market.

The active tradable index of North America reference entities is the CDX. The iTraxx index family consists of various indexes of the most liquid CDS contracts in Europe and Asia.[10] The North America CDX indices are portfolios of CDS designed to track 14 segments of the North American CDS market, including both investment-grade and high-yield reference entities. A consortium of 16 investment banks helps compose and price the indices. Each member bank of the consortium makes a market in the CDS index. The CDS index is freely tradable with low bid-ask spreads of ½ to ¼ of a basis point. The Investment Grade CDX (CDX.NA.IG) is intended for mitigating trading exposure in the credit risk of North American investment-grade firms. The index is made up of 125 firms with the most liquid investment-grade credits and the composition is determined by the member banks. CDX.NA.IG is an equal-weighted index with each

---

[10] Bystrom (2005).

credit initially making up 0.8% of the index. The High Yield CDX (CDX.NA.HY) is intended to reflect multiple industry sectors and provide a broad exposure to the North American high-yield credits. CDX.NA.HY is an equal-weighted daily index composed of 100 high-yield entities domiciled in North America. It includes CDX.NA.HY. BB and CDX.NA.HY.B depending on the rating of reference pools. The CDX index further splits into several sector indices (autos, financials, etc.), a *crossover* index comprising the most liquid sub-investment grade non-financial names, and a *HiVol* index that consists of names with the widest CDS spreads. There are also quotes of CDS indices for emerging markets (CDX.EM) and diversified emerging markets (CDX.EM.Diversified).[11]

Figures 3.1 and 3.2 depict the price movement of the investment-grade CDS indices/speculative-grade CDS indices and the S&P 500 index for the period between January 2001 and December 2006. Both CDS indices are negatively related to the S&P 500 index, but the high-yield CDS index has a much wider credit spread than the investment-grade CDS index. Fung *et al.* (2007) study the market-wide lead-lag relations between the US stock market and the CDS indices for the period of 2001–2005. They find significant mutual feedback of information between the stock market index and the high-yield CDS index in terms of pricing and volatility, while the stock market leads the investment-grade CDS index in the pricing process. The CDS market seems to play a more significant role in volatility spillover than the stock market. The implication for investors is that the stock-market participants would gain leading and incremental information from the CDX market when they are about to engage in trading and/or hedging.

4.5   *Other Products*

Other less common but growing products include CLNs, options on CDO tranches, CDOs using CDO tranches as collateral (also known as CDO-squareds), and CDOs embedding equity default swaps. The

---

[11] Source: www.markit.com/information/affiliations/cdx.html.

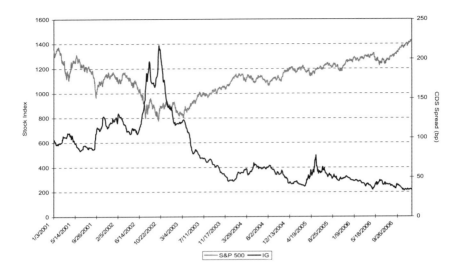

Figure 3.1. Investment-Grade CDS Index vs. S&P 500 Index.

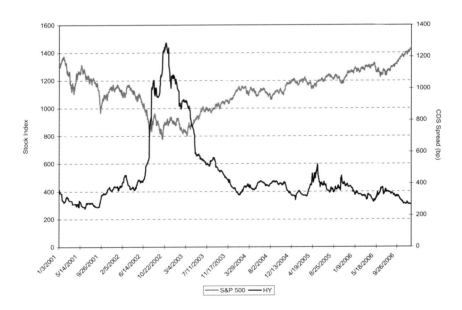

Figure 3.2. High-yield CDS Index vs. S&P 500 Index.

pricing and risk management of these more complex products and strategies require reliance on credit risk models and in particular on assumptions about the extent of default correlation between different reference entities.[12] According to Joint Forum (2005), many portfolio swap products reflect investors' increasing desire for portfolio diversification and enhanced yield, particularly during the recent low-yield environment.

5. Risks and Challenges

As in other derivatives market, the fast-expanding credit derivatives markets are confronted with various risks. Evaluating, managing, and ultimately reducing risk represent a key challenge for investors, as well as for supervisors. First, CDS contracts are still an over-the-counter (OTC) market only, except for the limited retail market in Australia. The greater number of products but less liquidity leads to a potential liquidity crisis. Second, back-office processing and documentation failures caused long delays in settlement. The US Fed Chairman issued an edict to major credit market players to clean up documentation and settlement procedures or face a halt in trading. Third, the Delphi default in 2005 uncovered significant counterparty risk and problems with price squeeze on defaulted bonds used for physical delivery.[13] Several hedge funds and broker-dealers take large losses as buying of defaulted bonds for physical delivery. Fourth, questionable risk management of complex strategies, interlocking ownership, high leverage, and secrecy of the hedge fund industry lay the groundwork for potential market shocks. We focus on liquidity risk, operation risk and market risk in this section.

5.1 *Liquidity Risk*

Liquidity is not consistent across all segments of the credit derivatives market. Market liquidity has improved rapidly for index products. The

---

[12] Das *et al.* (2007) and Jorion and Zhang (2007) represent the recent efforts that investigate default correlation.

[13] See www.ft.com/cms/s/850bd646-b467-11da-bd61-0000779e2340.html. Other top credit events in 2005 include Calpine, Delta Airlines, Northwest Airlines, Collins & Aikman, and Winn Dixie, reflecting difficulties of two depressed sectors, autos and airlines.

emergence of standardized CDS indices has attracted a variety of new participants to credit markets, resulting in an increasingly liquid market for index tranches, which are relatively inexpensive tools to trade and hedge credit. Two-way liquidity seems to be readily available for on-the-run tranches of standard CDS indices.

The single-name CDS market comprises more than 2,000 reference names, including a growing number of high-yield and EM names. However, only a fraction of the CDS names are traded regularly and in sufficient size to represent a truly liquid market. Liquidity in emerging CDS markets is even more limited, with mostly sovereigns, trading on a regular basis. Liquidity in single-name CDSs tends to evaporate quickly with increased market volatility, even for the most liquid names. During such periods, protection buyers often significantly outnumber protection sellers. This highlights an important feature of the CDS trading activity, i.e., many market participants often do not proactively hedge credit exposures, and typically seek to hedge positions in reaction to unfolding events. In doing so, they will be confronted with disappearing or very costly liquidity upon events (IMF, 2006).

The "primary" risk transfer CDO tranche market has a limited diversity of participants within the different tranches of a CDO. Buy-and-hold investors tend to dominate the senior and mezzanine tranche markets. However, secondary market liquidity is limited. More tailored credit exposures such as single-tranche transactions have generally little or no secondary market liquidity.

5.2 *Operational Risk*

Another major risk in the credit derivatives market is operational risk, evident in the mounting backlog of unconfirmed trades and the management of trade reassignments, as well as the need to improve settlement procedures. This is largely due to the rapid growth in trading volume and in the complexity of many new products, as well as the entry of hedge funds as active participants in the market.

The Delphi bankruptcy in 2005 highlighted the potential risks and challenges in the settlement processes. The deliverable-bond-market squeeze pressures arose when the notional value of outstanding CDS contracts far exceeded the outstanding amount of deliverable obligations, given the requirement of physical delivery. The Delphi experience had induced the industry and regulators to reexamine the existing settlement procedures and to consider the greater use of cash settlement.

Moreover, some hedge funds had delays or incorrect notification procedures for reassignments of credit derivative contracts. Some had reportedly executed trades without seeking the approval of the original counterparty. Such delays in confirming and executing reassignments apparently raised counterparty risks and introduced operational uncertainty.

The good news for investors were that regulators and supervisors, particularly the Federal Reserve Bank of New York and the UK Financial Services Authority (FSA), had sought to ensure that banks and dealers implement adequate systems. The major credit derivative dealers committed to significantly reduce the number of confirmations outstanding. The dealers were also committed to: strengthening their operating efficiency; improving information systems; automating more back-office procedures, including electronic matching platforms; and making proprietary platforms conformable to the Depository Trust & Clearing Corporation systems, which offer industry-standard processing platforms for other financial instruments.[14] As a result, the Dura default and auction in November 2006 went smoothly, showing the value of improved standardized industry procedures and clear documentation.

5.3 *Market Risk*

Significant movements in credit spreads had occurred over the past five years. The demand for credit protection grew substantially in the wake of the increase in investment grade default rates witnessed in the years from 2000 to 2002. This created an environment where default risk was a tangible event and the cost of hedging was a rational expense in relation to the potential losses. At the end of 2002, the CDX.NA.IG

---

[14] Source: IMF (2006).

index was traded at approximately 160 basis points, meaning that the average cost of credit protection on the names in that index was 160 basis points per annum. Over the course of 2003, however, perceptions of credit conditions improved considerably, leading to the same index falling to approximately 55 basis points, or nearly two-thirds. The narrowing of the credit spread could be attributed to both the supply and demand factors. On the demand side, banks became more reluctant to buy credit protection to hedge as credit conditions were perceived to have improved. On the supply side, the larger spreads in prior years had induced additional sellers of credit protection to enter the market. Narrow spreads made it harder to structure traditional CDOs with investment grade credits as collateral. In response, underwriters shifted to new collateral types and single-tranche deals.

Company idiosyncratic risk is another major market risk. It is more difficult to anticipate because it can occur abruptly, compared with a deterioration of the company's business over time. The change in firm-specific risk can be brought about by the credit cycle. A widening of credit spreads for specific firms can spread to specific industries (automobiles and airlines industries) and to related companies (supplier, lender, customer, etc.)[15] If such a company-specific deterioration in credit quality were to affect a very large name in the fast-growing market for credit derivatives and structured credit, this may upset the complex correlations. A contagion process may start if hedge funds are under pressure to liquidate other assets.

A growing tendency to releverage balance sheets recently may also lead to sharp deterioration of credit quality of the companies. These actions benefit shareholders at the expense of creditors — such as higher dividend payouts, large share buybacks, and merger and acquisition (M&A) activities. In particular, leveraged buyouts (LBOs), facilitated by a significant increase in the volume of LBO loans in the US and Europe, could significantly weaken the credit quality of the acquired company. Overall, however, given the healthy corporate sector balance sheet and the low default rates, the broad corporate spread is expected to change more moderately.

---

[15] Jorion and Zhang (2007).

6. Opportunities

Credit derivatives provide valuable investment and hedging opportunities to international investors. Given the difficulty in shorting bonds, hedging or investing through credit derivatives is attractive for credit market investors. This is particularly important for emerging market investors. CDS and CDS indices provide the market with a very accurate indicative measure of the credit risk of individual firms and the overall market. Investors can use CDS premiums to evaluate the fair value of bonds/loans, while debt issuers can use them in pricing new bond issues. Investors with a different opinion of the direction of the market can sell credit protection and earn the CDS premium on an unfunded basis, which is a high leverage and lucrative investment if the bet is in the right direction. Market investors are able to use credit derivatives to exploit relative value arbitrage opportunities in different markets, for example, in the stock and CDS markets. Banks are able to use credit derivatives to hedge loan portfolio exposure to achieve better use of credit lines, maintain customer relationship, and reduce risk capital requirement.

6.1 *Credit Risk Transfer*

The development of the credit derivatives markets has facilitated a material amount of credit risk transfer for domestic investors and international investors. It helps to enhance the geographic diversification of the credit risk profile. For example, banks in one state may gain exposure to other states in America by selling credit protection. Similarly, banks in Europe and Asia have been net sellers of credit protection, particularly in relation to highly rated products involving North American reference entities. This should offer a dominant risk-return profile relative to domestic market opportunities.

6.2 *Price Discovery*

As the credit derivative markets become more liquid, large banks now rely on these markets to actively manage their credit risk profiles and an increasing number of banks and other investors are using CDS markets for both pricing and price discovery. According to the IMF (2006), credit derivatives improve the availability, quality, and timeliness of information in credit markets, thereby enhancing price discovery and reducing adjustment lags.

The growth of credit derivative trading and the information advantage of market participants have provided better and more timely information regarding credit market conditions. Credit derivatives improve price discovery and may even be more efficient than bond markets. Recent research provides evidence that changes in CDS spreads lead to changes in bond spreads in the short run, and thereby increasingly set the marginal price of credit.[16] In short, the effectiveness of market prices would appear to have been enhanced by credit derivatives. Figure 4 shows that CDS spreads had begun to widen in anticipation of WorldCom bankruptcy in 2002, providing an early sign for investors to take their positions.

6.3 *Credit Risk Diversification*

Credit derivatives offer a highly attractive mechanism for managing exposure concentrations for international investors. In the wake of high-profile investment-grade defaults in the US, the largest banks have become increasingly concerned with exposure concentrations to individual names. Their credit portfolio management arms have therefore used credit derivatives as a way of bridging the gap between the credit extensions needed by their corporate customers and the bank's own desires with respect to exposure concentrations. Geographic diversification is made more likely with the development of credit derivative products, particularly with the envisioned growth of the emerging credit derivative market.

---

[16] Blanco *et al.* (2005) concluded that CDS spreads lead changes in bond spreads. Zhu (2004) and Norden and Weber (2004) arrive at a similar conclusion. Fung *et al.* (2007) find that there are two-way interactions between the equity market and CDS indices.

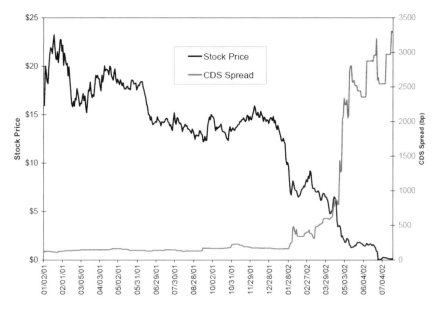

Figure 4. CDS Spread and Stock Price of WorldCom

6.4 *Credit Provision*

Credit derivative products influence credit provision to international investors in that the extension of credit by large banks has become much more dependent on market prices, and less on traditional limits related to a particular client, sector, or geographic region. Indeed, credit derivatives allow banks to preserve customer relationships, while risk managers may simultaneously adjust total or specific credit exposures. In other words, these markets enable banks to optimize their credit portfolios according to a chosen risk management strategy, and to more proactively and gradually adjust credit exposures.

6.5 *Financial Stability*

In the past, credit risk on bank balance sheets often contributed to volatility and failures during credit downturns. Such failures can lead to instability in the financial system and the economy. By dispersing risk to a more diverse group of market participants, larger banks have been able to improve the liquidity and resilience of their balance sheets. Transferring credit risk from banks via the credit derivatives markets helps to make the banking system, including smaller banks, less vulnerable to credit shocks.[17]

With the growing credit derivative markets, banks and supervisors may be able to identify credit-turning points at a much earlier stage in the cycle, signaled by noninvestment-grade spread widening and various broad market and idiosyncratic event risks rising (e.g., bankruptcies, increasing LBO activity, declining corporate earnings growth, rising M&A activity, and increased dividends and share buy-backs, etc.). As such, international banks are able to manage credit risk in a more timely and gradual manner.

6.6 *Opportunities to Individual Investors*

In terms of retail investors in the credit derivatives markets, some private banking clients are involved in various structures, but there is little in the way of broader direct retail involvement. However, dealer firms are reported to make efforts to develop product structures appealing to a broad retail market. In addition, retail investors may be participating indirectly through investment managers, if mutual finds or hedge funds that specialize in fixed-income related products invest a portion of their funds in credit derivatives.

The index products are particularly attractive to international retail investors given its liquidity and standardized contract. They can use the new and more liquid index products both to gain credit exposure and/or to hedge positions. Such proxy hedging may help to protect position against unfavorable spread movements.

Furthermore, international individual investors in other security markets (equity market, bond market) can gain more market insights by spanning the credit derivatives market at home and abroad. Indeed, the financial industry has already started to take advantage of the possible link between the CDS and stock markets by offering new products that help investors make better investment decisions.

---

[17] IMF report (2006).

For example, the GFI group, a leading inter-dealer brokerage, designed the MarketHub for cross-asset analytics between the credit and equity markets. The GFI group believes that equity-holders should pay attention to activities in the CDS market because the CDS market provides the real time assessment of credit risk, acts as an occasional leading indicator, and delivers greater efficiency than the equity market.[18]

7. Conclusion

Since its debut in 1995, the global credit derivatives market has witnessed an exponential growth in size and complexity, attracting large institutional investors such as banks, insurance companies, mutual funds, and hedge funds. Recently, the indices and index-related products are driving the growth and liquidity of the market. Despite the ongoing debate on the effect of the credit derivatives market on financial market stability and efficiency, the credit derivatives market will no doubt continue to grow at a rapid rate in the near future. The market provides international investors valuable investing and hedging opportunities, and also present challenges facing all participants in the market. Presumably, as the market matures, exemplified by standardized ISDA documentation and greater liquidity and depth, some challenges will be replaced by new challenges. Given the high leverage and fast-evolving product profile in this derivative market, international investors are advised to have a good understanding of the market before they tap into this fascinating market.

References

Acharya, V. and T. C. Johnson, 2007, Insider trading in credit derivatives, 84(1), 110–141.

Blanco, R., S. Brennan, and I. Marsh, 2005, An empirical analysis of the dynamic relationship between investment-grade bonds and credit default swaps, *Journal of Finance*, 60, 2255–2281.

---

[18] Source: www.gfigroup.com/portal/index.jsp?pageID=def_mdata_markethub.

Bystrom, H., 2005, Credit default swaps and equity prices: The iTRXX CDS index market, working paper, Department of Economics, Lund University.

Dages, B. G., D. Palmer, and S. Turney, 2005, An overview of the emerging market credit derivatives market, Federal Reserve Bank of New York, May.

Das, S., D. Duffie, N. Kapadia, and L. Saita, 2007, Common failings: How corporate defaults are correlated, *Journal of Finance*, 62(1), 93–117.

Fitch Ratings Special Report, 2006, Global credit derivatives survey: Indices dominate growth as banks' risk position shifts, September.

Fung, H. G., G. Sierra, J. Yau, and G. Zhang, 2008, Are the US stock market and credit default swap market related? Evidence from the CDX indices. *The Journal of Alternative Investments*, forthcoming.

Hirtle, B., 2007, *Credit Derivatives and Bank Credit Supply*. Federal Reserve Bank of Staff Reports, No 276, February.

IMF Global Financial Stability Report, 2006, A report by the international capital markets department on market developments and issues. Chapter 2, The influence of credit derivative and structured credit markets on financial stability.

Jorion, P. and G. Zhang, 2007, Good and bad credit contagion, evidence from credit default swaps, *Journal of Financial Economics*, 84(3), 860–883.

Lehman Brothers, 2005, CDO/structured credit annual 2006, Lehman Brothers Structured Credit Research, December.

Minton, B. R. Stulz and R. Williamson, 2006, How much do bank credit derivatives to reduce risk, Working paper, The Ohino State University.

Norden, L. and M. Weber, 2004, The comovement of credit default swap, bond and stock markets: An empirical analysis, Working paper, University of Mannheim.

Ranciere, R. G., 2002, Credit derivatives in emerging markets, IMF Policy Discussion Paper, April.

The Joint Forum, 2005, Basel committee on banking supervision, credit risk transfer, Working Group on Risk Assessment and Capital, Basel: Bank for International Settlements, March.

Zhu, H., 2006, An empirical comparison of credit spreads between the bond market and the credit default swap market, *Journal of Financial Services Research*, 29(3), 211–235.

Chapter 11

Currency Derivatives and Emerging Market Currencies: Strategies, Perspectives, and Trends

Anthony L. Loviscek

Emerging markets have delivered significant double-digit returns to foreign investors for more than a decade, clearly outpacing the returns from developed markets. The gains, however, have come with a price: high risk. In particular, political instability and erratic macroeconomic policies have caused wide swings in local currencies. Although these swings have mitigated in recent years, it behooves foreign investors to use currency derivatives to limit their impact. This article provides an overview of currency derivatives and strategies to hedge currency risk in emerging markets, including developments in currency derivatives in selected emerging economies in Asia, Africa, Europe, and Latin America.

Keywords: Forward; futures; option and swap.

1. Introduction

Since 1990, investor interest and participation in emerging markets have dramatically increased. As evidence, according to the International Finance Corporation, equity market capitalization among emerging

Department of Finance and Legal Studies, Stillman School of Business, Seton Hall University, South Orange, NJ 07079, USA. Email: loviscto@shu.edu.

economies climbed from approximately US$250 billion to over US$5 trillion by the end of 2006, an annual growth of 19.1%. During the same period, international and domestic debt issuance by emerging market sovereigns and corporations increased by 12.5% per year from 1995 to over US$4 trillion by 2004. Moreover, international interest in emerging market local currency investments has shown impressive growth, with US mutual fund investments jumping nearly tenfold to over US$230 billion in 2006 from US$27 billion in 2000.

Given these levels of activity, it is not surprising that Morningstar, a US-based mutual fund rating service, reports that the number of US emerging market mutual funds increased from under ten in 1990 to over 200 by 2006. And these numbers by no means reflect all of the interest in emerging market investments because they do not account for the interest of hedge fund investors, whose managers may find even greater interest in emerging markets than mutual fund managers because they have more freedom and flexibility to pursue emerging market investments than their mutual fund counterparts.

The reasons for the growing interest in emerging markets are apparent and straightforward. First, monetary and fiscal authorities have positioned the economies of these markets to register robust growth at comparatively low rates of inflation, a reversal of fortunes when noting the runaway inflation and debt burdens that plagued these economies worldwide during the 1980s. Second, the push toward globalization has promoted the integration of financial markets, permitting a free flow of financial capital that is inhibited only by limited government decree. Third, the rates of return on investments in the emerging markets of developing countries have been far superior to those in the developed world. For example, between 1999 and 2006, the S&P 500 returned 3.3% annually compared to 18.5%, as reported by the Morgan Stanley Capital International Index, a difference that is even more significant from 2003 through 2006, in which the S&P 500 registered an annual
        5% to the 36.4% jump enjoyed by investors in emerging

However impressive the rates of return from emerging markets, they have come with a price: higher risk. It is common to find standard portfolio risk measures to be from 50% to over 100% higher than found in the markets of developed countries. As evidence, from 1997 through 2006, the standard deviation of the S&P 500 is approximately 15%; that for the average emerging market mutual fund is about 23%. From 2003 through 2006, the difference increases to over 100%, or from 7 to 16, as witnessed, for example, between mid-May and mid-June of 2006, in which a worldwide equity market correction caused emerging market returns to plunge by as much as 30%.

The sources of this higher risk are not hard to find. Although emerging markets have significantly advanced in depth and breadth of activity since 1990, they are prone to bouts of inflation, fiscal imprudence, current account deficits, political turbulence, corruption, terrorism, and contagion effects. In addition, they are not nearly as deep compared to the markets in the US, Japan, and Europe, implying sensitivity to shocks that developed markets more easily absorb. As well, they are subject to "hot money" episodes, in which investors either infuse into markets or withdraw from them large sums of capital, and sometimes quickly do both, which are known to destabilize financial markets and precipitate a crisis of confidence in the developing country's currency that often spreads to currencies of neighboring countries.

Even when these problems are not present, however, emerging market economies suffer from what Eichengreen *et al.* (2003) term "original sin." The governments of these economies — in fact, all governments except the issuers of the US dollar, Euro, Yen, pound sterling, and Swiss franc — cannot borrow abroad in their home currencies. This leads to a much higher percentage of emerging market debt being denominated in foreign currencies than in local currencies. Thus, any significant and negative event can trigger a twofold crisis of confidence in the emerging market currency that can easily feed on itself: a surge in financial capital outflow and a rising debt payment burden.

In a series of papers, Calvo and Calvo and Reinhart (1998, 1999, 2000, 2002, and 2005) argue, among other points, that these problems can sometimes be outside the control of a country's financial authorities. He shows that investors in developed markets might misread and misinterpret investor behavior in emerging markets, leading to what he refers to as a "sudden stop" in capital inflows that virtually paralyzes emerging markets and carries contagion effects. For example, he demonstrates that the Russian debt crisis of 1998 triggered a financial and economic crisis in Latin America, and one from which Argentina is still trying to recover, exacerbated by a unilateral devaluation in the Brazilian real that reduced Argentinian exports. In addition, as McFadden (2004) observes, the Asian financial crisis of 1997 spread from Thailand to Malaysia, Indonesia, the Philippines, and Korea, forcing Korea to lose six months of potential output.

Concerning political unrest, Crowley and Loviscek (2002) use daily data to demonstrate the impact and lingering effects of it on Latin American currencies, illustrating the sharp and prolonged decline that occurs in the value of the currency against the US dollar with the announcement of a coup attempt, terrorist attack, or episode of political corruption. Regarding "hot money" and capital flight, Claessens and Naude' (1993) illustrate that their impact extends well beyond the Latin American financial markets, which often receive the brunt of the impact, to those in Egypt, Nigeria, Poland, and Turkey. Das (2003) extends their work by discussing how macroeconomic instability and unsettled exchange rate policy can cause boom-bust cycles in capital flows, creating "jump risk," which precipitates wide swings in currency values and illustrates a "downside" of globalization.

McFadden (2004) also points out that the source of emerging market risk need not be confined to developing economies; in fact, it can be precipitated by developed ones. He points out that the international financing of loose fiscal policy in the US carries a currency risk that "can ignite a financial storm that could sweep across the entire international market system and do great damage to unwary emerging economies." In this regard, he cites five risks (p. 4):

- Exchange rate risk, in which depreciation of the local currency occurs relative to a developed currency, causing loan payment problems in the local currency;
- Maturity risk resulting in an overweighting of short-term debt, or hot money, that easily leaves the country;

- Interest rate risk that manifests itself in the fluctuation of LIBOR rates;
- Service risk in which an economic contraction leaves the home country vulnerable to debt service difficulties; and
- Speculative risk that increases the volatility in securities markets, leading to capital flight that further pressures domestic currency values.

If the past is a precedent — the Asian currency crisis in 1997, the Russian debt crisis of 1998, and the Argentinian crisis in 2002, to name three within the past ten years — the outcome of these risks becoming reality is very likely to be a severe step back in the progress toward open markets, which would stifle investments and slow economic progress worldwide.

Both McFadden (2004) and Calvo (2005) propose to deal with these risks through policies promoted in conjunction with developed economies. For instance, McFadden calls for greater supervision of financial intermediaries, including substantive banking regulations that are applied consistently by strong, independent regulators, compliance with international accounting standards, and tight lending standards that incorporate early-warning systems for troubled borrowers. Calvo recommends the creation of an emerging market fund that would serve as a lender of last resort to support the bond prices, or spread index, of emerging economies.

Even if fully implemented, these approaches would not be set up to handle the daily, week-to-week, and month-to-month fluctuations that accompany the currencies that underlie the value of emerging market prices of securities. Moreover, the integration of financial markets worldwide calls into question the efficacy of even the most efficient form of portfolio diversification, as Bhargava *et al.* (2004) find in their study of four major indices over two decades. This leaves currency risk management as the only solution.

Currency risk, the chance that the actual return from a currency will fall short of the expected return, can be complicated to manage, and therefore is not without some controversy. For international fixed-income portfolio managers, for example, currency risk has typically accounted for about two-thirds of portfolio volatility, nearly double the risk of international equity fund portfolios. Thus, the motivation to hedge currency risk would appear to be greater for fixed-income managers than for equity analysts. However, the currency component of international investing can contribute significantly to the performance of the portfolio. Thus, the inclination of managers is to maintain the position on directional carry trades and not hedge away the risk. By hedging the risk, whether in fixed-income securities, equities, or commodities, a fundamental reason to invest internationally is eliminated.

At some point, however, risk aversion, especially in emerging markets with fragile financial systems, begins to dominate, and the need to hedge at least some risk becomes prudent, an observation that motivates this article. Its aim is twofold: to provide an overview of how currency risk in emerging markets may be managed by using currency derivatives and to point out some of the latest trends in currency derivative developments in emerging markets worldwide. In what follows, Section 2 provides an overview of currency derivatives. Section 3 discusses some traditional hedging strategies. Section 4 looks at some recent foreign exchange and derivative developments in emerging markets of specific countries. Section 5 discusses additional trends in emerging markets with respect to exchange rate and interest rate movements. Section 6 concludes the study with perspectives on future developments in emerging markets.

2. Currency Risk and Currency Derivatives

By allowing for the unbundling of currency risk, currency derivatives represent a big step forward in currency risk management. By increasing the liquidity of investments beyond that offered by the cash markets, they offer three benefits: hedging, price discovery, and transactional efficiency. By using currency derivatives to hedge risk, emerging markets investors can shift unwanted exchange rate risk either to speculators who are willing to assume the risk or to currency traders who possess a higher tolerance for risk. Through price discovery, currency derivatives provide emerging market investors with exchange rates that reflect current and future demands for and supplies of a currency. In fact, they offer dynamic price discovery by revealing future, or expected, exchange rates at a series of future delivery dates. By enhancing transactional efficiency, currency derivatives provide an efficient mechanism for dealing with counter-party risk.

Following Soendoro (2007), we begin by providing an overview of currency derivatives:

- Forward. Frequently used by large multinational corporations to hedge currency risk, this is a financial contract that requires the buyer either to purchase or sell the currency at a specific price and at an agreed-upon date and amount. Traded over the counter, it is priced in terms of the interest differential between the currencies involved in the transaction. A forward has a high degree of liquidity and is easy to follow. There are two kinds of forwards, "foreign exchange" and "flexible forward," with the latter carrying the flexibility to profit from favorable exchange rate movements.
- Futures. More liquid than a forward contract, a futures contract involves the purchase or sale of a currency based on an order that is placed in advance, with the payment required on the delivery date. The buyer is required to show liquid assets, such as cash or Treasury securities — called "margin" — that demonstrate the ability to honor the contract. Futures differ from forwards because they contain standard contract terms that enable them to be traded on exchanges worldwide. With currencies, the futures contract involves a fixed price at which a foreign currency can either be bought or sold in the future. It is used not only for hedging but for speculation in an attempt to profit from fluctuating exchange rates. Investors are permitted to close out a contract at any time prior to the delivery date specified on the contract.
- Spot Foreign Exchange. More liquid and risky than a futures contract, spot foreign exchange binds the buyer or seller of the currency to a specific amount that is marked for settlement in two business days.

- Option. An over-the-counter derivative that is more expensive than either a forward or a futures contract, a currency option is a contract that gives the investor in the currency the right but not the obligation to either buy or sell the currency at a pre-determined price. A call gives the holder the right to buy the currency under contract; a put gives the holder the right to sell the currency. As extensions, there is a forward start option and a ratchet option, with the former being a forward on an option in which the buyer pays the premium in advance and the latter representing a series of forward start options.
- Swap. Another over-the-counter currency derivative, it represents an agreement between two investors to exchange the principal and interest on one currency for another currency at fixed intervals. Available for short- and long-term maturities (up to ten years), a swap contains the concept that the present value equals zero. Variations on it include the following:

  ○ Forward swap. It is a combination of a forward contract with a swap. The agreement is set at the current time with the provision that the swap begins at a specified future date.
  ○ Currency swap/fixed rate currency swap. This involves the purchase of a currency for spot settlement and, at the same time, the sale of the same currency for forward settlement.
  ○ Interest rate swap. It represents an agreement between investors to exchange interest payments on currency principal, which is known as the "notional" principal.
  ○ Currency coupon swap. It combines the interest rate swap and the fixed-rate swap and involves a fixed-rate interest in one currency that is traded for a floating-rate interest in another currency.
  ○ Swaption. It incorporates an option into a swap. The purchaser of it has the right, but not the obligation, to invoke a swap at agreed-upon terms at a specified date in the future. There are three categories of swaptions depending on whether the holder can enter into the swap at almost any time (i.e., American

swaption), during a limited time (i.e., Bermudian swaption), and only on a single specified date (i.e., European swaption).

o Quanto swap. A complicated swap, it contains three features, currency, interest rate, and equity, and the payments are based on the interest differentials between the interest rates of two countries. One investor agrees to pay another investor an interest payment based on the foreign currency but the notional amount is in the domestic currency.

o Exotic options. More complex and sophisticated than the above instruments, they incorporate special features that extend the fundamental contracts discussed so far. Some examples include Asian options, lookback options, and barrier options, each of which has a payoff that depends on both the value of the underlying currency and the values at various intervals across the life of the agreement.

Relying on Henderson (2002), we provide an overview of the following characteristics that complicate currency risk management in emerging markets:

- Significantly higher forward premiums than developed country currencies. Although inflation has dropped from the double-digit, and in some cases triple-digit, levels during the last decade, the threat of structural inflation is not insignificant, especially considering that political unrest can give way to unstable governments that pursue a very loose monetary policy.

- Negative correlation between the future spot rate and current forward premium is low. The threat of inflation and its impact on interest rates reduces the negative correlation that is observed for the more stable currencies of developed economies.

- Options market complications. The high forward premiums lead to high implied option volatilities and risk-reversal skews.

- Capital inflows and inflation differentials. It is not uncommon for the effect of the capital inflows that pursue the high emerging market returns to more than offset the effect of the depreciation in the home currency resulting from inflation differentials.

- Capital inflows and the central bank. Large and variable capital inflows and outflows complicate central bank monetary management, leading to interest rate volatility.

- Event risk. Sudden and unexpected events, such as political unrest or corruption, can lead to wide currency swings, which is also called "jump risk."

- Liquidity risk. Emerging market economies are not as deep as their developed counterparts, and therefore their currencies can be thinly traded, presenting investors with potential liquidity problems.

- Capital account risk. All developed country currencies are freely floating and fully convertible, unlike some emerging market currencies that are not convertible on the capital account (and a few that are not convertible on the current account).

- Exchange rate controls. Exchange rate controls, such as pegging currencies to a price, as still practiced in some emerging market countries, can upset financial and economic exchange, leading conceivably to capital flight as the pressure to change the controls increases.

- The options market can be a poor predictor. Unlike the markets of developed countries, in which option pricing can indicate future direction of the price of a security, the same does not hold well in emerging markets, especially when a crisis is imminent.

- Low implied volatility may be a buy signal. If emerging market implied volatility drops below that of developed market volatility, it is probably a good time to buy the emerging market currency because emerging market volatility tends to increase whenever the currency is depreciating.

3. Hedging Strategies and Perspectives

Although currency derivatives of emerging markets do not begin to match the depth and liquidity found in developed markets, there are not only signs of ongoing progress but also the appearance of a discernible maturity. For instance, bid-ask spreads are narrowing and large risk-reversal skews are becoming less common. As broad evidence, swap rates have dropped dramatically between 2003 and 2007 in South American markets, especially in Brazil, where rates have fallen from nearly 40% to about 12%. In addition, over the same period, swap rates in Asia have moved in step with US rates.

What are some common and exotic strategies for hedging currency risk in emerging markets? What are their advantages and disadvantages? Although not all of the strategies to be mentioned are available in every emerging market, owing to different degrees of market development and government decrees, the following discussion, which draws heavily on the work of Henderson (2002, pp. 9–11), outlines a sample of effective approaches, including a brief statement of the advantage and disadvantage of each approach:

- Plain vanilla call. This involves the purchasing of an upside strike in a currency, such as the Mexican peso, without having the obligation to exercise it. Its advantage is that it is simple. However, it can carry a higher cost than more complex products.

- Plain vanilla forward. As mentioned previously, an investor who purchases this contract is waiting for future delivery of a currency based on an agreed-upon price today. It offers the advantage of total risk reduction. However, it also runs the risk of the exchange rate moving against the investor's position, not an uncommon occurrence with emerging market currencies.

- Call spread. This deals with the purchase of a call at-the-money and selling a call that has a low delta, or hedge ratio, which measures the relationship between the change in the emerging market foreign exchange rate compared to the change in price of the derivative. The advantage of this position is that it carries a lower cost than a plain vanilla call. Its disadvantage is that an investor can exercise the written call at any time.

- Calendar spread. This strategy involves, for example, the simultaneous purchase and sale of call options on the currency that differ only in their time to maturity, such as the buying of a three-month call and the selling of a one-month call. It has the advantage of allowing for modest exchange rate appreciation depending on the exercise price, which can easily occur with an emerging market currency. Adverse moves in a currency, which can be common in an emerging market, leave the investor subject to downside risk.

- Risk reversal. This approach concerns the purchase a 25-delta call and a 25-delta put simultaneously (where "25" refers to the degree to which an exchange rate of the underlying emerging market currency exceeds its exercise price). Investors interested in gleaning information on the likelihood of a large currency appreciation compared to a large currency depreciation will engage in a risk reversal, enabling them to gain insight into the skewness of the emerging market's foreign exchange rate. The disadvantage is that the delta put leaves investors vulnerable to losses in the event of adverse and undiversifiable moves in the spot rate.

- Seagull. In this method, investors purchase an at-the-money forward call while simultaneously selling a low-delta call and a put. This move can reduce costs to zero, but unless carefully structured, can leave investors uncovered against an adverse move in the spot market, such as what occurred during the Asian financial crisis of 1997–1998.

- Knock-out. With this strategy, an investor could buy a 30-delta call that has a downside knock-out, which limits the upside potential of a vanilla call. It significantly reduces the cost of the call, however, which has been no small matter with emerging market currencies. However, it can leave investors open to losses from a sudden reverse spike in the exchange rate, as seen, for example, in the large drop in the Venezuelan bolivar between 2002 and 2007.

- Knock-in. This approach is the same as a knock-out, but the 30-delta call has an upside knock-in. It significantly reduces the cost of the call because the investor does not participate until he is "knocked in." However, once knocked in, the investor is subject to the risk of a significant reversal.

- Range binary. This method is defined as the purchase of double knock-out, which permits investors to lever their investments against the exchange rate as long as the rate is expected to remain within a trading range. The down side of this position occurs if the spot rate exceeds the barriers — again, as seen in the case of the bolivar — forcing the investor to hedge again but at potentially unattractive prices. The bigger the change, the more costly the new hedge will be.

- Window option. A flexible approach that allows an investor the right, but not the obligation, to buy a 30-delta call at any time within a pre-determined number of periods during the life of the option. It gives an investor the freedom to have an incorrect forecast of an emerging market currency during the time in which the option can be exercised. However, it comes with a price: a higher cost than a vanilla option.

- Fade-in option. This method allows for a gradual move into a call option during the time in which it can be exercised, allowing the investor the advantage of flexibility that vanilla calls do not have. Yet, the approach fails to capture much of the profits from a quick and significant move in the spot rate.

- Convertible forward. In this situation, an investor buys a vanilla call and, at the same time, sells a down-and-in put. It converts to a plain vanilla forward during the exercise period, positioning the investor to profit from a contrarian move in the spot rate. However, the forward is cheaper than the strike, a difference that an investor must pay if the agreement gets knocked in.

- Cross-currency coupon swap. It permits an investor to move from a fixed-rate commitment in one currency — for example, an emerging market currency — to a floating-rate commitment in another currency, say, the US dollar, allowing the investor to control currency risk and interest rate risk in markets that offer the greatest return-to-risk ratios. This appealing approach, however, leaves an investor open to both currency and interest rate risk.

- Cross-currency basis swap. In this move, an investor purchases a standard currency swap while simultaneously receiving a floating interest rate in one currency (e.g., US dollar) for a floating rate in another currency (e.g., Brazilian real). This position allows an investor to profit from interest rate differentials while assuming no more risk than found in a basic currency swap. However, the risk is no longer in the currency but in the interest rate.

4. Trends in Emerging Markets

As expected, the derivative instruments available for managing currency risk inherent in emerging markets depend on the degree of development of these markets — their respective depths and breadths — and the degree of openness of their respective governments to foreign investment and floating exchange rates. As also expected, the variation is wide. This section follows the lead of Soendoro (2007) by reporting on trends in derivatives markets in selected countries in Asia, Africa, Eastern Europe, and Latin America.

4.1 *Asia*

Owing to robust economic growth and expansion, Asian markets represent the world's fastest growing region for the development of currency derivatives. Expectedly, these markets have come a long way over the last two decades, led by developments in Singapore and Hong Kong, each of which is active in forex trading, holding and offering a wide range of financial instruments within fairly deep capital markets. In fact, among emerging markets, they have the most liquid over-the-counter currency derivative markets.

In early 2007, the Monetary Authority of Singapore increased its net forward and futures positions in foreign currencies from US$26.6 billion to US$66.6 billion, a jump of 150%. As one of Asia's anchors for currency trading, Singapore accounts for about 7% of the approximately US$2 trillion per day traded in the world forex markets in 2007. In addition, Hong Kong has the well developed Hong Kong Exchanges and Clearing for handling forex and their associated derivatives. Although restrictions were imposed after the Asian currency crisis of 1997–1998, trading of futures and options jumped to an all-time high of nearly 25 million contracts. Like the Singapore market, the Hong Kong exchange offers a full range of currency options, swaps, and exotics.

The same does not apply to the closely followed Chinese financial markets. Although its GDP growth has been estimated to be well over 10% per year for the last several years, as of 2007 the forex market was still under a fixed regime. Although the pressure to liberalize is strong, especially with respect to the US dollar, given China's huge current account surplus with the US, the process is slow and deliberate. Initial experiments with currency derivatives went badly, in part because the banking system was not set up to handle them. As a result, the China Banking Regulatory Commission has issued the edict that Chinese banks need to restrict their trading in derivatives transactions because bank managers to date have not acquired the acumen necessary to trade them properly. Nonetheless, it is possible for an investor to hedge currency risks with a forward contract, currently known as the Chinese Yuan Non-Deliverable Forward Contract. Begun in late 2005, the contracts run from periods of one, two, three, six, and 12 months and can be purchased for as little as US$10,000. The reference currency is the Chinese yuan and the settlement currency is the US dollar. More than US$1 billion of yuan forwards are estimated to be exchanged daily, a significant increase from an overseas market that did not exist as late as 1992. As China gradually and deliberately moves to a more open economic and financial system as it attracts capital worldwide from the rapid expansion of its economic and financial markets, only legal restrictions can prevent the development of an on-shore market for currency derivatives. In support of this view, in 2006 Chinese government officials announced that they are considering the formation of a futures market in Shanghai, a component of which would consist of currency derivatives.

By comparison, the Indian forex market has grown significantly in the last ten years. As explained below, however, it has a long way to go before it catches up with large international markets. Although forward trading in commodities began in the nineteenth century, the derivatives market was closed for over 40 years until the late 1990s when the government began to allow limited derivatives trading. Despite the fact that growth in the derivatives market in general, and currency derivatives in particular, is still significantly restricted by government decree — in this case, the Reserve Bank of India — there is active trading in the non-deliverable forward market on the rupee price of the US dollar. Most of the trading, however, takes place outside India; as much as US$1 billion a day is estimated to change hands.

Currency derivative trading is active and available across a number of instruments, such as options, forwards, swaps, forward swaps, swaptions, quanto options, and ratchet options. However, beyond basic currency derivatives, such as vanilla options and forwards, sophisticated instruments and exotics apply only to foreign currencies, not to rupee-generated transactions. This is despite the upsurge in currency volatility that has hit the rupee between 2006 and 2007, a fluctuation against the US dollar of more than 10% as of the second quarter of 2007. Given India's strong economic advances and its increasing presence in the global economy, it appears that the development and growth of the currency derivatives market in the rupee will continue to advance in markets outside India, such as in London and Singapore, with or without the Reserve Bank of India. It would appear only a matter of time before investors and other agents are permitted to apply more sophisticated currency derivatives to rupee-generated transactions. In fact, as of early 2007, the Reserve Bank of India held over US$200 billion in reserves, exposing itself to significant exchange rate risk if the US dollar were to appreciate. As a step toward allowing more currency derivatives, during the first quarter of 2007, the Reserve Bank announced that it will be allowing the creation of credit default swaps.

An emerging market that has attracted a lot of international investor attention during the last two years is Vietnam. With an economy that reportedly expanded by nearly 8% in 2006, which coincided with a surge of 126% in its equity market, Vietnam has begun gradually to loosen currency controls. This has led to a drop of 30% in the dong price of the US dollar, finding a floor at about 16,000, as the government continues its restrictions on loans for investments in securities. As another restraint against the value of the dong, investors interested in trading it need derivatives to do so because the government only allows the purchase of the dong for specific purposes, such as the purchase of equipment and the construction of plants. As of early 2007, despite these restrictions and restraints, two things appear to be almost inevitable: the appreciation of the dong as investor interest in the country accelerates and the emergence of a standard futures contract as currency controls are loosened.

In contrast to currency derivatives markets in China, India, and Vietnam, the market in Korea is more open and attracts worldwide interest. Prior to 1999, however, the growth and development of the on-shore currency derivatives markets were hindered by the legal requirement that a forward contract had to be hedged against future current account flows. This changed in 1999, with the launching of the Korea Futures Exchange, or KOFEX. Linked to the world's most heavily stock index option, the "Kospi 200," the KOFEX leapt to a record of nearly 2.6 billion contracts by 2004. Among the traded products were won/US dollar futures and options. As globalization advances and the market for KOSPI 200 index futures and options saturates, it is difficult to envision anything but the KOFEX being part of an increasingly open financial system of sophisticated currency derivative products, especially as Korea dismantles barriers to foreign exchange trading.

Thailand has had its share of crises, from the devaluation of the baht in 1997 that triggered the Asian financial crisis to a political coup late in 2006. In addition, it has not been slow to impose capital controls, restrictions on currency trading, and limits on the formation of the currency derivatives market beyond basic forwards, futures, and swaps. This was seen in early 2007 as the Bank of Thailand sought to protect the baht from devaluation as it strengthened by 12% against the US dollar. It imposed a requirement of having 30% of a total investment deposited with a Thai bank, with the additional requirement of forcing investors in stocks, bonds, and foreign direct investment to hold the deposit for at least three months and have the investment hedged with currency swaps that would prevent investors from profiting from a fluctuating baht. These controls were soon relaxed, a sign that as the economy expands and financial markets mature, currency derivatives may become an increasingly important tool in currency risk management, especially as neighboring countries adopt them. As evidence of a first step in this direction, Thailand has agreed to contribute to a pool of currencies aimed at reducing the likelihood of repeating the Asian currency crisis of 1997–1998.

4.2 *Africa*

South Africa, far and away, is the standout player in foreign currencies and currency derivative developments among African nations, having one of the most liquid currency derivative centers among emerging market economies. However, in many countries, such as Nigeria and Togo, financial markets lack the development to carry out anything beyond basic forwards, futures, and swaps, and in Zimbabwe, progress has been hampered by hyperinflation — a rate exceeding 50% per month. Not surprisingly, as these observations suggest, institutional and managerial support is weak in most African markets.

Next to the Singapore dollar, South Africa's rand is the world's second most actively traded emerging market currency. Its degree of recognition and sophistication parallels that of developed economies. It offers a deep currency derivatives market, and is part of a fluid standard settlement system that promises market clearance and settlement that effectively reduce settlement risk to zero. Interestingly, though, unlike in Asian markets, investors here, not unlike investors in neighboring countries, appear to stick to basic hedging and speculative instruments, avoiding exotic ones. With domestic economic growth on the upswing coupled with the integration of global financial markets, it is only a matter of time before more sophisticated currency derivatives products become commonplace.

Kenya should not be overlooked as a center for forex and currency derivatives. Serving as a center for multinational corporations, Kenya has the financial traction to advance currency derivative products. At this time, however, most of the trading occurs in basic forwards, futures, and in vanilla options, with no foreign exchange protection available for more than one year. One obstacle to the development of more sophisticated derivative instruments is that they are under the control of Kenya's central bank, and until this control is relaxed, it is unlikely that Kenya's financial markets will offer any exotic currency derivatives.

4.3 *Eastern and Central Europe*

rn Europe, we find a wide variation in currency derivative ments. For example, when the Russian Federation lifted controls on the ruble in July of 2006, it allowed it to float more freely, making it fully convertible. This is paving the way for the ruble to become a world-trading currency. Coupled with the country's sound macroeconomic fundamental position and with an upturn in investment spending, the Russian Federation offers international investors solid opportunities, leading to significant and steady interest in currency futures. This has stimulated trading in currency derivatives on the Moscow Interbank Currency Exchange, or MICEX. In early 2007, the volume of trading in standard contracts on the MICEX reached US$14.0 billion, more than double the amount year over year. In February 2007 alone, the volume of trading in US dollar futures reached a record-high of US$5.57 billion and a daily high of US$910 million. At this time, with economic growth and development in a take-off phase, and with the ruble at floating rates, it seems that the Russian Federation is not far away from more sophisticated currency derivatives.

Since 2000, when the Warsaw Commodity Exchange became private, Poland has advanced in its use of futures and options, beginning with the use of four currency pairs: Polish zloty-euro, zloty-US dollar, zloty-Swiss franc and the euro-dollar. Each of these pairs was begun at a contract size of 10,000 units, settled by cash, and delivered by the end of the respective year. These small contracts were linked to larger contracts of 50,000-unit nominal value that are deliverable. In 2005, two more currency pairs were added: zloty-Czech korona and Hungarian forint. All six currency pairs serve as a strong foundation for further developments in currency derivatives, as already seen in the availability of forward and options contracts for up to five years and cross-currency swaps for at least ten years.

The Hungarian forint became fully convertible in 2001, leading to higher currency risk, fostering the development of basic currency derivatives, which are traded on the Hungarian OTC market. Not surprisingly, the most widely traded products are based on the euro and the US dollar, with currency futures being the most popular contract. Moreover, the demand for central and eastern European currencies is fairly strong, showing the strength of the OTC market in Hungary and the influence of the forint. In fact, the Bank of International

Settlements reported that currency derivative activity likely doubled between the third and fourth quarters of 2006. Strengthening the demand for these derivatives during 2007, Russian investors have been investing in Hungary because interest rates are higher there than in their country. Based on these trends, it is safe to say that the market for currency derivatives in Hungary will broaden and deepen at a solid pace.

The currency derivatives market of the Czech Republic is small compared to those of developed nations, but its currency derivatives market is active, stable, and tightly regulated by the Czech National Bank, the nation's central bank. It is driven by a floating koruna, which the central bank has allowed to float since 1997. Currency derivatives activity has been significantly advancing since May of 2004, when trading began to center on the euro. In particular, the volume of currency forwards has been relatively large for the last several years because international investors have sought the higher interest rates in the Czech Republic, motivating them to exchange their home currencies for the koruna to buy Czech bond issues. As these differences persist, the currency derivatives market will, in all likelihood, advance beyond basic forwards, futures, and options.

4.4 *Latin America*

This is an area long marked by political and economic instability, across all the countries, especially among the most developed ones — Argentina, Brazil, Colombia, and Mexico. Like their Asian counterparts, such as Korea and Thailand, they often bear the brunt of capital flight whenever an episode of political instability, including coup attempts, assassinations, government takeover of private industry, and political corruption, occurs.

As of 2007, Argentina is still recovering from the lingering effects of a prolonged financial crisis that began in 2002, one that has significantly affected the currency derivatives market, as the link between the peso and the US dollar became untenable. As the peso was allowed to float, an active spot market rapidly developed, along with forwards and futures. Non-deliverable forward contracts are available only in large amounts; in fact, most hedging instruments are generally unavailable to small investors. Although the freely floating peso is likely to lead to further advances in the currency derivatives market, it seems safe to say that these advances will be limited until the financial crisis of 2002 is safely behind the country.

As its economic progress marches forward, and with its bonds moving closer to an investment-grade rating, Brazil has the most advanced capital markets and most sophisticated currency derivatives market in Latin America, with both basic hedging and sophisticated instruments available. As such, the Brazilian Mercantile and Futures Exchange, where currency derivatives and other instruments are traded, is considered to be one of the leaders in currency derivatives development among western emerging markets. Currently, over US$2 billion a day is traded in currency derivatives and about US$1 billion alone, according to the Bank of International Settlements, in single-currency interest rate derivatives. As a result, the connection between raising capital in international markets and hedging the associated risk through the currency derivatives market is strong. It is common to find investors infusing capital into investment opportunities by using the Brazilian real and then using a basic strategy of swapping out the risk through the US dollar or the euro. In fact, and as a sign of progress, five-year swap rates are down from 39% in 2003 to less than 13% by the first quarter of 2007. It is safe to say that Brazil is well on its way toward establishing itself as a world-trade center for currency derivatives. In fact, it is already ranked as one of the ten largest derivative trading centers in the world.

Chilean authorities have recently chosen to move from a managed floating system for the peso to a freely floating one, leading to well over US$1 billion a day traded in currency derivatives (an amount that does not include off-shore transactions in developed markets, such as in New York and London), with an annual trading volume estimated at over US$400 billion in 2006. Unlike Brazil, however, hedging instruments are centered on basic forwards, futures, and swaps, and are mostly devoid of exotic contracts, although it is not uncommon for some hedging to be done by using knock-in and knock-out options. By far, the most common currency derivative traded is the forward. Beyond this contract, a common move, for example, is for risk-taking investors to avail themselves of cross-currency swaps — as opposed to a currency exchange swap — by borrowing money in a foreign currency at a lower interest rate than offered in Chile and then swap out of the foreign currency risk back into the peso, locking in the lower rate. It is a safe bet that the floating peso, along with continued economic growth and derivative advancements in neighboring Brazil, will deepen and broaden Chile's currency derivatives market.

In Mexico, given the history of the volatility of the peso and the country's propensity for corruption — reportedly worse than the world average, according to the Heritage Foundation's Index of Economic Freedom — investors have always had the incentive to hedge currency risk. As the peso was unlocked from a fixed rate to a floating rate, the currency derivatives market was born, growing to over US$700 billion by 2006. Moreover, Mexican authorities have successfully reduced inflation and promoted economic growth, leading to an investment-grade bond rating of "A-" by Fitch in the second quarter of 2007, attracting worldwide interest in its debt from investors. Expectedly, these developments have led to Mexico's capital markets commonly using traditional forward, futures, options, and swaps. Exotic contracts are not nearly as common, however. Nonetheless, the growth in option and swap contracts has been outstripping the increase in forwards since 2002, a trend that will continue as Mexico's economic growth and financial market development continue to advance.

Colombia has progressed away from its image as a location for drug cartels in the 1980s and 1990s, emerging as a center and clearing house for foreign exchange. As a part of financial regulation, all exchanges in foreign currency are monitored by the central bank, Banco de la Republica, and since 2005, all foreign currency trades of at least US$200 have to be reported to the Financial Analysis Unit. These regulations stem from the country's role for years as a haven for drug smuggling and money laundering. Basic hedging contracts, such as forwards, futures, and swaps, are common and have been growing. For example, forward contracts have increased from about US$420 per month in 1997 to over US$6 billion by 2006. More sophisticated instruments, involving options and exotics, however, are still relatively rare. It would behoove monetary authorities to promote further development of them. In addition, unlike in Brazil, Chile, and Mexico, contracts are almost always short-term at this time. With further progress in and development of its financial markets, coupled with significant economic growth, Colombia's market for currency derivatives will continue to expand and derivatives contracts will lengthen.

4.5 *Additional Developments*

Three additional developments among emerging markets deserve mention: cross-hedging, currency portfolios, and portable alpha. First, it is not uncommon for international investors, when invested in portfolios of emerging market securities, especially with emerging markets in early stages of development, to be unable to implement a hedge directly; that is, they cannot take out a forward or futures contract to reduce currency risk. In this situation, investors might still be able to hedge their currency risks through cross-hedging: risk reduction by taking an offsetting position in another currency, say, a forward or futures contract, with similar price movements. Although it does not provide as much risk reduction as a direct hedge, it may be more liquid and less expensive (i.e., lower transactions costs) than an OTC position, and it expands the universe of hedging tools available. For example, DeMaskey *et al.* (2003) demonstrate that the yen can be an effective cross-hedge for mutual funds invested in emerging Asian economies, and Chang and Wong (2003) demonstrate that cross-hedging can reduce currency risk by up to 56% compared to a non-hedged position.

Currency portfolios can also be used to hedge currency risks. Chincarini (2007) shows how a portfolio of currencies can be an effective way, in terms of higher Sharpe ratios, to hedge the currency risk inherent in global portfolios. Campbell *et al.* (2007) demonstrate that an investor can minimize portfolio risk by shorting the Australian dollar, Canadian dollar, the pound, and the yen while going long on the US dollar, the euro, and the Swiss franc. They further show that this portfolio of currencies is nearly equivalent to a full-currency hedge. They also uncover the interesting finding that a long position in the US-Canadian exchange rate is an effective way to mitigate the volatility of equity investments. These findings could well lead to the creation of a global currency portfolio, which would include both developed and emerging market currencies.

Since the emergence of hedge funds during the 1990s and the globalization of financial markets, it appears that hedge funds and corporations have been aggressively seeking ways to enhance portfolio returns through foreign exchange. As a result, currency returns have become the focus for enhancing a "portable alpha." This concept involves portfolio managers who preserve the beta of the portfolio while seeking above-average returns from a portfolio that represents a different asset class or even a different market. For example, a portfolio manager of US equities may be tracking stocks in the S&P 500, and, as a result, may doubt her ability to outperform the S&P 500, the alpha effect. Writing call options on her security selections, she might use the proceeds to invest in Latin American markets that she expects will outperform the S&P 500. In addition, because an index fund of currencies is rare and because a wide variety of strategies exists across developed and emerging markets, the manager's alpha is considered to be almost "pure," and offers the added benefit of having nearly zero correlation with other asset classes.

5. Additional Trends

The dramatic increase in investor participation in emerging markets, along with the developments in emerging market currency derivatives, has moved lock-step with several other trends as follows:

- An appreciation of emerging market currencies against the US dollar
- A drop in volatility of emerging market currencies
- A convergence of interest rates

As evidence of the appreciation of emerging market currencies against the dollar, as reported by the International Monetary Fund

(2002 and 2007), Table 1 shows the emerging market price per US dollar for 14 currencies from January of 2002 through May of 2007. With the exception of the Mexican peso, all the currencies show significant appreciation against the dollar. The Czech Republic's koruna shows the largest percentage appreciation, from approximately 37 to 21 units, while South Africa's rand has the smallest increase, from 7.77 to 7.11.

These appreciations have not met with as much volatility during the most recent five years compared to the last five years of the twentieth century, which include the Asian and Russian financial crises. This is evidenced in Table 2, which shows the volatility of the same emerging market currencies in Table 1. The data come from the Oanda Corporation (www.oanda.com/convert/). The comparison is between two five-year periods, from 1996 through 2000 and from 2002 through May of 2007. With the exception of the Brazilian real, the Chilean peso, and the South African rand, each of the currencies

Table 1. Selected Emerging Market Currencies against the US Dollar, 2002–2007

Currency	2002 I	2007 II
Brazil, real	2.41	1.95
Chile, peso	704.55	524.58
Colombia, peso	2347.30	1997.49
Czech Republic, koruna	37.04	21.13
Hungary, forint	283.04	186.98
India, rupee	48.56	40.53
Mexico, peso	9.15	10.78
Poland, zloty	4.23	2.85
Russia Federation, ruble	30.72	25.90
Singapore, dollar	1.84	1.53
South Africa, rand	7.77	7.10
Korea, won	1314.40	928.00
Thailand, baht	44.07	32.55

This table illustrates the appreciation of emerging market currencies against the US dollar from the beginning of the first quarter of 2002 through May of 2007. All currencies show significant appreciation except the Mexican peso.

Table 2. Volatilities of Emerging Market Currencies, 1996–2000 and 2002–2007

Currency	1996 I–2000 IV	2002 I–2007 II
Brazil, real	0.141	0.221
Chile, peso	2738.0	5719.40
Colombia, peso	165220.60	66271.22
Czech Republic, koruna	17.17	15.78
Hungary, forint	2161.63	555.82
India, rupee	14.99	3.52
Korea	53102.90	13151.30
Mexico, peso	0.800	0.365
Poland, zloty	0.350	0.182
Russia, ruble[a]	72.77	3.191
Singapore, dollar	0.018	0.007
South Africa, rand	1.07	2.51
Thailand, baht	50.56	7.17

[a] Applies from 1998 through 2000 because the Russian government divided the current ruble price of the US dollar by 1000 on January 2, 1998.

This table provides volatility estimates of emerging market currencies measured against the US dollar for two five-year periods, from the beginning of the first quarter of 1996 through the fourth quarter of 2000 and from the first quarter of 2002 through May of 2007. With the exception of the Brazilian real, the Chilean peso, and the South African rand, all currencies show a significant reduction in volatility, as measured by the variance in the exchange rate of each currency against the US dollar.

has experienced notable drops in volatility between the two five-year periods. For example, the volatility of the Hungarian forint against the US dollar fell from 2161.63 to 555.82. For the Thai baht, the drop was even more noticeable, from 50.56 to 7.17. Even the Colombian peso, while still experiencing tremendous volatility compared to that of the other emerging market currencies, has begun to settle down somewhat, experiencing a drop in volatility from 165,220.60 to 66,271.22, a decline of 60%.

The appreciation in emerging market currencies and the decline in their volatilities have moved in step with decreases in interest rates across emerging markets. As seen in Table 3, every interest rate of the 14 emerging market countries, as reported by the International

Table 3. Selected Emerging Market Interest Rates, 2000–2007

Country	2000 I	2007 II
Brazil	60.18%	47.20%
Chile	14.04%	8.34%
Colombia	17.29%	13.31%
Czech Republic	7.32%	5.65%
Hungary	13.60%	9.30%
India	12.50%	12.00%
Mexico	18.23%	7.44%
Poland	19.40%	5.50%
Russia	31.70%	9.90%
Singapore	5.83%	5.33%
South Africa	14.50%	12.50%
Korea	7.70%	6.30%
Thailand	8.00%	7.50%
United States	6.56%	8.25%

This table illustrates the convergence in lending rates in emerging markets by using the lending rate in the US as the benchmark. The period is from the beginning of the first quarter of 2000 through May of 2007.

Monetary Fund (2002 and 2007), has experienced a drop in interest rates, as measured by lending rates, reflecting an improved business climate and a drop in inflation risk. For example, Mexico registered a drop in its average lending rate from 18.23% at the beginning of the first quarter of 2000 to 7.44% by the first quarter of 2007. The decline in the average lending rate in Poland is even more impressive, from 19.40% to 5.50%, as is the fall in interest rates in Russia, from 31.70% to 9.90%.

6. Summary and Additional Perspectives

Undoubtedly, emerging economies have made substantial progress since the troubled years of the 1980s and 1990s, and it would seem that many of them are beyond the threshold of fragility. With higher bond ratings driving emerging market debt premiums to all-time lows, leading to robust borrowing in international capital markets, the notion of "original sin" seems an outdated thought. This is certainly the view advanced by Cooper (2005). He sees the current environment as a largely uninterrupted period of prosperity that is ushering in a new world order, one in which, for example, "Asia miracle" stories will be the norm rather than the exception, offering rates of return significantly higher than those of more advanced economies and without the volatility that often plagues emerging market returns. Other observers, such as Dooley *et al.* (2004) and Bernanke (2005), offer a different but still optimistic scenario. Succinctly, the world is awash in a savings glut. Coupled with falling inflation rates, real interest rates are low and will likely stay there. Because savings behavior tends to be long-term, the present expansion of financial opportunities and derivative instruments in emerging markets has only just begun.

Agreement about the direction, however, is far from complete. Rogoff (2006) offers the alternative, and perhaps more mainstream, view that the world is on a cyclical upswing, and the fact that emerging markets are doing well economically and financially does not preclude another series of crises. For one thing, the ongoing and sizeable US current account deficit means that the US dollar will have to depreciate significantly, on a trade-weighted basis by as much as 25%. Depreciation of this magnitude can be avoided only if the deficit reverts to near zero very slowly, say, by 2020, an unlikely occurrence. While a weaker dollar implies a stronger emerging market currency, it is fair to say that a large and a sudden drop in the value of the dollar will rattle financial markets worldwide, possibly unraveling much of the current global financial order, especially if economic growth slows. Viewing this scenario in the light of political instability, which has a long history in emerging markets, international investors will be well served to adopt a prudent plan of hedging currency risks by using currency derivatives.

References

Bernanke, B., 2005, The global savings glut and the US current account deficit, Sandridge Lecture, Virginia Association of Economics, Richmond, VA, www.federalreserve.gov/boarddocs/speeches/

Bhargava, V., D. K. Kohku, and D. K. Malhotra, 2004, Does international diversification pay? *Financial Counseling and Planning*, 15, 53–62.

Calvo, G. A., 1998, Varieties of capital market crises, in G.A. Calvo and M. King, *The Debt Burden and its Consequences for Monetary Policy*, London: MacMillan.

Calvo, G. A., 1999, Contagion in capital markets: When Wall Street is a carrier, www.bsos.umd.edu/econ/ciecrp8.pdf.

Calvo, G. A., 2002, Globalization hazard and delayed reform in emerging markets, *Economia*, 2, 1–29.

Calvo, G. A., 2005, Crisis in emerging market economies: A global perspective, Frank D. Graham Memorial Lecture, March 30, Princeton University, Princeton, NJ.

Calvo, G. A. and C. M. Reinhart, 2000, When capital flows come to a sudden stop: Consequences and policy, in P.B. Kenan, M. Mussa, and A.K. Swoboda (eds.), *Reforming the International Monetary and Financial System*, Washington, D.C.: Brookings Institute.

Campbell, J. Y., K. S. Medeiros, and L. M. Viceira, 2007, Global currency hedging, National Bureau of Economic Research, Working Paper 13088.

Claessens, S. and D. Naude' 1993, Recent estimates of capital flight, World Bank Policy Research Working Paper Series, 1186, Washington, D.C.: World Bank.

Chang, E. C. and K. P. Wong, 2003, Cross-hedging with currency options, *Journal of Financial and Quantitative Analysis*, 38, 555–574.

Chincarini, L. B., 2007, The effectiveness of global currency trading after the Asian Crisis, *Journal of Asset Management*, 8, 34–51.

Cooper, R., 2005, A glimpse of 2020, in M. Porter, K. Schwab, X. Sala-i-Martin, and A. Lopez-Claros (eds.), *The Global Competitiveness Report, 2004-2005*. New York: Palgrave MacMillan.

Crowley, F. C. and A. L. Loviscek, 2002, Assessing the impact of political risk on currency returns, *Quarterly Review of Economics and Finance*, 42, 143–153.

Das, D., 2003, Emerging market economies: Inevitability of volatility and contagion, *Journal of Asset Management*, 4, 199–216.

DeMaskey, A. L., W. L. Dellva, and J. L. Heck. 2003, Benefits from Asia-Pacific mutual fund investments with currency hedging, *Review of Quantitative Finance and Accounting*, 21, 49–64.

Dooley, M., D. Folkerts-Landau, and P. Garber, 2004, The revised Bretton Woods system: The effects of periphery intervention and reserve management on interest rates and exchange rates in center countries, National Bureau of Economic Research, Working Paper 10332.

Eichengreen, B., R. Hausman, and V. Panizza, 2003, Currency mismatches, debt intolerance, and original sin: Why it matters, National Bureau of Economic Research, Working Paper 10036.

Henderson, C., 2002, Editorial: Hedging emerging market currency risk, *Derivatives Use, Trading & Regulation*, 8, 5–12.

International Monetary Fund, 2002 and 2007, *International Financial Statistics*, Washington, D.C.

McFadden, D., 2004, Hot money and cold comfort: Global capital movement and financial crises in emerging economies, presentation at ANEC Conference on Globalization and Development, Havana, Cuba.

Rogoff, K., 2006, Will emerging markets escape the next big systematic financial crisis?" *Cato Journal*, 26, 341–357.

Soendoro, M., 2007, Foreign exchange risk management in developing countries, International Trade Centre UNCTAD/WTO, Trade Finance Programme, 2–8.

Index

DH

332.
673
ADV